Also by H. Arthur Klein and Mina C. Klein

Peter Bruegel the Elder, Artist of Abundance
Great Structures of the World
Surf's Up! An Anthology of Surfing
Hypocritical Helena
Max and Moritz

by H. Arthur Klein

Graphic Worlds of Peter Bruegel the Elder
Masers and Lasers
Bioluminescence
Fuel Cells
Surfing

Bruegel's Seven Deadly Sins (a motion picture)

TEMPLE BEYOND TIME

The portals of the "Temple Beyond Time" as built under Herod on Mount Moriah.
(From a reconstruction on the grounds of the Holyland Hotel in modern Jerusalem.)

TEMPLE BEYOND TIME

The Story of the Site of Solomon's Temple at Jerusalem

Mina C. Klein and H. Arthur Klein

VNR VAN NOSTRAND REINHOLD COMPANY
New York Cincinnati Toronto London Melbourne

Van Nostrand Reinhold Company Regional Offices:
Cincinnati • New York • Chicago • Millbrae • Dallas
Van Nostrand Reinhold Company Foreign Offices:
London • Toronto • Melbourne

 Manufactured in the United States of America. Library of Congress Catalog Card No.: 75-88674.

Published by Van Nostrand Reinhold Company
450 West 33rd Street, New York, New York 10001
Published simultaneously in Canada by
D. Van Nostrand Company (Canada), Ltd.
16 15 14 13 12 11 10 9 8 7 6 5 4 3 2 1

Book design by Howard M. Burns
Printed and bound by Mahony & Roese, Inc.

Dedicated to devoted archeologists,
professional or part-time, who,
from many parts of the world
have come to the region
of the Temple Beyond Time,
and there have helped
to reconstruct a rich past,
strikingly relevant to the present.

"... in these ancient lands
Enchased and lettered as a tomb
And scored with prints of perished hands,
And chronicled with dates of doom ...
I trace the lives such scenes enshrine
And their experience count as mine."

— THOMAS HARDY

Acknowledgments

Studies underlying this book began about five years ago, well before the outcome of the "Six Day War" focussed new attention on the site of the *Temple Beyond Time*. During our labors we consulted hundreds of books, articles, and pictures in such rich collections as the Library of Congress, Washington, D.C.; the New York Public Library; the British Museum; the Bibliothèque Nationale, Paris; the Israel Museum, Jerusalem; and, much closer to home, the friendly libraries of UCLA and Los Angeles County. As more than once before, our thanks to many staff members of the latter two, via Dr. Robert Vosper, UCLA Librarian; and Mrs. Deborah B. Wilds, Regional Librarian, Los Angeles County system.

While working during many memorable days in Jerusalem, fall, 1968, we were fortunate in being guided at times by Dr. Michael Avi-Yonah, eminent art historian and archeologist of the Hebrew University there. In 1969, during an all too brief visit to California, Dr. Avi-Yonah helped us again with invaluable advice and insights on a number of points. We hope the finished book will be worthy of such aid, as generous as it was authoritative and intelligent.

For kindness connected with illustrations, we thank Mrs. E. Cherni of the management of the Holyland Hotel, Jerusalem; and Mrs. Elishiva Cohen, acting chief curator of the Israel Museum there; also Mrs. Hermione Pappas of the Israel Information Service, Los Angeles office; and Miss Anit Kali, of the New York office.

In the effort to let the Bible speak today in language as fresh, forceful, and meaningful as when its books were first written, several recent translations were consulted, though no one of them was followed throughout. Bible passages in this book can be considered as late twentieth century paraphrases. We trust they will be found faithful both to the sense and the spirit of the originals.

Finally, our warm thanks go to Dorothy S. Briley of the Van Nostrand Reinhold Company for her constant encouragement, understanding, and practical aid.

MINA C. KLEIN AND H. ARTHUR KLEIN

CONTENTS

TEMPLE BEYOND TIME

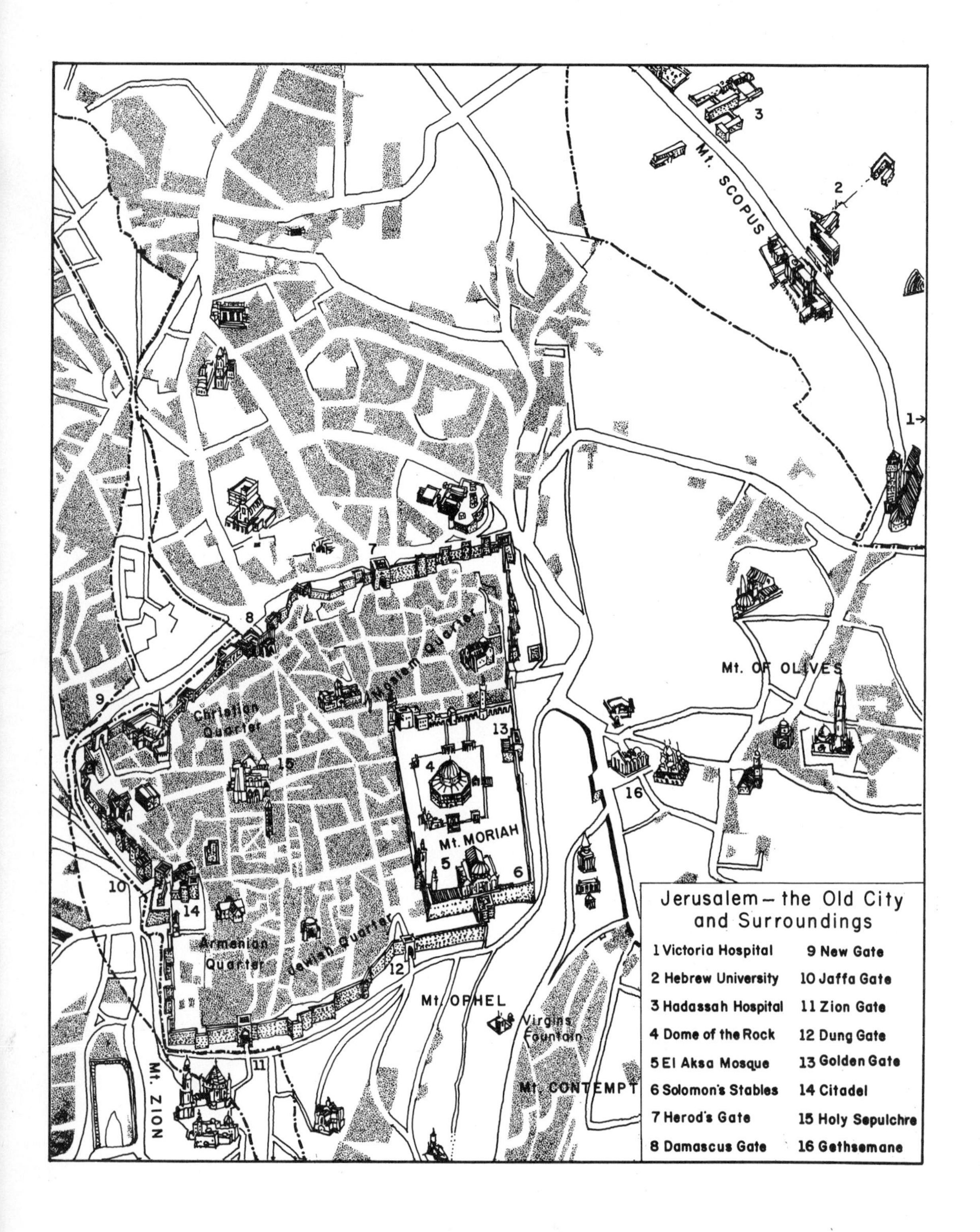
Jerusalem — the Old City and Surroundings
1 Victoria Hospital
2 Hebrew University
3 Hadassah Hospital
4 Dome of the Rock
5 El Aksa Mosque
6 Solomon's Stables
7 Herod's Gate
8 Damascus Gate
9 New Gate
10 Jaffa Gate
11 Zion Gate
12 Dung Gate
13 Golden Gate
14 Citadel
15 Holy Sepulchre
16 Gethsemane
Mt. SCOPUS
Mt. OF OLIVES
Moslem Quarter
Christian Quarter
Armenian Quarter
Jewish Quarter
Mt. MORIAH
Mt. OPHEL
Virgins Fountain
Mt. CONTEMPT
Mt. ZION

1

War, Peace, and an Old Wall

(Mid-1967 and 1968)

The first shells were fired just after 11:30 the morning of Monday, June 5, 1967. They vaulted through the air over one Jerusalem, then held by the nation of Jordan, and landed with loud explosions in the other Jerusalem, held by Israel and serving as its capital.

On the way they passed above a strange and ugly boundary, a barbed-wire and barrier-created no-man's-land that ran like a jagged gash between the two sectors of Jerusalem.

Those historic first shells caused no great amount of physical destruction. They damaged some Israeli residential dwellings near the boundary barrier. But they shattered more than Jerusalem stone, wood, and glass. They broke the uneasy truce that until then had existed between Israel and its neighbor to the east, known as The Hashemite Kingdom of Jordan.

Those Jordanian shots into Jerusalem came not as a surprise, but as a disappointment to leaders of the government and military forces of Israel. They had hoped that somehow the Jordanian government could be persuaded to refrain from attack, while Israel was occupied in fighting the United Arab Republic (Egypt), and other allies in the coalition of Arab powers dedicated to the elimination of Israel from the Near East.

Actual combat in that war, now known to the world as the Six Day War, had begun at dawn that same Monday, with surprise attacks by the Israeli air force on airfields in Egypt. Threats and aggressive acts had begun earlier still. Egyptian war vessels had blockaded the Gulf of Akaba, Israel's channel of access to the Red Sea and waters to the south. Arab troops had moved into positions menacing Israel's borders. The ominous prelude to the Six Day War and its swift, startling outcome have been told in some detail elsewhere. Here we follow only one amazing aspect of the days from June 5 to 7, which brought the capture of Jordanian-held Jerusalem including the historic "Temple mount" and the reuniting of all Jerusalem, a city sacred to myriads of mankind.

Israel's war plans had not included this action and outcome. It had to be improvised, beginning in the afternoon of Monday, as Jordanian shells and bombs continued falling into Israeli Jerusalem, while from Amman, the capital of Jordan, came announcement that Jordanian troops had occupied Mount Scopus, commanding all Jerusalem from the northeast.

Plans based on the hope that Jordan would remain out of the fight now had to be given up. Counter-action was planned in a hurry as the only possible answer to the attack from Jordan. By 5:30 that Monday afternoon, Israeli mechanized forces entered a sector of Jerusalem that had long been under Jordanian rule. Additional Israeli ground forces, including tough paratroopers, were on their way to Jerusalem by about seven that evening. The first objective was to gain control of Mount Scopus. It was from there that Jerusalem had been attacked and captured a score or more of times during three thousand years of varied, tragic, and bloody history.

A task of tremendous difficulty was assigned to the Israeli forces. They had to fight their way into closely built and strongly defended areas, yet spare selected sites from harm as they did so. Though combat now raged on many fronts, this divided small city of Jerusalem was like no other. It was, as one observer noted, "the focus of Israeli hearts and those of Jews around the world." And for millions of people, neither Israelis nor Jews, Jerusalem was in the spotlight, for it was the city where David and Solomon had ruled, where Jesus had taught and died, where the prophet Mohammed had gone to make his miraculous ascent into Heaven itself, and where had stood the most famous temples and religious shrines in the world.

The sites most renowned and revered stood in the sector of Jerusalem that had been held by Jordan during the years since 1948. This was the eastern part of Jerusalem, containing the Old City with its ancient gates, walls, narrow streets, markets, shops, mosques, and churches. Jordan had not permitted Jews from Israel to visit there. Jordanian Jerusalem had been divided from Israeli Jerusalem by a no-man's land of barbed wire, guns, and patrolling soldiers. Residents of one Jerusalem could see the other; but they were separated by the ugly gash across the sacred city.

Had the Israeli commanders sought to take the rest of Jerusalem with least sacrifice of their men and materials, they would have ordered artillery barrages and airforce bombings to flatten walls and buildings and drive out the stubbornly defending Arab legionnaires. There was, however, no hesitation: the Old City was to be taken, not destroyed; not even harmed, if possible.

The racket of mortar and artillery tore through the darkness that night.

Then, about 2 A.M. the morning of June 6th, Israeli paratroopers with tank support cut their way through barbed-wire barriers and began moving into Jordanian sectors of Jerusalem north of the Old City itself. The advance was slow, for the Jordanian forces defended their positions bravely. Fighting was house to house, door to door, but it moved always deeper in the direction of Israeli objectives. The Jordanian Police School, a prime objective, was taken before 4 A.M., the Ambassador Hotel by 6 A.M., and soon afterward the so-called American Colony sector. Now the fighting men of Israel controlled a route that led all the way to strategic Mount Scopus itself.

Between nine and ten that morning an historic order was given. Brigadier General Uzzi Narkiss, head of the central Israel command, instructed Colonel Mordecai Gur, leader of ground forces, to make preparations to penetrate into the walled Old City itself. Just after noon of that day, Narkiss and General Moshe Dayan, recently appointed Minister of Defense for Israel, stood on Mount Scopus together and looked intently down toward the southwest where lay the historic Old City.

In preparation for the final thrust in that direction, Israeli forces slowly eliminated Jordanian sniper and mortar positions from heights further south, including mainly the Mount of Olives due east of the Old City.

By nightfall of June 6, the armed men of Israel held the slopes from which they could clearly see westward across the Kidron Valley the walls and towers of ancient "Jerusalem of Gold." They rested then during a night torn by gunfire and flare-lights, preparing for what most of them knew might be the greatest — or the last — day of their lives. The military "order of the day" left no doubt as to the import and burden of their task. It demanded that "the greatest respect" be shown the holy places, for ". . . we are about to take the Temple mount. This is an historic task. The Jewish people are praying for our victory. All Israel awaits it. . . ."

Dawn diluted the dark over Jerusalem. The light, coming from behind them now, was reflected from the golden cupola of the Dome of the Rock, and from the silver cupola of the el Aksa mosque, both atop the old Temple platform on Mount Moriah at the eastern side of the Old City. (Meanwhile, far to the south and west, Israeli fighters had reached the banks of the Suez Canal itself.)

The awaited command came early, and by 8:30 the morning of June 7, the action began with half an hour of artillery barrage and aerial bombing. Colonel Gur cut it short, for he felt not a moment could be lost. The advance began. Israeli tanks moved down the slopes toward the Old City. They were "firing in every direction" said one observer — but they managed to avoid the most sacred sites.

Colonel Gur himself dashed across the valley in his command halftrack. Ben Tsur, his massive, bearded driver, disregarded the speedometer needle that at times indicated 90 kilometers per hour as they swayed past firing tanks, wrecked Jordanian rolling stock, and Israeli troopers hurrying to keep up with the pace of the advance.

A few minutes before ten in the morning, Gur and Tsur reached the eastern wall of the Old City itself. Before them now was the great gate of St. Stephen, known also as "the Lion's Gate." Somehow its door stood ajar. Jordanian rocket-launchers and some of their ammunition were still visible on the walls around the gates. But Jordanian soldiers were not then in sight.

Commander Gur took a long chance. Using the halftrack as a tool, his driver pushed open the great gate. They drove on, into the Old City itself.

Stones lay scattered past the gate along the narrow street called in English "The Road of the Gate of our Lady Mary" and in Arabic the *Taria Bab Sitt Maryam.* The halftrack pushed on, passing a Jordanian soldier stunned and stupefied by the onslaught. A riderless motorcycle blocked the way about 500 feet west of the St. Stephen Gate. The halftrack, however, rolled right over it, in rash disregard of the danger of landmines.

Thus they reached and entered the great paved courtyard, atop the Temple mount, known as the *Haram esh-Sherif.* Then there was an end to firing, "for it is a Holy Place."

Tanks could not follow into the Haram itself, but foot soldiers did. Before eleven that morning, the forces of Israel were firmly in control, not only of the great Haram but of all the Old City. Only some clearing out of scattered snipers remained to be done.

As soon as possible, and even before it was safe, officers and men began to leave the Haram itself. They made their way down to the foot of the massive retaining wall that formed part of its western side. Drenched with battle-sweat, dirty, dishevelled, or bloody, they stood there, acting as if they had suddenly gone mad. They laughed, wept, stroked, embraced, or kissed the great stone blocks from whose crevices grew a few stubborn green plants. Some men, still clutching guns or bazookas, repeated old prayers in Hebrew.

A colonel had been the first to reach the foot of that Western Wall and greet it with tears. A corporal, who followed him, was cut down by a sniper's bullet as he dashed down the last steps that led from above. His blood still lay dark on the ground. Ever greater numbers of the fighting men of Israel gathered now, celebrating the first return to a Wall most of them had known all their lives, yet never before seen.

Thus, following battle and bloodshed, came their first return to the sole remnant of what had been the Temple — a Temple beyond the reach of time, because of mankind's memories and dreams. Above this old retaining wall had once stood the sanctuaries for the God of Israel built by Solomon, by Zeru-babbel, and by Herod. And here for nearly nineteen hundred years the children of Israel had come only as mourners — when they could come at all.

Ceremonies mingling joy and grief began that afternoon of June 7. They have seldom halted since, for the Western Wall and its surroundings remain a recognized place of worship and of pilgrimage — a synagogue without roof and without enclosure.

In the first traditional observance, the uniformed and bearded chief rabbi of the army of Israel, Brigadier Shlomo Goren, carried the traditional

Worshipers gathered before the Western Wall. A wooden fence divides the men's section from the women's (nearer.) Lockers at intervals along the base of the Wall hold sacred scrolls for prayers and rituals. The large lower stones date from the days of King Herod. The smaller blocks above were placed in the nineteenth century, during repairs to the Wall.

Scrolls of the Law and sounded the ancient *shofar*, the ram's horn of ritual and repentance. Its crabbed, mournful tones were reflected by huge stone blocks that had borne their burdens before the time of Jesus and his disciples.

Before mid-afternoon, leaders of the nation of Israel began to arrive to do homage at the Wall. Defense Minister Moshe Dayan made a challenging prediction before he left: "We have returned to the holiest of our holy places, never to part from them again."

The people of Israel — all ages, conditions, colors, and backgrounds — now poured through the narrow, gun-blasted streets to come to the clearing at the foot of the Wall, standing in wonder and worship. They came long before it was safe or officially allowed to do so. They came by scores, by hundreds, by thousands. They, and citizens of other lands, near or far, have been coming ever since to visit the extraordinary, unique site.

Active, open warfare between Israel and Jordan did not continue long after all Jerusalem was in the hands of the forces of Israel. By 10 o'clock that same evening of June 7 a ceasefire had been arranged and approved by both sides.

The Six Day War ended in a great victory for Israel on all fronts. Perhaps *paused* rather than *ended* would be the safer term, for sporadic conflicts continue, and threats of another major outbreak seem stronger now, as these lines are written, than they were when the Jews of Israel and elsewhere first regained their ancient rights of access to the Wall.

If sheer disaster is not to be the outcome, some tenable and lasting settlement must be worked out — not just an uncertain deadlock punctuated by violence and new outbreaks of declared or undeclared war. An essential ingredient of any such lasting settlement must be assurance that people of all faiths have access to the Wall, and that all Jerusalem's historic great shrines, venerated by Moslems, Christians, or Jews, shall be accessible to all who come in peace to worship or observe.

Jerusalem is embedded in the memory and the hopes of a world. Its fascination is not limited to visitors of any one, or even any, religious attitude. In this city of not yet 300,000 inhabitants, the past, the present, and the future all seem to jostle each other. Its history emphasizes the need for a unified, open, and peaceful Jerusalem.

When the authors in the autumn of 1968 visited the no-longer-divided Jerusalem to gather material for this book, they saw and studied with equal fascination the lovely Dome of the Rock and el Aksa mosque above, the Wall below, and the entire complex of historic remains associated with the site.

An ancient custom is still observed by many who today come to visit and pray at the Wall. They place in its crevices messages expressing their most profound hopes, written on small bits of paper. One of the authors, in autumn of 1968, approaching its massive old stones, beside which so much blood and so many tears have been spilled, felt moved to insert such a message. Just one word seemed to suit the place and occasion: *Shalom*, which is to say: Peace!

Its cupola atop an octagonal base, the Dome of the Rock dominates the Haram esh-Sherif on the Temple Mount. In its shadow (to right) is the smaller Dome of the Chain. Closer to us stands the el Aksa Mosque. Paved area to its right lies over the great vaults called "Solomon's Stables." Through the Kidron Valley (far right) runs the Jericho Road. In the distance stand the white buildings of the Rockefeller Archeological Museum.

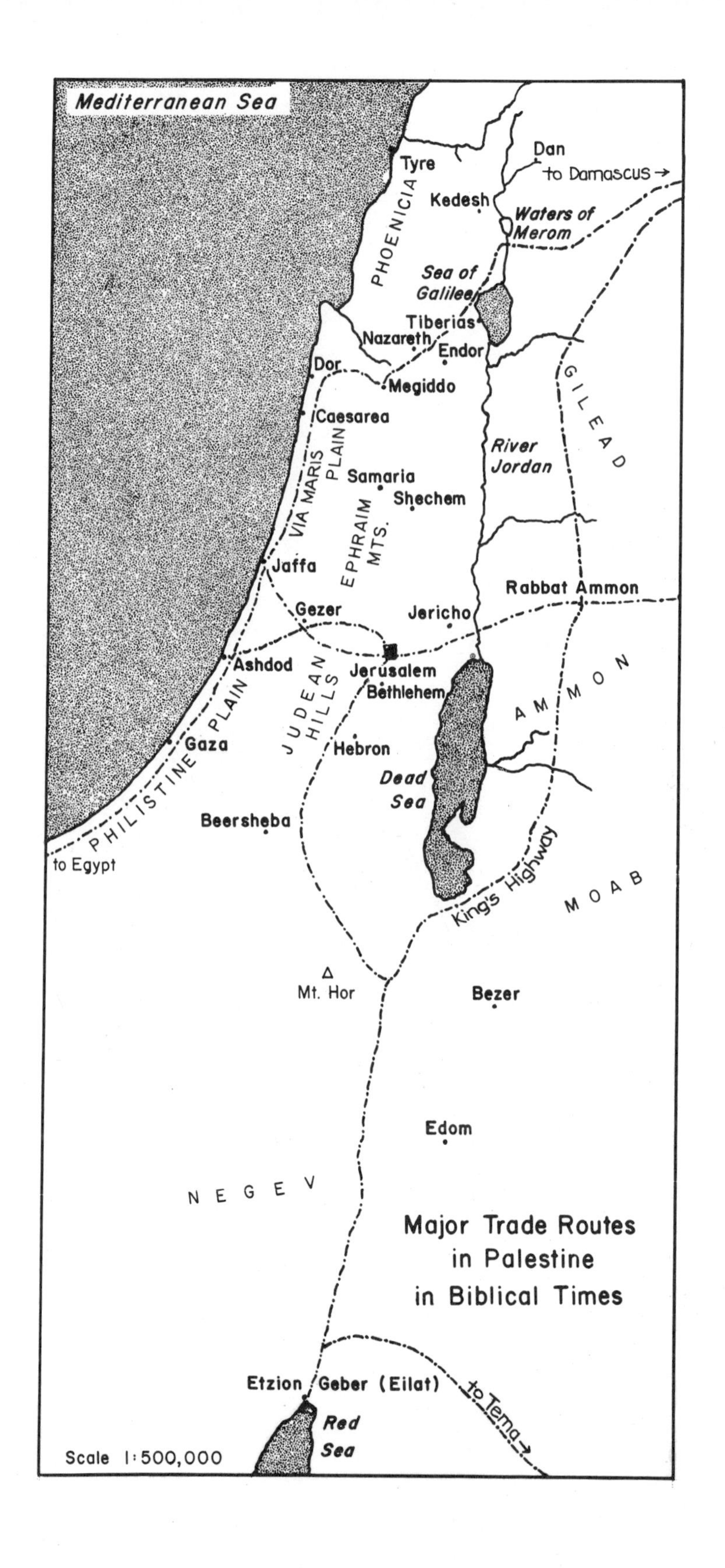

Mediterranean Sea
Tyre
Dan
to Damascus →
Kedesh
Waters of Merom
PHOENICIA
Sea of Galilee
Tiberias
Nazareth
Endor
Dor
Megiddo
Caesarea
GILEAD
River Jordan
VIA MARIS
PLAIN
Samaria
Shechem
EPHRAIM MTS.
Jaffa
Rabbat Ammon
Gezer
Jericho
Ashdod
Jerusalem
Bethlehem
JUDEAN HILLS
AMMON
Gaza
Hebron
Dead Sea
PHILISTINE PLAIN
Beersheba
to Egypt
King's Highway
MOAB
Mt. Hor
Bezer
Edom
NEGEV
Major Trade Routes in Palestine in Biblical Times
Etzion Geber (Eilat)
to Tema →
Red Sea
Scale 1:500,000

2

King David and His City

(1000–962 B.C.E.)

How did an old wall become a shrine so revered and longed-for? What made the broad Haram area above it a treasury of tradition for three great faiths of the western world? For the answers, we trace back three thousand years.

The origins here, like their outcomes, are associated with a tiny segment of the earth's land area — a segment called by such names as Canaan, Palestine, the Holy Land, *Eretz Yisroel*, or simply Israel; a mere sliver of land, combining coastal plains, hills, valleys, and waste places — at the eastern end of the Mediterranean Sea.

Though small, it is the most crucial part of the Middle East. In the true sense of the word *crucial*, or crosslike, it became the first great crossroads of man's world. It lies where two regions of utmost importance adjoined, and where their major roads merged.

This becomes clear when we trace in both directions the Way Beside the Sea, later known by the Latin name of *Via Maris*. Followed toward the south and west it led to the Nile River valley, at the Egyptian city of On. Followed from Egypt, it brought travelers along the coast, to Gaza, the famous Philistine city; then northward to the center of Megiddo. There it split into two branches. The more important of these led to Damascus. From there the caravans followed the trail that ran in great sweeping arcs through the richest parts of the sector called "the Fertile Crescent," moving into the region of the Euphrates River, to Accad, to Babylon, and finally to Ur, where the waters flowed into the hot Persian Gulf.

In that Fertile Crescent, as in a curved green frame, arose the first extensive agriculture, the first great cities, and important early empires such as Babylon, Assyria, and others. Palestine itself, from one point of view, provided the westernmost horn of the Fertile Crescent, which arcs up and over the great Arabian Desert.

Palestine not only stood astride the great links between Fertile Crescent and Nile Valley; it also included other roads that reached finally into the forbidding Arabian desert itself. Down the center of Palestine, like a great gash from north to south, ran the valley in which flows the Jordan River, into the exitless Dead Sea, lowest land level on earth. East of this rugged valley ran the trail called later "the King's Highway." Its route could be traced from Damascus in the north all the way down to the Gulf of Akaba, where today is found the Israeli port of Elath, or Eilat.

Not far north of Elath, caravans could turn off the King's Highway and move southeast across a trail to the town of Tema. From there they could continue due south into the great desert. Not far north and east of the upper end of the Dead Sea, another trail branched eastward from the King's Highway at Rabbath-bene-ammon. It led caravans to Karkor and then to Dumah. From there they could either turn left (northward) and cross the great desert all the way to Babylon itself; or they could turn right (southward) on a trail that led down to Tema.

Palestine thus commanded not only the juncture between the great roads to Egypt on one hand and the Fertile Crescent on the other, but also in another sense served as a gateway between the eastern end of the Mediterranean Sea and the vast Arabian desert.

In Palestine met and merged influences emanating from all these important cultural regions: from the Fertile Crescent empires; from Egypt; and from the Arabian desert in still another direction. Thus Palestine became important and immortal in human history not from mere size or sheer richness of natural gifts, but by virtue of a unique location. Only in this light can Palestine's history be understood.

Into this very special region, drawn by promise of more abundant and settled living, had come tribes of nomadic peoples called sometimes the Habiru and more often the Hebrews. They had entered Palestine, fought for it, settled according to their tribes where they could, become farmers, orchardists, tenders of vineyards, herdsmen, and small craftsmen.

Some two hundred years after they had moved in, a remarkable man whose name was David, son of Jesse of the tribe of Judah in the south, had become king of these Hebrews. First he had made himself king of his own kinsmen of the tribe of Judah. Then he gained the crown also of eleven other tribes whose lands lay north of Judah.

Once king over all these Hebrew tribes, David launched further bold, aggressive moves. He marshalled his men and captured a little hill-girt town known as Jebus, site of an alien non-Hebrew people. It had projected like a wedge between the two areas that he ruled: the region of Judah to the south and that of the other tribes to the north. But David, in taking Jebus, was not mainly seeking to remove this dent in his boundaries. Rather, he was carving out for himself a royal city, free from the Hebrew tribal traditions that prevailed elsewhere in his realm. Later developments made the site of Jerusalem (Jebus) seem to be part of the land of the tribe of Benjamin; but when David besieged and took it, it belonged not to the Hebrew Benjaminites, but to the Jebusites, a small Canaanite people.

The taking of Jebus alarmed the Philistine chieftains. Till then they had assumed there was little to fear from David who, only a few years before had served them while he was an outlaw and fugitive from Saul, first king of the Hebrews. The Philistine forces marched to punish this rash upstart David. But they were too late. He defeated them soundly in two battles not far from Jebus, and they fled toward their own fortified towns along the seacoast.

David wasted no time in pursuit. He turned back to building his center, which soon became known as "the city of David." From the beginning he shaped it as the capital for his expanding realm. He built it outside the control of the twelve-tribe pattern of the Hebrew people. In much the same way, twenty-eight hundred years later, the Founding Fathers of the United States of America set up the capital in a "District of Columbia" created outside the boundaries of any one of the states of the new union. To this extent, King David freed himself from inter-tribal rivalries and jealousies.

Jebus had a rich history when David took it. It had been the site of an ancient worship center called Salem. It is tempting to suppose that its eventual immortal name of *Jerusalem* arose from a combination of *Jebus* and *Salem*, related to the Hebrew word *Shalom*, meaning peace. However, more likely seems to be an origin in a combination of the word *Yarah,* meaning to found or lay the foundation for, and *Salem*, the name of a western Semitic god from the early days before the rise of monotheistic religion. Thus Yarah-Salem would signify that "the god Salem founded (it)". And this became the word still pronounced in Hebrew like *Yerushalayim*, though we are used to the Anglicized form of Jerusalem.

No city name in all man's history is more famous than Jerusalem — not even Rome or Athens or Babylon. Yet in the land of David, during his day and for long generations later, the capital was often called "the city of David." So powerful had been the impress of his personality and purposes.

Lying high in the hills, Jerusalem had a more pleasant climate than most of the rest of David's growing realm. Yet his primary motive in creating his capital was political advantage, not comfort or even commerce. This was unusual for that era. The site of Jerusalem, when David took it, lay far from principal highroads, camel trails, harbors, or navigable rivers. Neither of the great trade routes through Palestine passed through Jerusalem. The Via Maris, or seaside road, ran along the coast of the Mediterranean, sometimes branching into two, then reuniting. It was nearly two days journey to the west of David's new capital. In the opposite direction, east of the Jordan River, lay the "King's Highway," even more distant. It connected Damascus in the north with the upper end of the Red Sea (at Elath) in the south.

In its origins, Jerusalem was the only one of the major cities of the ancient world that owed little or nothing, in location or later greatness, to established travel routes in land or sea. The trails for camel caravans, mules, or foot travelers that later passed Jerusalem, linking the Via Maris and the King's Highway, arose largely because of the growth of Jerusalem as center of rule and worship.

Even after it became the important City of David, the new center was for years relatively small, limited, and difficult to get to. But this did not lead to obscurity. On the contrary, Jerusalem survived repeated ravages, destructions, and long periods of ruin, arising ever again to win new and greater import in men's minds. Jerusalem, the City of David, became and remains an inseparable part of the history and culture of our world. Many a legend or folktale illustrates and embroiders this striking development.

> One of these, told long afterward, said that the site on which David built Jerusalem had been partly within the lands of the tribe of Judah, partly in those of Benjamin, so that the Temple when finally built stood half in Judah, half in Benjamin. This was not true, but it suggests the tribal claims that David sought to evade.

David was beyond doubt a genius of strategy — both military and political. He continued attacking until he had firm control of the rest of Palestine west of the Jordan River. Even his former hosts, the Philistines, ceased to be a serious threat. He drove deep into areas still held by Canaanite peoples who had lived there when Hebrew tribes began moving in from the desert. In these areas, David acquired attractive parcels of land which became his personal estates, much as Jerusalem had become his personally owned city. These crown lands brought revenue to his royal coffers. Thus David paid and enlarged his armies of professional fighters, something new among the children of Israel.

This warrior-king extended his sway, subduing the Ammonites beyond the Jordan and the Moabites beyond the Dead Sea as well as the Arameans in what is now Syria. A successful campaign in Edom made David master of all Trans-Jordan. By about 990 B.C.E., he either ruled outright or dominated a realm that would seem extensive even by modern standards in that part of the Middle East. And before he died, David's control reached all the way from the banks of the Euphrates River to the north, down to the Red Sea in the south. He dominated the areas that on a modern map would make up almost all of today's nations called Israel, Jordan, Lebanon, and also a great part of Syria.

From his new capital, Jerusalem, David exercised a fourfold rule: first, over his "private property," his city, estates, and royal enterprises; second, over the twin but merged kingdoms — Judah on the south, and Israel on the north; third, over conquered regions of non-Hebrew population, which he ran as if they were his own, not part of Judah-Israel; and finally, over subject lands nominally still ruled by their kings, but who nevertheless paid tribute to him.

Outside of these four categories remained the coastal wedge of the Phoenicians, or Sidonians. This region extended south to the great port of Tyre, its busy capital and shipping center. Hiram, the king there, was friendly and useful to David. Their interests coincided rather than conflicted.

David was thus the first really strong king of the Hebrews in Palestine. His predecessor, Saul, had been more the leader of a somewhat united people's militia than a real empire-building monarch on the Egyptian style. Saul's weak son, Esh-baal — called Ish-bosheth in the Bible book of II Samuel — had barely become king over the northern tribes of Israel when David, already at the head of Judah, had defeated and disposed of him, thus acquiring a double crown.

A map alone cannot show all the major changes wrought by David. Steadily and purposefully he altered relationships between himself and his Hebrew subjects in Judah-Israel. The land, before David was born, had been a loose confederation of tribes, led by elected "judges" or chieftains, assisted by councils of elders. Their positions were not hereditary, and their powers over their fellow tribesmen were limited. Tribal traditions and taboos provided much protection for the small farmers, orchardists, and handworkers who made up most of the population. The same leaders who held this limited civil authority in time of peace, commonly led the voluntary militia in time of war, or chose its officers.

King David in Jerusalem assembled increasing numbers of full-time military men, tax officials and treasurers, scribes and administrators, agents and envoys. No longer did he need to depend on citizen armies supplied on a quota basis by separate tribes. Nor did he have to solicit approval or supplies from judges or elders.

His new corps of officers and inspectors journeyed from Jerusalem throughout his lands, dependent on him for appointment and continuation in their positions. He would promote them, fire them, or even find ways to get rid of them altogether if they seriously offended him. David's Jerusalem-based "establishment" thus gathered taxes, ferreted out opposition, and maintained law and order — the King's law and order, to be sure. As a result, traditional tribal safeguards and protections were much weakened.

The pattern emerging under David was new in the history of the children of Israel in Palestine. But it was not new in the world around them, for it more and more resembled the absolute kingships that dominated Egypt. Jerusalem, though so far from navigable rivers or well-trod caravan routes, was becoming the Thebes of a semi-pharaoh, King David I. Until then the top leaders of the land had made their headquarters or capitals in their tribal home towns. But David had created his own city and citadel. He had placed in it his own offices and officers, his men at arms, storerooms and treasuries, his wives, concubines, harem attendants, children, nurses, cooks, cupbearers, and the rest.

Yet one aspect of the absolute monarchies of Egypt or Mesopotamia was still lacking. The center of exclusive royal rule had not yet become the exclusive center for approved religious worship in the realm. David moved in this direction also, with the imagination and enterprise that marked most of his efforts.

The traditional tabernacle camp may have looked like this when nomadic Hebrew tribes were moving from the desert into the land of Canaan. The banners mark the places of assembly of the twelve tribes of Israel. To the east are the standards of Issachar, Judah, and Zebulun. To the west: Manasseh, Ephraim, and Benjamin. South: Naphtali, Dan, and Asher. North: Gad, Reuben, and Simeon.

The most sacred object, to the Hebrew tribesmen, was neither an idol nor an image. It was not even fixed in one place. It was compact, small, and purposely portable. Known as *the Ark*, it was a small box fitted with handles for easy carrying by means of long poles. As a symbol, the Ark had been carried by the Hebrews into the Battle of Eben-Ezer, about 1050 B.C.E. The outcome was not only destruction by the Philistines of the traditional Hebrew ritual center of Shiloh, but the capture of the Ark. It reposed for a time in the Philistine city of Ashdod. Later recovered by the Hebrews, it was kept first at Beth-shemesh and later at Kiriath-jearim, near the border separating the tribal territory of Benjamin from the northern tribes.

Now with pomp and rejoicing, King David conveyed this historic Ark to his Jerusalem. He mustered a force of thirty thousand men to make that procession memorable. The Ark was carried in a new cart drawn by handsome oxen. David and all the male members of his family, including his many grown sons, accompanied it. Led by David, they danced, sang, and made joyful music with harps, lyres, cymbals, castanets, and tambourines. En route, David himself, clad in the priestly *ephod* or apron, sacrificed fat cattle to the Lord, whose Law and Covenant with the Children of Israel was symbolized by the traveling Ark.

At Jerusalem a suitable resting place had been prepared for the Ark. This was a fine tent or tabernacle, strictly a portable, temporary structure. Such tents for worship had been traditional with the Hebrews since their

Singing and dancing, David leads his people to bring the Ark to Jerusalem. Infant cherubs atop the carved Ark are a seventeenth century artist's misunderstanding of the Hebrew *cherubim* (winged lions.) Below the Ark lies a man, stricken when he touched it to steady it. None but the ordained priests might touch so sacred an object.

nomadic days, long before they entered Canaan-Palestine. Never had their tribal traditions included a fixed sanctuary built by men, or an established, immovable Temple. Their rites of worship were held in high places, often under the sky itself, or under some frail fabric shelter.

When at last the Ark stood in the tabernacle prepared for it at Jerusalem, King David himself led in making the burnt-offerings and prayers of thanks. Then to the assembled people, "both men and women," this priest-king gave loaves of bread, meat, and raisin cakes. Feasting and rejoicings followed, after which the people returned to their homes outside the city of their king.

Though this most sacred symbol of the worship of his people now rested in Jerusalem, David was not yet content. He spoke about it to his advisor, Nathan, today usually called a "prophet." David pointed to the palace he had built for himself of noble cedar wood from trees that grew in the mountains of Lebanon, in the land of his friend, King Hiram of Tyre. "Look," said David, "I live in a house of cedar wood, but God's Ark is kept under the curtains of a tent."

That night, we are told in the book of II Samuel, Nathan thought about David's obvious wish to build a Temple. The divine voice spoke to Nathan, telling him: "Say to David: Should you build me a house to live in? For I have not lived in a house since the day when I brought the Israelites out from Egypt, nor to this day. Rather, I have made a tent my dwelling place."

In fact, the voice concluded, "did I ever say to one of the leaders of Israel, 'Why have you not built me a house of cedar wood?' "

Clearly, the writer of II Samuel, setting down the story long after the first Temple had been built, regarded the traditional tabernacle as closer to the Lord's wish than the Temple. This, however, is not the only reason mentioned in the Bible why David did not build a Temple.

The other reason, as given in I Chronicles, is rather different: because David in all his warring "had shed much blood on the earth," the Lord would not allow him to become the builder of the house of God.

Yet that same book of the Bible tells that David made many preparations for the Temple, which had been long in existence when Chronicles was written. First came the site on which it would later rise. David one day went from his small city, which stood on the hill of Zion, and further north along the same ridge came to the elevation now called Mount Moriah. There, Ornan, a Jebusite and survivor of the people who had once held this region, was threshing wheat. As threshing floor he used a great rock, a natural outcropping on the hill.

David said Ornan, "Let me have the site of this threshing floor in order to build an altar to the Eternal." And he added, "You must take the full price for it." Ornan offered to give it to him, but David insisted that for this purpose he would not take without payment what belonged to another. The story in I Chronicles says that David finally paid 600 shekels of gold, but another version in the book of II Samuel speaks of only 50 shekels. In any case, David built an altar on the site, on which he offered sacrifices to the Eternal. It was an open altar, with no temple near by.

However, according to I Chronicles, David did gather materials to be used by his son in building a Temple later on. The king is said to have ordered all aliens in his kingdom to be called together. Those among them who had skill as stonemasons he put to work cutting building stones, no doubt from the abundant tan-golden limestone that lies around Jerusalem and provides the golden hue for which the city became famous. Other craftsmen, with ability as smiths, prepared iron from which to make nails for doors to the gates of a temple, and clamps for holding stones together in walls. David

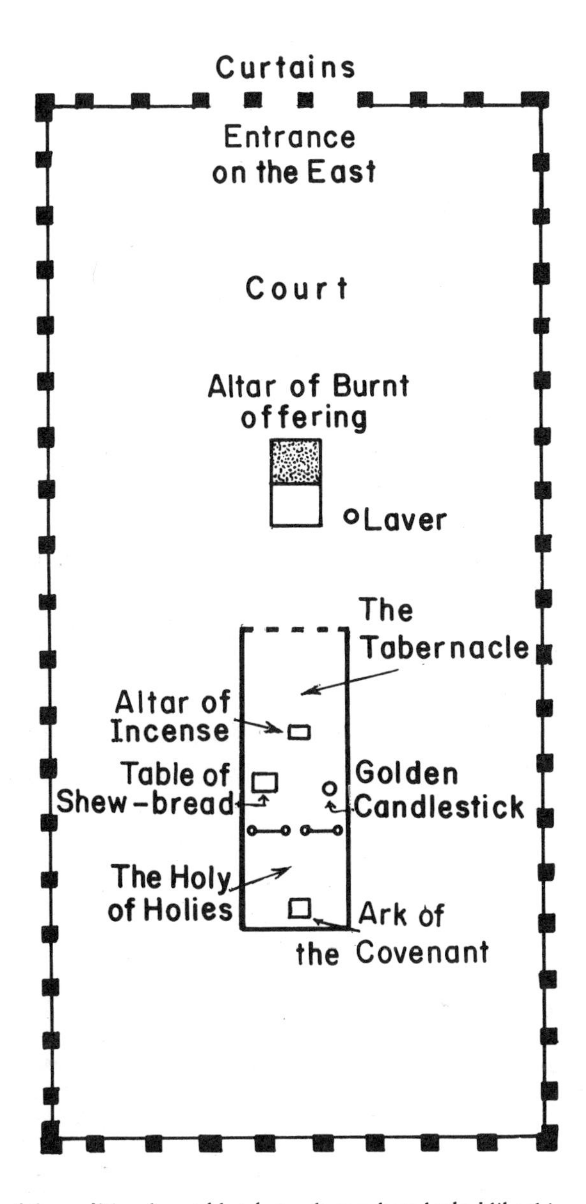

The ground plan of the traditional portable tabernacle may have looked like this.

also ordered the stockpiling of quantities of bronze and "innumerable" cedar trees from the forests of Lebanon. The Bible story says that David reflected, "Because . . . my son is young and inexperienced, and because the house which is to be built for the Eternal must be magnificent, far-famed, and glorious beyond compare . . . I must make preparations for it."

And indeed he had made ample preparations when at the age of seventy, he closed his restless eyes and died after a life that left a deep imprint on his people and all following history. I Chronicles is here concerned to show that the later building of the Temple was not only approved in principle, but actually prepared for, by David, a king whose prestige grew from decade to decade after his death.

Legends and myths crystallize around the memories of great men. The dynamic life of David of Jerusalem, the king who ruled from Zion, has accumulated many such fabulous evidences of his power to excite men's imaginations.

David was one day wandering through his domain, says a Jewish tale, when he began to climb the sloping sides of what he thought was a mountain. It was actually, however, a sleeping beast of monstrous size, the *Ray-em* or *Reëm*, which suddenly awoke and reared up. David found himself high in the air on its horns, and in danger of falling. Quickly he begged the Lord to rescue him, promising that if spared he would build a Temple 100 ells (375 feet) high, which was in fact the height of the *Ray-em*'s horns from the ground. Suddenly, a lion appeared, divinely sent. Awestruck by its majesty, the *Ray-em* knelt, and David safely descended. Thus originated his obligation to see that the Jerusalem Temple would be built.

A Moslem story tells how David, wishing to learn whether common people were content under his rule, disguised himself and went among them. He met a man (in reality an angel, in disguise) who replied to David's question, "Something is wrong. This David lives off the public treasury instead of earning his living by the labors of his own hands." David, impressed, begged Allah (God) to teach him a trade, and Archangel Gabriel was sent to train the King to make coats of mail, as an armorer. In his spare time the great King worked in his armory, and because no weapon could harm the wearer of one of his suits of mail, they were much in demand. Each working day David completed one such suit, which sold for 6000 gold dinars. His earnings he divided into three equal parts — one to support himself and his family, another for alms to give to the poor, and the third to buy materials for the Temple.

A Jewish legend pictures David as determined that the Temple must be built on pure, virgin soil untainted by human hands. He dug under the stone threshing floor, and went down, down, down to 2200 feet, finding no trace of previous human presence. At that level he struck something hard — a shard or fragment of ancient pottery, that by miraculous power could speak and so explain, "I did not lie here originally, but only since the earth was split in twain." (That was when the Lord gave the Law to Moses on Mount Sinai). "If you doubt," the shard continued, "look for yourself. Even now the great Deep, called Tehom, lies just beneath me."

David picked up the shard and—behold!—up rose the waters of Tehom, the Deep, to engulf him. David called out a great curse: "May suffocation slay anyone who remains silent, knowing the word that will halt this Tehom!" This forced the powerful spirit Ahitophel to speak that mystic word, thus halting the rise of Tehom, the Deep.

Variations of this tale appear in the Babylonian Talmud and other Jewish lore. Often it is linked to the great stone on which the Temple's most sacred chamber, the Holy of Holies, was said to have stood. This Tehom, the subterranean sea, was believed to remain from the days of the great Flood, survived by Noah and his Ark. As those floodwaters subsided, they drained back into the earth's interior, waiting.

One variation says that David, when threatened by Tehom, asked Ahitophel what to do, but got no reply, for that malign spirit wanted David to drown, so as to usurp his place as king. David then took a stone and on it engraved the so-called Tetragrammaton, the mystic and ineffable name of God, in form of the letters YHWH (now vocalized as Yahweh, or Jehovah.) This forced Ahitophel to tell David what to do, and so the Deep subsided again into the bowels of the earth. Ahitophel, however, in rage and spite, hung himself.

David's rule pushed his kingdom far in the direction of empire. He set up a dozen administrative districts, but these were quite different from the traditional regions of the twelve tribes, for they were run by the king's own officers.

Resistance to the King's demands showed itself even during his lifetime. About 978 B.C.E. a serious revolt broke out, led by one of his sons, Absalom, who had support not only from discontented elements in Israel to the north but also from Judah to the south. Forces loyal to David killed Absalom, but even after that the King felt compelled to make concessions to pacify leaders in his native Judah. Barely a year later, another revolt flared up in Israel, whose people now demanded treatment equal to that given the people of Judah, whom David was constantly suspected of favoring.

However, imaginations seem to triumph over memories. After David's death, the descendants of his subjects looked back with pride and longing to the power, the glory, and the prestige attained under his rule. The time came, too, during days that had become bitter or even intolerably hopeless, when prophets predicted the coming of a hero-savior, or *Messiah,* to the children of Israel. Such a Messiah would set them free from the heavy oppressions which they suffered, whether from their own native rulers or from alien conquerors or occupiers of the land. By the time of those dark days it had become inevitable that such prophecies should picture the Messiah as a direct descendant of the great king who had first established Jerusalem, the City of David.

The Messiah, it was foretold, would be of "the seed of David, son of Jesse" — the monarch who had ruled from the Mount of Zion and who had himself secured the site on Mount Moriah where, not along after he had ceased to live, rose the unforgettable Temple beyond time.

3

Solomon in All His Glory—and the Temple

(About 962–922 B.C.E.)

Solomon, who took and kept the throne after David, was not an eldest son. He had not even been regarded as the "heir apparent" until a short time before his aged father died. Solomon was in fact surprisingly young, when by successful scheming on his own and his mother's part he managed to make himself the next monarch. He was certainly less than twenty, and there are reasons to believe that he was even in his earliest "teens."

Solomon's mother, the beautiful Bathsheba, had not been *the* Queen in the royal city. She was one among many wives who passed through David's harem, though she had the advantage of being a special favorite during the last ten or fifteen years of his life. A dramatic and guilty romance had joined them. David, walking on his palace roof one hot day, caught sight of Bathsheba bathing. Struck by her beauty, he sent for her, though she was the wife of Uriah, one of David's warriors residing at Jerusalem. Keeping Bathsheba with him, David secretly ordered Uriah sent to certain death in battle. The King thus took first the wife, then the life, of one of his men.

Young Solomon and his mother Bathsheba went to great lengths to secure the kingship for him. The heir apparent had been Adonijah, an elder son of David's, by a wife married some time before Bathsheba. A move had already been made by Adonijah's supporters to designate him as the man to take the throne when aged David died. Bathsheba and Solomon were able, however, to outmaneuver Adonijah. Several allies helped them: Zadok, a priest ambitious to become high priest in place of Abiathar, David's man; Benaiah, who wanted the office of Joab, David's top general; and, not least in influence, Nathan, the royal advisor.

It was Nathan who had presided when Bathsheba's son had been given his "birth name" of Jedidiah, meaning "beloved of God." He is known to

Gustave Doré (1832-83) pictured men of Israel in the hills of Lebanon felling great cedar trees for the Temple and other royal buildings of their demanding monarch, Solomon. The trees were hauled to the coast, floated down the Mediterranean, dragged overland to Jerusalem, and finally to Mount Moriah, on which stood Solomon's palaces, courts, harems, and Temple.

history, however, by his "crown name" Shelomo, or Solomon, formed from the same root as *Shalom,* the word for "peace."

Solomon was not more than twelve to fifteen years of age when David, old and failing in health, was persuaded to consent that Solomon be anointed. Thus Bathsheba's son was established as the next-in-line for the throne, while his father was still alive.

When Adonijah heard what had happened, he was properly terrified, and rushed to the altar — probably the very same altar that David had built for sacrifices on Mount Moriah. So long as Adonijah clutched its "horns" or handles, he was assured of sanctuary. But he knew that his life was in danger.

David died, and Solomon was crowned. Believing himself safe now, Adonijah made a misstep. He asked to have for his wife Abishag of the tribe of Issachar, a beautiful young girl who had belonged to David in his final days. It was the custom that only he who succeeded to the kingship might inherit the harem of his predecessor. Solomon ordered Adonijah slain at once.

Solomon continued swiftly making a clean sweep of all real or suspected foes. He ousted Abiathar and installed Zadok as high priest. Here, as so often elsewhere in history, the monarch dominated the priesthood. Now Zadok, beholden to Solomon for his position, presided over sacrifices and rituals at the tabernacle in Jerusalem, and also handled the contributions collected for its support. Benaiah also took the place of Joab as chief of the armed forces.

Solomon went on, remolding his realm from top to bottom. His policies were quite different from those of David, the warrior and man of conquest. Solomon was an eminently peaceful potentate, preferring prestige, profits, and splendor to the clash of arms. David has been said to have ruled like a successful oriental sheik. Solomon now ruled like a combination of pharaoh and merchant prince. To do so, he had to tear up by the roots still more of the tribal traditions from the bedouin-like past of his subjects.

Since he considered a show of military might better than warfare, Solomon assembled an imposing striking force built around a new highly mobile weapon, designed for an early kind of *blitzkrieg* — the war chariot. David had used them little or not at all. Solomon had fifteen hundred built and manned by skilled drivers. He maintained some twelve thousand horses to draw his chariots. His elaborate stone stables for these steeds have been unearthed in Israel at Megiddo and elsewhere. They were finer than the housing for the poorer people and the state slaves who labored for the great King.

Solomon in fact became the great horsetrader of that ancient world. He bought horses mainly in Asia Minor, kept his own breeding farms, and sold the trained animals to Egypt or other neighboring countries. To Egypt, he also sent men to labor as slaves or servants. The Bible book of Deuteronomy, set down long after the end of Solomon's reign, contains a telltale commandment directed at kings. It is placed in the mouth of Moses: "He (the king) shall not multiply horses for himself, nor oblige the people to go back to Egypt in order that he may multiply horses." Memories of Solomon must have been behind that warning of a later date.

With Jerusalem as his improved and glorified capital, Solomon set up his own shipping and transport enterprises. Until recently it was widely believed that he developed the "King Solomon's mines" for copper near the southernmost end of the Negev desert, and worked them and their smelters with the labor of state slaves. He took taxes from caravans carrying goods across his land between Egypt and the Fertile Crescent countries, which for

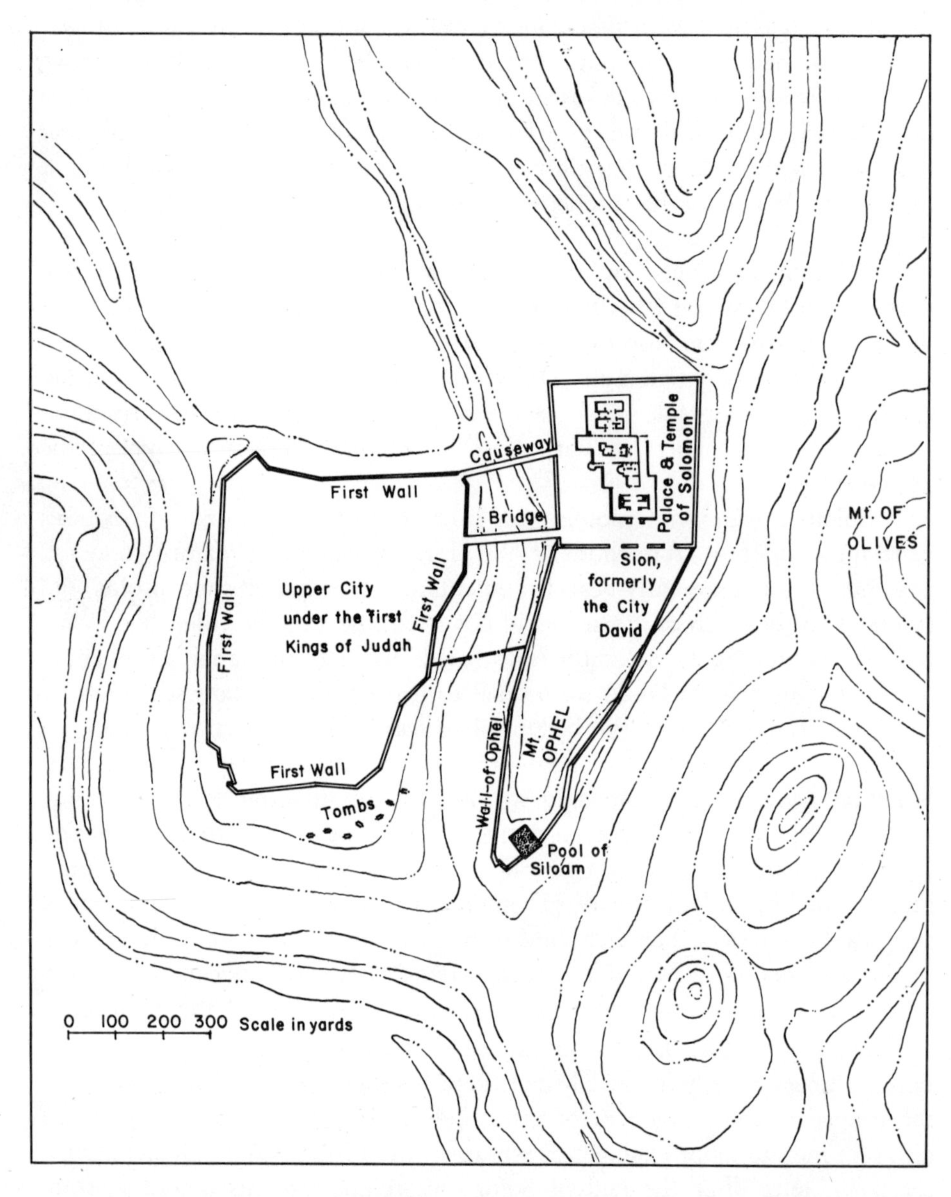

This map shows "Sion" or the city of David as a triangle pointing in a southerly direction. North of it is the enclave in which Solomon erected his royal buildings and the Temple. After Solomon's death the "Upper City" was developed under the first rulers of Judah.

the time being were not strong enough to endanger his rule. Slow donkies once had carried this overland traffic; now the relatively new camel caravans were under way, their half-wild beasts able to haul heavy loads twenty-five or thirty miles a day, day after day, under the most difficult conditions.

Solomon traded with Phoenicia, southeastern Asia Minor, and southern Arabia. The celebrated visit of the Queen of Sheba was made not so much to drink of his "wisdom," as to produce mutually beneficial trade pacts. Many of Solomon's profitable agreements with neighbor kings were sealed with the help of a royal marriage. So Solomon's harem grew, filled with daughters of kings or nobles, whose favor or toleration Solomon sought.

The treasure that flowed into his Jerusalem treasuries from commerce abroad and taxation at home did not long remain idle. Much of it went for materials and imported craftsmen, resulting in imposing new buildings that transformed Jerusalem and made the name Solomon a synonym for glory and luxury.

In his royal city, two well-defined valleys met in a great V. To the east lay the Kidron valley; to the west Hagai, meaning the valley. Much later it became known by the strange name of Tyropeon or "valley of the cheese-makers." The southern part of the ridge between them, known as Zion or Sion, was the site of David's city. Now Solomon went further north along this rising ridge, and toward the former stone threshing floor of Ornan, now an altar. Here he cleared an additional area, more or less level. It became the new and far grander City of Solomon, and its hill was called Mount Moriah.

Solomon built his palace, so much more elaborate than David's, on the western side, closer to Hagai Valley, than to the Kidron valley. Beside it, but further east, stood his great new throneroom and judgment hall. Still further east, and close to the slope down to the Kidron, rose the impressive Hall of Pillars. North of that hall, but separated from it by an open courtyard, appeared the House of the Forest of Lebanon. All this was built by the experts and with the materials supplied by Hiram, King of Tyre, who was even more useful to Solomon than he had been to David. And since Hiram was a canny trader, Solomon had to pledge to send him in payment much olive oil, grain, and other products that the Phoenicians wanted. These payments were raised by taxes-in-kind on Solomon's subjects, who still were mostly farmers, stock-raisers, and orchardists. The luxury-loving monarch on Mount Moriah thus drained his people of large amounts of food, flocks, and fibers.

Even more burdensome to them was another kind of royal levy. This was the draft of labor, sometimes called the *corvee.* State slaves had toiled on many projects during the last years of David's reign, and continued to do so under Solomon, but his commercial, industrial, and building enterprises demanded more and ever more labor. It was drawn, by royal decree, from the villages and countrysides of his own kingdom. In great and unwilling labor battalions, the children of Israel were marched off — not by some pharaoh but by their own king — to labor in the hills and highlands of Lebanon, hewing and hauling great cedars for beams and columns. They

worked by a rotating plan: a month of hard toil for his majesty, then two or three months off to tend their fields and flocks at home, if they had any. The scale was great, considering the size of the kingdom. It was as if in the modern United States six to seven million citizens were to be drafted for work in the forests of Canada!

To carry out all these systematic innovations, Solomon re-districted his kingdom. The new boundaries differed even more than the old from the former tribal territories. The districts quite ruthlessly cut across traditional relationships. The administrators were Solomon's own viceroys or prefects, owing obedience only to him. At least two were among his many sons-in-law. All were part of his "establishment." These district-rulers gathered taxes to send to Jerusalem, and oversaw the drafts of manpower for the King's purposes.

One officer found useful by Solomon was the able Jeroboam of Ephraim, one of the tribes of Israel, the northern section of the kingdom. He was placed in charge of the labor draft from the important tribes of Ephraim and Manasseh comprising the tribal group called "the house of Joseph." While Jeroboam was traveling in this part of the land he encountered a spokesman for the growing popular resentment against Solomon's high-handed policies.

This prophet, or "agitator," was Ahijah, from Shiloh, the shrine city in the land of the tribe of Ephraim. He told Jeroboam that the Lord would "tear the kingdom from the hand of Solomon" after the great King's death. According to the story in the Bible, Solomon had built for his many foreign wives and harem women, altars or shrines for the worship of their deities. These included the Ammonites' Milcom, the Moabites' Chemosh, and the Sidonians' godess Astarte, called Astoreth by the Hebrews. Apparently Solomon himself had joined in worshiping these alien idols, and in punishment divine vengeance would leave his son and heir with only Judah to rule. (By this time Judah included also the tribal areas of Benjamin.)

The remaining ten tribes — later known as the kingdom of Israel — would be given to Jeroboam, said Ahijah. Thus what was lost to the dynasty of David and Solomon would pass into the hands of Jeroboam, the future king.

Informers perhaps carried word of this meeting between Ahijah and Jeroboam to the palace on Mount Moriah. Solomon issued an order to slay Jeroboam, who managed however to escape to Egypt. There he took refuge with Shishak, a new, more aggressive ruler who had unseated the previous weak pharaoh, father of Solomon's Egyptian wife. Pharaoh Shishak saw in Jeroboam a pawn he might possibly use later against King Solomon of Jerusalem.

These and related events indicate that all was not wisdom, glory, and peace during the final phases of the forty-year rule of Solomon, in spite of what many admiring folktales suggest. On the outskirts of his realm serious setbacks took place. He lost the allegiance of Edom, the Damascus (Syrian) kingdom, and other lands that David had subdued. Solomon's wealth, though great, lagged behind his expenditures. Unable to raise funds to meet his debts to Hiram, Solomon was forced to turn over to him portions of land, complete with their inhabitants, one encompassing as much as twenty towns! Hiram, however, was not satisfied that even this made a sufficient payment.

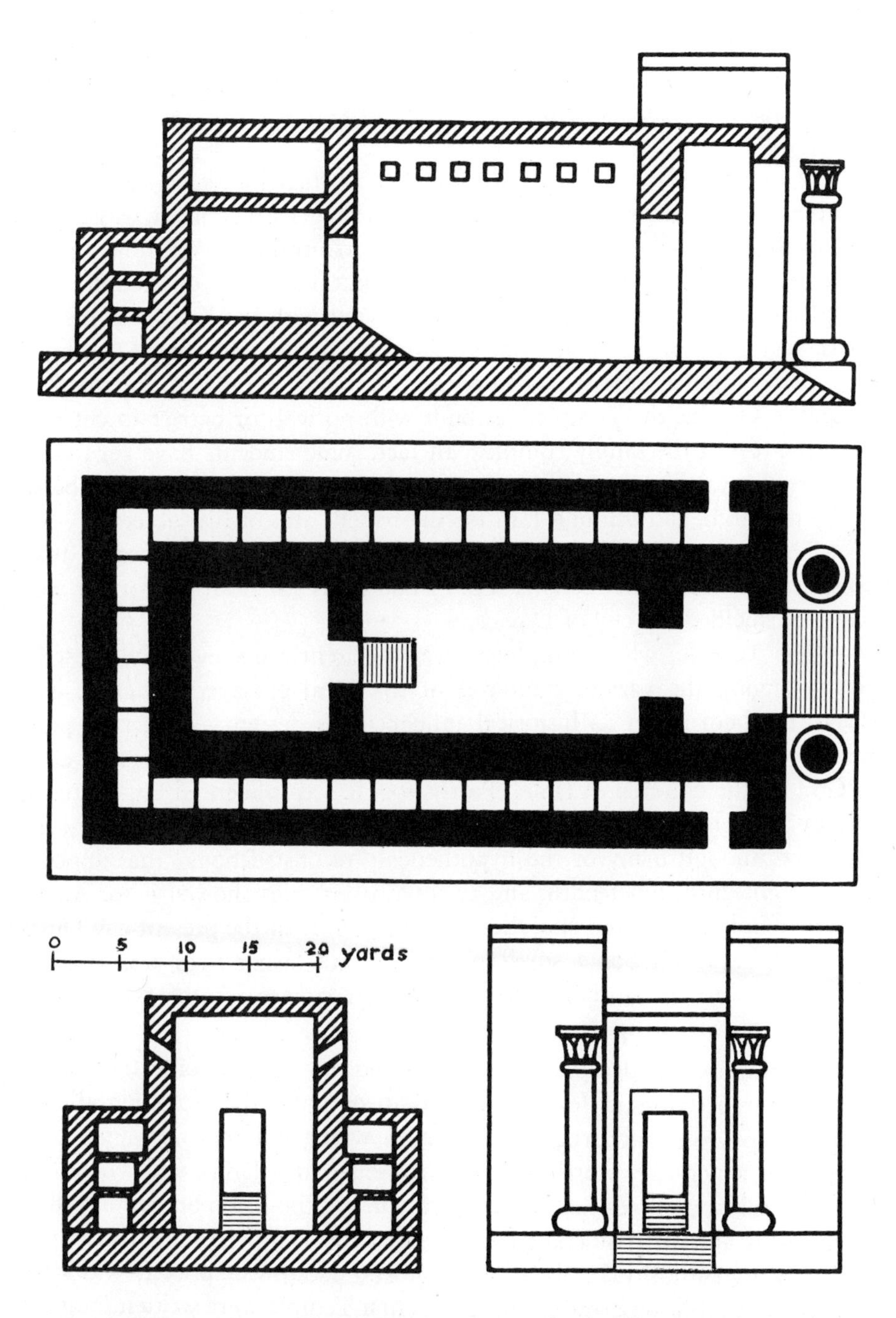

Four views of Solomon's Temple, based on C. Watzinger's *Denkmaler Palastinas.* Top: Lengthwise cross section, as if seen from the south. Middle: Ground plan, as if from above. Bottom left: Cross section, as if from the front. Bottom right: Main entrance, with free-standing pillars, Jachin and Boaz.

Solomon thus appears to have had flawed and faulty wisdom. Yet he did not lack a clear and stubborn policy — to form in his land a full-fledged absolute monarchy on the Egyptian model. The religious control essential to that Egyptian pattern had been lacking. To supply it, Solomon early undertook his greatest, most memorable building project. Next to his own palace complex, and in fact as part of it, he erected the first permanent central religious sanctuary for the once-nomadic children of Israel, the sanctuary that became the Temple beyond time.

Solomon had been king only four years when he began to build the Temple, and seven years were taken up with its construction. It was used as the royally-ordained place of sacrifice and worship during the final twenty-eight or twenty-nine years of his reign. Its location and its dedication, when completed, showed how closely it was connected with the King and his concerns. Just north of his palace, not far from his harem and other royal buildings, a rectangular area was cleared and elevated slightly above the level around it. On this the Temple was built with no wall or barrier to cut it off from the rest of the kingly complex. In fact, some students have regarded it as a sort of royal chapel, in which sacrifices and rites were conducted on behalf of the monarch, and through him for the benefit also of his subjects.

The protective walls of the city had been moved northward to make possible these new constructions. They stood fairly far from the former walls that had shielded the city of David.

The Temple, when completed, was apparently not even the most imposing among the various buildings of the royal enclave, though it overshadowed them all in its historical influence. Its design was derived partly from the tentlike tabernacle which till then had been the traditional abode of God for the children of Israel. Partly, too, it was influenced by sanctuaries already built by Canaanite and Syrian neighbors. It was neither large nor elaborate, though many of the hypothetical "reconstructions" that appeared in the eighteenth, nineteenth, and twentieth centuries showed it so. Among the two hundred thousand churches and synagogues in the present-day United States, probably all but a small percentage are larger than was this first Temple on Mount Moriah — larger, whether square feet of floor area or cubic feet of interior space are measured.

During its first decades, this Temple did not even become the sole site for religious activities in Jerusalem. It has been noted that Solomon allowed, and perhaps even encouraged, his foreign wives and their servants to use chapels in which they worshiped gods of their native lands, and where Solomon himself sometimes took part. It was among the common people subject to the King and his aristocratic courtiers that the Temple gained its exclusive and growing authority. Its rise to supreme and nationwide priority was a long process. The biblical narratives about this first Temple were written long after it was completed. They reflect many attitudes that evolved in the intervening years. Jerusalem, when Solomon began to build the Temple, was relatively new as the shrine center for the children of Israel.

The first sanctuary for the worship of the God of the Hebrews had been a simple tabernacle among oak trees at Moreh, near a site today called Balata, close to Nablus, but then known as Schechem. It was Schechem that Joshua had made his capital and there he divided among the Hebrew tribes the territories they had won during the conquest of Canaan under his leadership. Later, and for nine or ten generations ending about 1050 B.C.E., the Ark itself had been kept at Shiloh, midway between Schechem and Bethel. Then in a great battle won by the Philistines in 1050, Shiloh had been destroyed and the Ark itself captured. The Philistines held it for about seven months. Then it was regained by the people of Israel and kept first at Beth-Shemesh in Judah, later at Kiriath-jearim from which David brought it to Jerusalem.

That Ark, as the abode of divine law, retained the supreme place of honor in the new Temple. The architects borrowed from the King of Tyre had made a simple but practical plan. The Temple faced east, toward the rising sun. It was built on an ascending pattern. First the steps up to the platform on which it stood, then at the main entrance further steps led into a small vestibule or enclosed porch, called in Hebrew the *ulam.* Next came a main hall or holy chamber, the *hekal.* And finally, past another short flight of steps and a wall, a small unlit chamber, the Holy of Holies, or *debir.* There, at the western or inmost end of the interior was sheltered the sacred Ark.

It was not accidental that a series of ascents led from the level of worldly splendor to the supreme sanctity within, or that the Temple was erected on a hill or mount. In their worship the children of Israel had long associated holiness with high places. The Law itself had been given to Moses on Mount Sinai.

This tradition has lived on, as in the words of Psalm 121, which in modern language, asks and answers:

> I raise my eyes to the hills;
> From where does my help come?
> My help comes from the Lord.

Or Psalm 123, which addresses the Lord:

> Toward you I raise my eyes,
> O you, who dwells in the heavens!

These psalms, among many others, were in fact great worship chants, known as Songs of Ascents, performed chorally by Temple priests and musicians — for the rites there were musical as well as sacrificial.

In spite of this emphasis on heights, Solomon's Temple was not itself lofty. There is no basis for reconstructions which portray it with a tall tower.

Its maximum height can hardly have exceeded 50 feet. Even this may have made it one of the tallest buildings in the land, for the children of Israel were not yet advanced in construction.

In other dimensions, the Temple framework was also rather small: about 33 feet in width, and 115 feet from front to rear. The floor area of the three interior chambers totaled between 3500 and 4000 square feet, no more; and most of this was in the central *hekal.* How could large numbers of worshipers gather in so small a building? They did not. It was never planned or used as a place for worshipers to congregate, or even as a building to house priests in numbers. It was the house for the Lord, the one God, and for the appropriate objects needed in the rites to glorify and worship him. Priests entered it only as required by those rites. The actual animal sacrifices took place in front of, not inside, the Temple.

To provide storage and repair space for its ritual tasks, the Temple had on three sides a belt or jacket made up of triple levels of small stone cells or rooms, about twenty-five or thirty of them in each level. The cells were low, perhaps not over 8 feet high, and most were between 8 and 12 feet long, with none over 15 feet. Together they extended about 30 feet up the sides and rear of the main Temple building. In these cells were stored priests' garments, utensils, oil for the Temple lamps, tools, ritual objects, and the Temple funds, or treasury, as well as supplies of nonperishable foods.

Stone and cedar wood were the two great building materials used throughout. The stone was quarried near Jerusalem and hewn into shape at the quarries, in order that the Temple site itself should not be profaned by such menial labors. The walls were formed of these stone blocks, reenforced by sturdy wooden beams. They supported stout, finely carved horizontal beams which carried the planked ceiling and roof.

The finest woodworking obtainable was used to make the interiors impressive. Skilled carpenters from Tyre, with local craftsmen working under their direction, had shaped the interior panels and doors. The doors of the main front portal were more than 20 feet high. They opened on the *ulam* vestibule which was an estimated 33 feet from side to side and 17 feet from front to back.

The door from *ulam* to *hekal* was formed from fir and olive woods. The *hekal* itself, some 33 feet wide and 66 long, was panelled in fragrant cedar carved into shapes of flowers, palm trees, and cherubim.

The *debir*, or most holy place, at the far end, was doubly screened, first by a fine veil of dyed fabrics, then by a wall with a door kept shut except at rare intervals.

That *debir* itself was cube-shaped, about 33 feet on each side. In its center stood the ancient "Ark of the Law of Yahweh." As if to guard it, on either side were placed the figures of two cherubim made of olive wood, overlaid with gold. Each had a height and a wingspan of about 16 feet. Since they were placed so their inside wingtips met over the Ark, their outside wingtips reached the walls of the room.

Cherubim is the Hebrew plural of the word for *cherub.* In the days of Solomon, this did not mean a cute, fat-cheeked cupid or child angel. That notion came from the later images of the love-god of the Greeks. The Temple's cherubim were much like the Egyptian figures which also joined human

CROSS-SECTION OF SOLOMON'S TEMPLE.

1. The Holy of Holies.
2. The Holy Place.
3. The vestibule.
4. The chambers.
5. The Jachin and Boaz.
6. The ark.
7. The altar of incense.
8. The table of shewbread.
9. The windows
10. The priests' court.
11. The Altar.
12. The people's court.
13. The pro-pylon.

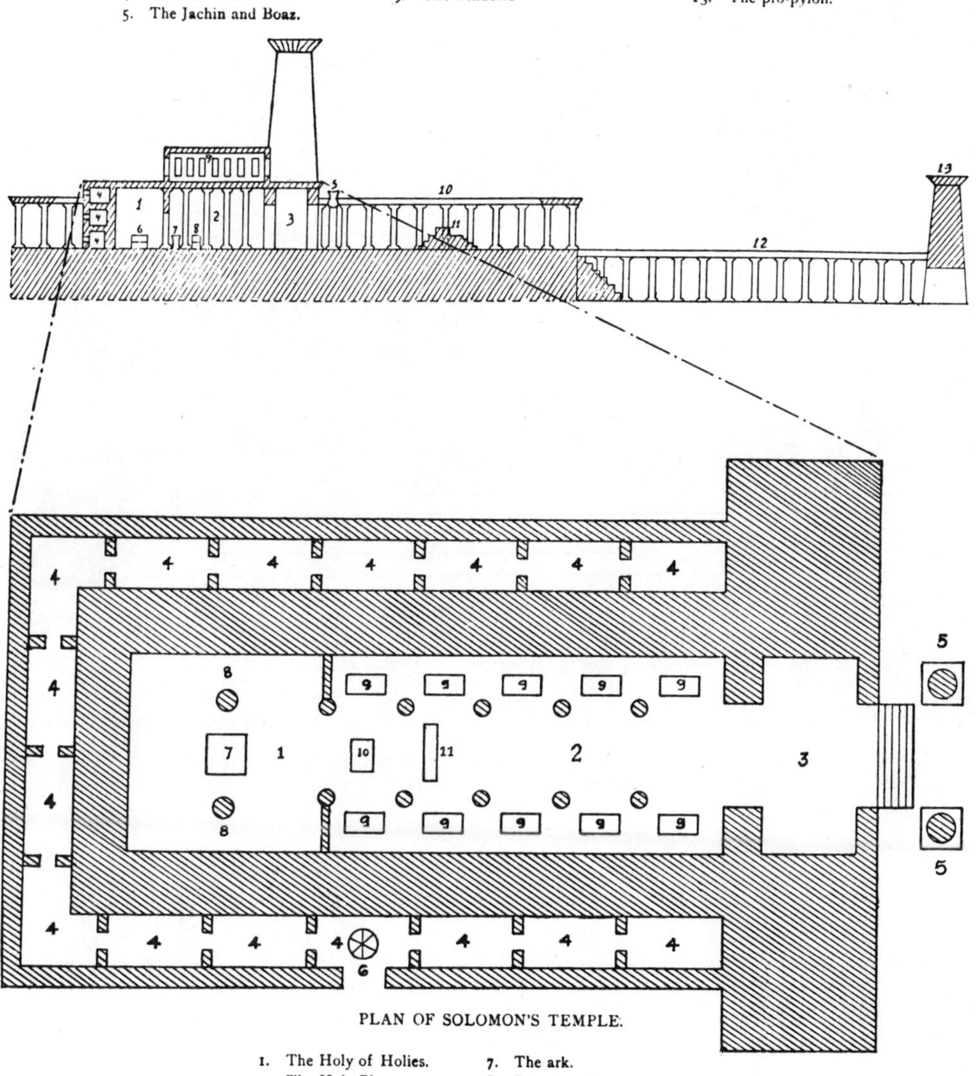

PLAN OF SOLOMON'S TEMPLE.

1. The Holy of Holies.
2. The Holy Place.
3. The vestibule.
4. The chambers.
5. Jachin and Boaz.
6. The winding staircase.
7. The ark.
8. The cherubim.
9. The tables for the candlesticks.
10. The altar of incense.
11. The table of shewbread.

The floor plan of *Solomon's Temple* was published in 1902. This plan, like others that differ from it in various details, is conjectural in many respects. It does, however, give a good guide to the major features of the Temple.

heads to lion bodies, as in the famous Sphinx — which however lacked wings. Cherubim symbolized divine power and majesty. Dieties were often imagined, or even pictured, as being carried or upheld by them. Influenced by the neighboring conceptions, the children of Israel also imagined Yahweh as enthroned on such a cherub, or even as standing on a golden bull.

Excavations in Palestine and nearby areas have revealed the images of

This reproduction of a Charles Chipiez reconstruction shows clearly the altar for burnt offerings, the stairs leading to its summit, and the entrance to the Temple with the bronze columns (Jachin and Boaz) on either side.

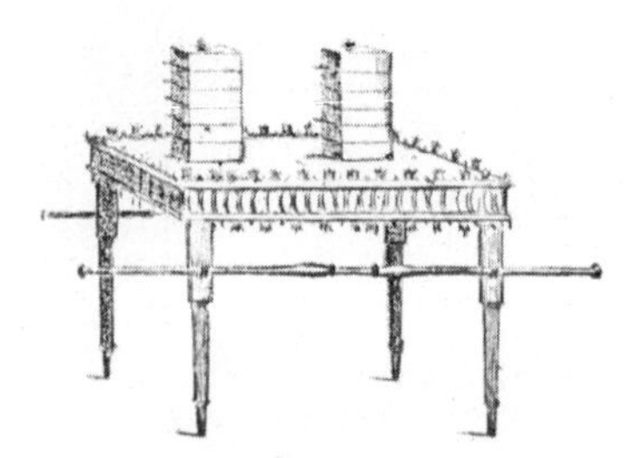

Within the Sanctuary stood the metal table bearing the sacred presence bread, or shew-bread, reserved for the ordained priests. Right: The seven-branched candelabrum, or *Menorah,* long identified with Solomon's Temple, was actually a later development, but was well-known by the days of Herod's Temple: It now appears on the shield of the nation of Israel.

human kings on thrones upborne by cherubim. In the Holy of Holies of the Temple of Solomon, the Ark itself served as a kind of throne or "mercy-seat" for the one God. And the cherubim here served as the supporters and upholders of this divine seat, reserved solely for the invisible God.

In the book of II Samuel, King David sings a hymn of joy on being rescued from his enemies. It has been identified as a very old one, from a period prior to most of the writing in the Bible, and it includes this: "I . . . called to my God for aid. He . . . heard my voice . . . down he came . . . He rode on the flying cherubim, and swooped with the wings of the wind. . . ."

Thus we see that the figures of the cherubim, here and in many other

Another nineteenth century scholar, Calmet, pictured in this way the bronze altar for burnt offerings. Sacrificial animals were led up the sloping ramp to the summit where the rites were performed. At right is the altar for incense offerings as Calmet envisioned it. It was kept within the Sanctuary and carried by means of the poles along the sides.

places in the Temple interior, were not *idols.* They were traditional symbols of divine power and glory.

Immediately in front of the Temple, and flanking its main entrance, were two free-standing columns of bronze, about 6 feet in diameter and 30 feet high. Their shafts were topped by massive capitals carved to suggest lilies or lotuses, garlanded with pomegranates. The importance of these columns is revealed by the fact that they had names: *Jachin*, on the north signifies "establish," *Boaz,* on the south indicates "power." Did the twin columns suggest that by his power Solomon had established this sanctuary? Today scholars can only guess.

These and other great bronze castings for the Temple were made by a wonderful craftsman named Hiram — not the King of Tyre, but the son of

This elaborate reconstruction of the interior of the Temple of Solomon was offered by Charles Chipiez, a French scholar of the nineteenth century. Here we look westward toward the Holy of Holies.

a Tyrian father and a Hebrew mother of the tribe of Naphtali. Brazen castings so massive show that metal technology was advanced in the era of Solomon, copper king of the ancient world. These columns remained standing during more than 365 years, till King Nebu-chadnezzar, when he took Jerusalem, had them cut down and carried off.

Famous, too, was the Temple's interior altar used for offerings of incense. It was plated with gold over a wooden frame. A fine metal table, probably also overlaid with gold, was provided for the sacred presence-bread, or "shewbread," which only the priests might eat. Five golden candelabras stood inside toward the right, and another five toward the left. The *menorah* or seven-branched candelabrum was a later development.

Many utensils and tools of bronze or gold were at hand for the Temple's daily rituals of sacrifice and worship. The most impressive single objects, however, stood in the court in front of the Temple. There, either next to or perhaps even on the great Rock, was erected a brazen altar, some 16 feet high by 33 feet long and wide. To reach it for the making of burnt offerings, priests ascended a ramp or stairway. And on the top, to elevate them still higher, stood a bronze platform, nearly 5 feet tall and more than 8 feet long and wide.

Not far away stood a huge basin called "the Brazen Sea." It was a water-bowl more than 16 feet in diameter and about 8 feet high, upheld by a dozen bronze oxen, placed in groups of three facing east, north, west, and south. Total capacity has been estimated at between 10,000 and 16,000 gallons. This water was used for purification and cleansing in the bloody rituals of sacrifice. The Brazen Sea survived a long time. Nearly two hundred

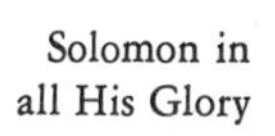

Sacrificial animals were taken up the imposing stairway to the great bronze altar for burnt offerings, in front of the main entrance to the Sanctuary. At right is a great wheeled laver, or portable water basin, for purification purposes. At upper left, the Brazen Sea, supported by its dozen metal oxen. Reconstruction by the nineteenth century scholar Mangeant.

years after Hiram first cast it, a king of Judah had its bowl shifted onto a mere stone base, so that he might use the metal forming the dozen bulls to help pay tribute he then owed to the King of Nineveh.

During the constant sacrifices, cleansing waters were needed at various places at the Temple. They were moved by means of ten rolling "lavers," looking much like bronze teacarts, all richly ornamented.

To make all these major metal castings, Hiram had to work far from the Temple site, beside the Jordan River. There he had suitable clay for molds and plenty of water too. Transporting all these castings, cedar beams, and imported stonework up to Jerusalem and assembling them there required staggering amounts of human labor. And there was the vast toil of felling the great trees in the mountains of Lebanon, dragging them to the coast, floating them south, landing them again, and hauling the wood up to Jerusalem. Human muscles performed these giant tasks, with some help from oxen. The toilers were largely conscripted or even slave labor. So the Solomonic structures — the palaces, halls, stables, fortifications, and the new national sanctuary or Temple — required enormous outpouring of wealth, goods, and sweat.

That was the grim side of the coin. The other is the shining image that passed into future legend and folklore: the monarch of unparalleled wisdom, power, and even piety. For had he not built this first Temple, and did not its glory transcend time itself?

4

Dedication of the Temple—and Some Later Legends

(about 950 B.C.E.)

The Bible gives a vivid picture of the dedication of the completed Temple. Though written many centuries after the event, it shows the importance of this first permanent sanctuary for the worship of Yahweh, the one god of the Hebrews.

The time chosen was the feast of the year's seventh lunar month, called *Ethanim.* Assembled at Mount Moriah were tribal elders, judges, magistrates, and leaders, as well as the royal family, courtiers, officials, officers of the military, and the priesthood that was to preside at the new Temple.

First came the installation in the Holy of Holies of the sacred Ark containing "the two tablets of the Law which Moses had placed there . . . when the Lord made a covenant with Israel at the time they came out of . . . Egypt." Under the outspread wings of the guardian cherubim, the Ark and its two long carrying poles seemed hidden from sight.

As the priests left the Holy of Holies, the Bible tells, a mist arose out of that chamber and filled the entire Temple. This was the "glory of the Lord" made visible, and it was so thick that the priests were unable to perform rituals within the Temple itself while it lasted.

Then Solomon, acting both as king of the people and chief of all the priests, faced the altar and spoke. He recalled the Lord's preference for the obscurity symbolized by heavy mist and darkness: "The Lord established the sun in the heavens, but he himself said that he would dwell in thick darkness."

Facing the spectators, Solomon declared this Temple to be the realization of the divine decision that it should be built, not by David, but by the son of David, ". . . and I have built the house for the name of the Lord, the God of Israel. . . ." The authors of this part of the Bible thus stressed that the Temple was not to contain or limit their God. It was merely a house for "the name of the Lord," or sometimes a house called "by the name of the Lord." In Solomon's mouth they placed this explicit question and reply:

> "But will God indeed dwell on the earth? Behold the heaven and the heaven of heavens cannot contain thee; how much less this house that I have builded."

Solomon then begged the Lord from on high to look day and night toward the Temple, so as to hear "the prayer that your servant shall pray toward this place." (Solomon being that "servant"). Also, to hear "your people Israel when they shall pray toward this place . . . Yes, hear it in the heavens, your dwelling place; and when you hear, forgive."

Other words in this prayer refer to calamities that occurred long after Solomon's time: "forgive your people . . . grant them compassion in the eyes of those who have carried them (away) as captives. . . ."

After the prayer, Solomon blessed the assembly. Then he and all present offered sacrifices. In addition he made a special "thank-offering sacrifice" of twenty-two thousand oxen and a hundred and twenty thousand sheep! Even the great brazen altar did not suffice for these sacrifices, and that day it was necessary to make offerings also elsewhere in the Temple court.

Great feasting and festivities followed for a full week afterward. Only on the eighth day did Solomon dismiss his guests, and they went home "joyful and glad of heart. . . ."

Today most of us regard as barbaric and ugly the animal sacrifices at this and other temples in the ancient world. Such rites were common in the "civilized" societies in Solomon's time and long afterward. Centralized animal sacrifice was, in fact, an advance over human sacrifice which was practiced in many places then, and indeed far later than that. The ritual sacrifice of humans was not so much a part of very primitive and backward cultures, as of more "advanced" societies that were rigid, harsh, and repressive. For example, the Aztec civilization in what is now Mexico.

First the Hebrews had banned the killing or maiming of human beings as a means of wiping out guilt or winning divine favors for the survivors. Then they had regulated animal sacrifice so that it was not wanton nor accompanied by orgies or frenzies in which worshipers behaved in ways that were "beastly."

The role of the Temple in the following centuries needs to be made clear. Today a synagogue, mosque, or church may be located wherever its worshipers live or visit. The Temple at Jerusalem became, during the later reign of the king known as Josiah, the only place where according to the priests and the monarch acceptable sacrifices might be made to the one God of Israel. Josiah reigned about three centuries after Solomon. Thus about ten generations followed one another before the Jerusalem Temple attained the sole and exclusive monopoly in the rendering of approved sacrifices. From that time on, the individual worshiper brought to the Temple the animals for sacrifice, but only the ordained priests might complete the prescribed rites. Membership in the influential priesthood was restricted. Strict rules were set down as to the ancestry, age, and even physical condition of those who might be designated priests.

While the Temple of Solomon gained fame and following, the older sanctuaries and worship sites in Palestine retained some of their former followers. But more and more, despite upheavals and setbacks, the Temple on Mount Moriah was to gain precedence among the children of Israel and all their descendants, both within and outside of Palestine itself.

David, and to an even greater extent Solomon, made the priests a part of their royal establishments. The result was that the rites of the Temple helped strengthen the authority of the monarch. However, in time a more popular form of worship and religious activity emerged from the daily lives and needs of the people. Its spokesmen were bold, persuasive, and persistent men today known as *prophets.* They were not soothsayers or clairvoyants, as the name "prophet" might suggest. Rather, they were protestors, warners, denouncers, and agitators. They were concerned with foreign policy, with social justice, and with urgent problems of this earth. The story of the Temple as an enduring institution and as a great aspiration needs also to refer to these non-Temple or even anti-Temple voices sometimes heard among the people later known as Jews.

What of the population that lived outside Jerusalem? The Temple touched their lives, also. They visited it, for it became the destination of the great pilgrimage festivals and holidays which had originated even before the building of the Temple. These holidays arose from the annual cycle of important events in the lives of people dependent on agriculture and animal husbandry for their well-being.

First in the year came a spring or planting festival. Called *Pesach* (Passover) it commemorated the liberation of the children of Israel from their bondage under the Egyptian pharaohs and taskmasters. It took place on the fourteenth day of the seventh lunar month, called *Nisan*, and continued during eight days. It led later to the Christian Easter.

Then, just fifty-one days after Passover came the Shavuoth, or Pentecost. It usually fell on the sixth or seventh day of the ninth lunar month, called *Sivan.* Originally it had been a vintage festival.

The third holiday for pilgrimages to the Temple was *Succoth*, festival of tabernacles or booths, a true harvest Thanksgiving, celebrated from the fifteenth to the twenty-second of the month of *Tishri*, equivalent to our September or October. The most solemn holy days of the Jewish religion today, the *Rosh Hashana*, or New Year, and the *Yom Kippur*, or Day of Atonement, are observed in the month of *Tishri*. They were not, however, pilgrimage occasions to the Temple on Mount Moriah.

Myths and folklore cluster thickly around the Temple. Again and again they are linked to the idea that peace, and only peace, made pos-

The Temple courtyard during a solemn rite is imagined in this old engraving. This was the "Great Hosannah" of the eighth day of *Succoth,* when ordinary worshipers were admitted to the courtyard usually reserved for the priests. Bearing palm branches, citrons, and eshrogs (a fruit), they marched around the altar, exclaiming *hosh i'ah na,* meaning "Save Now!" (The Greek form: Hosannah.) At lower left: the Bronze Sea, upheld by brazen oxen. At right: one of the temporary booths erected for the Succoth harvest festival. Both right and left: ten wheeled "lavers" full of purifying water. Behind the altar: the Temple portal, flanked by the twin columns, Jachin and Boaz.

sible the completion of this first Temple. Solomon is said, in Jewish legends, to have been divinely warned to use no iron in the building of "the house of my peace." Iron was, after all, warlike, a substance associated with weapons and armor, with bloodshed and killing. At least it became so later, for in Solomon's day bronze was used for both building tools and weapons.

A thousand years later the Romans under Titus destroyed a great Temple on Mount Moriah, and thereafter arose the Jewish legend that since iron was the metal of Rome, Solomon had been divinely instructed to exclude it from the building of his Temple.

But how could one construct the Temple without iron tools? Solomon had assembled twenty thousand laborers and their overseers. They waited while the great King consulted Shimei the Doctor, his fabulous advisor, who prescribed the use of a mysterious something called the *Shamir*. It had been created by the Lord on the evening of the very first Sabbath. Moses had employed it to inscribe the Law in the form of the Ten Commandments on the stone tablets before he brought them down from Mount Sinai. But where now was the *Shamir*?

"Its location is known to no man," Doctor Shimei admitted. Solomon, however, was strangely wise, and knew the speech of the beasts. He consulted many animals, birds, and even insects. Then with his chief general, Benaiah, he sought out the nest of a sea eagle. While the mother was away from the nest, Benaiah covered it with a strong glass bell. The mother eagle, returning, found that neither with beak nor claws could she break through to her young. Giving a great cry, she flew high and vanished into the distance.

A full day later, she returned, and swooped down to her nest. She held a dark object firmly in her beak. She set the object down on the glass bell, and it shattered instantly. It was the *Shamir* at work.

"Where did you find it?" demanded Solomon. The eagle took her nest and young, then guided Solomon and his men to the Mount of the Sleepers. There they found quantities of the *Shamir*, little things, small as a grain of cereal. Some tale-spinners have called the *Shamir* a worm, others an insect, others a plant, and still others just "a creature." The early rabbis seem to have regarded it more as a form or center of sheer energy than as an object.

The stone masons for the Temple learned that they need only mark a line on the hardest rock, place a *Shamir* on that line, and — behold! — the rock was split, clean and polished where it was cleft. Thus did the tiny *Shamir* make it possible to build the great Temple without the use of warlike iron, the metal of hated Rome, a power which had not yet appeared in history.

The *Shamir* idea, like many another kind of magic or wizardry, seems to have come first from Persia, but traveled far, even appearing in Old English as the worm *Thumare.* Its potency was said to be so great that the men who used it had to shield themselves by wrapping the *Shamir* in wool and placing it within a leaden guard-case lined with flour of linseed. So much akin to nuclear energy may the *Shamir* seem to us in the twentieth century that we may wonder whether it was truly more innocent for men than warlike iron.

The trees on Mount Moriah figure in Arab legends that tell how Solomon's first efforts to erect the Temple were mysteriously blocked.

Foundations would be built, only to be destroyed by unseen hands. Solomon ferreted out the cause at last: hostile spirits had cast on the project an Evil Eye, a curse then as now much feared in the East.

Solomon thereupon planted among the many olive and cypress trees on Mount Moriah also nettle-trees, which had miraculous power to ward off the Evil Eye. The nettle-trees of Moriah became famous, and two thousand years and more after Solomon and all his glory had vanished from earth, Arabs still plucked nettles there and from them made good luck charms. Most effective, they believed, were those picked after the twenty-seventh of *Ramadan*, the Moslem month of fasting.

In both Jewish and Moslem tales Solomon often appears as a great wizard or enchanter. He is credited with enslaving *genii*, or *djinns*, potent demons, to erect the Temple with fantastic speed and splendor. Many of these tales resemble the *Arabian Nights*. Solomon could master these demons, for he knew the Unutterable Name of God. Among the princes of darkness he is said to have bent to his will were Beelzebub and Asmodeus.

A Jewish legend tells how the massive Brazen Sea was installed. No human hand strained to move it. Solomon, having given his dread and secret commands, sat high and stern on his judgment-throne. At the appointed time, in plodded the twelve bronze oxen bearing the great bowl on their backs. Still supporting it, they took their appointed places near the entrance to the Sanctuary. Only then did the eyes of men perceive that these beasts were brazen, not flesh and blood.

After years of labor the Temple stood all but complete, says another tale. Only the cornerstone remained to be placed. That massive stone had been shaped and brought to the site, but for some strange reason resisted all efforts to move it into position. Not even the *Shamir* would help here. At last Solomon sent his useful general Benaiah to a spot on the shores of the Red Sea, known as the Birthplace of the Winds. Benaiah, obeying Solomon's orders, spread out a wineskin made from the hide of a goat. When the oncoming wind had filled it full, Benaiah quickly sealed it with the magical Seal of Solomon, whereupon the swollen skin stood erect on four legs, and its head raised as if the goat were alive.

Led before Solomon, the wind-goat bent low and kissed the feet of the great King and told him, "I am Epiphas, the wind summoned by the Lord when he parted the waters of the Red Sea so the children of Israel could safely escape the Egyptian warriors."

Solomon led this obedient creature to the Temple site, commanded it to finish the task, and shattered his seal. The unseen wind rushed out, raised the massive cornerstone and gently slid it into its place. Thus the Temple, destined since the first days of Creation, stood at last complete.

That chief foundation stone was called in Hebrew the *Eben Shetiyah.* When the Lord created the earth, he began by forming this stone first of all. In fact, Mount Moriah was credited with being at the very center of Creation and all that followed.

During hundreds and thousands of years most men believed that the earth was at the center of the universe, and around it revolved the sun, moon, planet, and stars. But what was at the center of the lands of the earth? Palestine! And what was at the center of Palestine! Jerusalem! And what at the center of Jerusalem? Mount Moriah! And at the center of that Mount — of course, the Temple. Thus the Temple was the center of centers. Both Jewish and Christian traditions were strongly infused with such notions, though for different reasons.

Mount Moriah, or sometimes Mount Zion, were often called "the navel of the earth" to indicate that at Creation time, the divine nourishment from which all else was formed had flowed here first. Especially during the centuries from about 1000 to 1500 C.E. (Christian Era) maps were circulated showing Jerusalem at the center and the rest of the known world spread about it like petals of a flower.

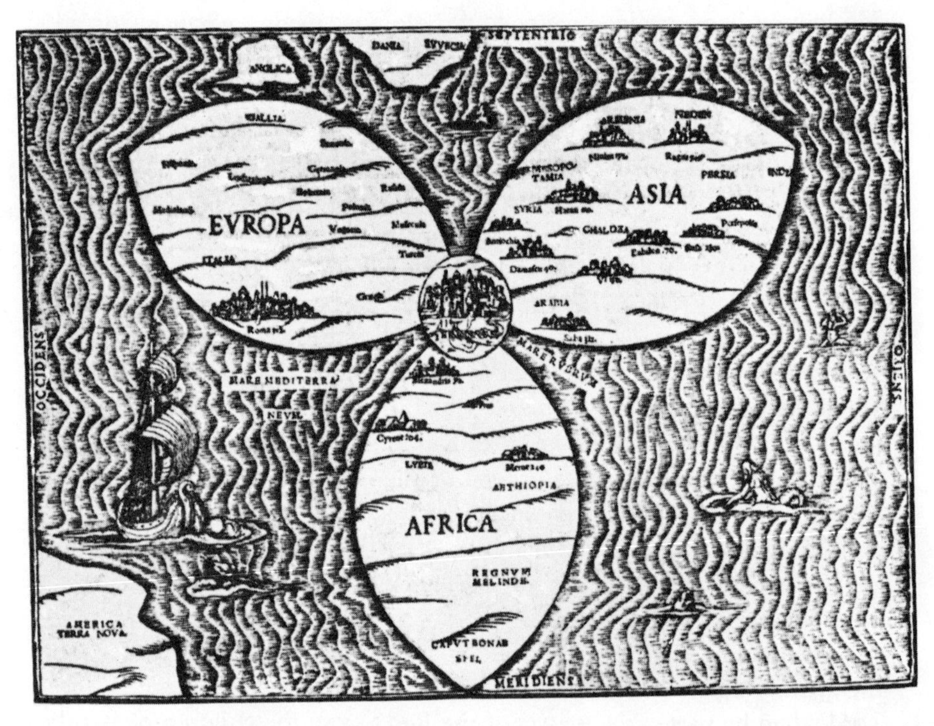

The known world, spread out like the petals of a flower, with Jerusalem at its center and the Temple as the center's center, is shown in this old illustration.

5

The Divided Kingdoms— Judah and Israel

(922–736 B.C.E.)

Solomon died about 922 B.C.E. after having ruled forty years. His son Rehoboam, reared in imperial luxury, had expected to become king without difficulty or undue delay. He did receive at Jerusalem the crown that made him ruler of the southern lands, including the tribal territories that had belonged to Judah and, in part, to Benjamin.

Then, in keeping with tradition that went back to his grandfather David, he went north to the old center of Schechem, for the formalities of receiving the crown also for the northern lands, which were larger than the southern both in area and population. Rehoboam and his closest companions at court, however, did not sense the bitterness seething among the people there.

The spokesmen for these northern peoples confronted him with demands that he promise to treat them better than Solomon had, "Your father, Solomon, made our burden bitter . . . But if you will lighten that burden and ease that yoke, we shall serve you."

Rehoboam restrained his rage, asked for three days in which to reply, then sought advice from elders who had served under Solomon. They urged that he ease, not escalate, the conflict: "If you help these people, and speak to them with kindness, they will be your faithful servants. . . ." Rehoboam turned in distaste from this council. Instead he listened to aristocrats who had grown up with him at the royal court. They urged that he humiliate these upstarts of the north.

Accordingly, Rehoboam uttered a scornful, provocative reply at Schechem: "My father made your burden heavy, but I shall add to that burden. My father lashed you with whips, but I shall lash you with scorpions!"

"To your tents, O Israel!" was the response, as the northern men left behind the king they now openly rejected. On hand, eagerly waiting to take over, was their own kinsman, Jeroboam, returned from his refuge at the Egyptian court. He became the first king of this new Israel, while Rehoboam went back to his palace in Jerusalem to rule over the much-reduced kingdom of Judah.

Possibly the military force he inherited from Solomon would have enabled Rehoboam to conquer Israel while it was still new and not organized. However, the policies and the fates of both these new rival kingdoms were now dependent largely on forces outside either. To the south lay the threat of an aggressive Egypt, and to the north and east other mighty powers were massing for conquest.

King Rehoboam soon found it advisable to build a defense line in hopes of protecting Judah and especially its capital, Jerusalem, against the aggressive Egyptian pharaoh, Shishak. This lesson was learned at great cost. In the fifth year of Rehoboam's reign, the Egyptian forces broke into and plunged deeply through Judah. Composed largely of "barbarian" troops from Ethiopia and Libya, the Egyptian forces destroyed much valued property, entered Jerusalem itself, and left only after taking large amounts of tribute from the Temple treasuries. They did not, however, at this time harm the Temple sanctuary.

Then they went on northward into Israel, though its new king Jeroboam had not long before been a political "guest" in Egypt. Egyptian forces withdrew only after heavy damage had been inflicted on both Hebrew kingdoms. This did not serve as a lesson to the leaders of those rival kingdoms, however, for during the next forty or fifty years their monarchs engaged in periodic costly warfare, Hebrew against Hebrew. Thus ended the expansive and powerful small empire of the periods of David and Solomon.

Nevertheless, this era of division and danger did not end the determination growing among increasing numbers of the people in both southern and northern kingdoms to retain their religious identities and to resist intolerable excesses by their rulers. Tough tribal traditions had been at work when the leaders of the north had rejected Rehoboam as their ruler. The same sort of resistance was to flare out again and again through centuries of unquiet history in this land of Palestine. It was directed sometimes against domestic tyranny, sometimes against aggression and domination from the outside, and sometimes against both.

The mighty monarchs of Egypt in the Nile Valley, and of the empires that arose within the Fertile Crescent including Mesopotamia, were commonly revered, or worshiped, by their subjects as gods-on-earth. Among the children of Israel, however, whether in their kingdom of Judah or of Israel, kings came to be regarded as merely human rulers, limited like their subjects by moral rules and religious taboos divinely handed down.

The many kings who occupied the thrones of Judah and of Israel during this era of division were seldom models of either virtue or compassion. They would have been as tyrannous as the most absolute monarchs of Egypt or Mesopotamia had they been able. However, the outside threats and the inner resistance set limits. Their subjects could be pushed or pulled only so far. A stubborn determination to maintain or regain certain minimal freedoms, including freedom to worship in traditional and engrained ways, remained, and even when it seemed sometimes to have been stamped out, would break out again in new forms or locations.

The Temple on Mount Moriah acquired rivals after the split into two unfriendly kingdoms. Jeroboam, as first king of Israel tried to establish central worship in his own land, in order to counter the spiritual and cult importance of Jerusalem. Such a worship-center was established at Schechem, where he made his capital as his rule began. Then, after moving his headquarters to Tirzah, Jeroboam promoted shrines in the ancient towns of Bethel and Dan. In Bethel lived priestly men who traced their ancestry back to the first "priest," Aaron, brother of Moses. In Dan were those who claimed descent from Moses himself. In these new "national" shrines for the kingdom of Israel, there was worship of the so-called "Bull of Yahweh," which is sometimes associated with the Golden Calf, prominent in the biblical narrative of the desert wanderings of the children of Israel after their escape from Egyptian bondage.

Yet Jerusalem seems to have remained the most widely accepted sanctuary for most people in Israel as well as in Judah. In fact, during his twenty-two-year rule, Jeroboam was obliged to station border guards to discourage his subjects from making their accustomed pilgrimages to Jerusalem at holiday times.

The following troubled years brought many alien influences to bear on worship at the Jerusalem Temple in Judah, and also at shrines in Israel. The many monarchs who occupied each of the rival thrones seem to have dominated priests and rituals in their lands. Again and again, a king of Israel or Judah, seeking to please a pharaoh of Egypt or perhaps a tyrant of Assyria, would import rituals or even idols from those countries for his court and subjects to worship. Thus the foreign policy shifts and plans of the kings were reflected not only by the new women in their harems but also by changing rites in the sanctuaries under their influence.

The biblical narratives concerning this period, written long afterward, express strong disapproval of these practices, denouncing them as idolatrous abominations. Jeroboam was followed by some eighteen other kings of Israel, while about twenty monarchs occupied the throne in Jerusalem. Among all these, only a few are credited with having truly "served Jehovah."

Rather early in the era of the divided kingdoms there seems to have been a strengthening of the Jerusalem Temple by the arrival of a number of priests and Levites (ritual aids) from Israel. They had apparently been driven away by idolatrous practices at the Dan and Bethel shrines. Yet defeat and degradation came also to the Temple on Mount Moriah. A king of Israel named Joash or Jehoash made war on Amaziah, king of Judah, captured him, tore down the defensive walls of Jerusalem, and plundered both city and Temple. For a time Judah was even a vassal to Israel. Then under following monarchs, peace and co-existence were restored, to the benefit of all.

Thus Uzziah, a later king of Judah, was able to rebuild the Jerusalem walls and renew its Temple defenses. However, a shocking story told in the Bible suggests that he may have clashed with the priests of that Temple. It relates that Uzziah, flushed with success, tried to prove himself on a par with David and Solomon by making with his own hands a burnt incense offering in the Temple. Its High Priest, Azariah, heading a staff of eighty lesser priests, protested: "Uzziah, it is not your place to burn incense. That may be done only by the priests, descendants of Aaron, consecrated for such service. Leave this sanctuary, where you are a trespasser!"

Uzziah, however, persisted until suddenly telltale marks of leprosy appeared on his forehead. From then till his death, the Bible story says, he remained a leper, and his son Jotham ruled as regent over Judah.

During the reign of King Ahaz, son of that Jotham, about 736 B.C.E., a new and terrible threat was felt in both kingdoms. Rule in Assyria to the north had been seized by Tiglath-pileser III, a formidable warrior, whose conquests established the Assyrian yoke over all the Fertile Crescent to the Persian Gulf itself.

Israel, lying north of Judah, stood in first line of danger. Its leading citizens were sharply divided as to the policies to be followed. Some, the anti-Assyrians, urged resistance. The pro-Assyrians, however, called for cooperation and even capitulation to Assyria. These disputes became so bitter that rulers were assassinated, their places taken by leaders of opposite policy, who were in turn assassinated — and so on, in violent and bloody cycles. Finally the crown of Israel was held by Pekah, who made an alliance with the king of Damascus (Syria) against Assyria.

These two rulers tried to persuade the current king of Judah to join them, and when he declined, they attempted to change his mind by attacking his territory. The armies of Israel and Damascus besieged Jerusalem. Though they were unable to take it, they plundered the country roundabout and took captives.

Within Jerusalem a powerful voice was raised against any such anti-Assyrian alliance. It was the voice of Isaiah, an eloquent and unforgettable prophet. He did not fear to attack even the rigid traditions and claims of the Temple. (He may have been responding to pro-Egyptian and anti-Assyrian policies of leading Temple priests.) Isaiah declared that right actions, not formal Temple rites, pleased the Lord. He attributed to the God of Israel such burning statements as these:

"Of what use to me is the multitude of your sacrifices? . . .
I am sated with the burnt-offerings of rams
  and the fat of fed beasts.
In the blood of bullocks and lambs and he-goats
  I take no delight . . .
Who demands this of you — the tramplings of my courts?"

That refers to visits to the courts of the Temple where the sacrifices were made. Then follows a direct command to give up empty fasts and sacrifices and instead to serve the Lord through righteous actions.

"Bring no more worthless offerings!
The odor of sacrifices is an abomination to me . . .
Fasting and festival I cannot endure . . .
Your hands are full of bloodshed —
  wash yourselves clean.
Remove the evil of your actions
  from before my eyes.
Cease to do evil. Learn to do good.
Seek justice. Restrain the oppressor.
Uphold the rights of the orphan.
Defend the cause of the widow."

The latter part of the book of Isaiah, probably written by a different person and at a much later date than the first part, is even more fiery in its attack, denouncing the very act of sacrifice as an offense:

"He who kills an ox is like one who kills a man.
He who sacrifices a lamb, it is as if he broke
  a dog's neck.
He who makes a flour-offering, as if he offered
  the blood of a swine.
He who makes a memorial offering of frankincense,
  as if he blessed [worshiped] an idol."

Isaiah was not the only prophet who preached in this vein. Thus Malachi, usually the final book of the Old Testament, speaks with scorn of the "dung of your sacrifices." And in Jeremiah the Lord is quoted in a denial that he had ever asked for sacrifices, ". . . when I brought your fathers out of the land of Egypt, I did not . . . give them command regarding burnt-offering or sacrifice. . . ." The only request, the Lord continues, had been the instruction to "Listen to my voice . . . and walk in all the ways that I command you, that you may prosper."

The well-known Psalms include one, the fifty-first, attributed to David himself, which tells the Lord:

"For you do not desire sacrifice,
And if I should give a burnt-offering
you would not be pleased.
The sacrifice for God is a broken spirit.
A broken and a contrite heart, O God,
you will not reject."

The thought has passed from the Bible into more than one work of literature. Thus, the deeply religious poet John Milton at the opening of his epic *Paradise Lost* invokes God's aid, addressing him in this way:

". . . O Spirit, that dost prefer
Before all Temples the upright heart and pure . . ."

And Rudyard Kipling, a very different kind of poet, in his well-known *Recessional* reminds the "Lord God of Hosts" that

"Still stands thine ancient sacrifice,
An humble and a contrite heart."

6

Destruction of the Temple—and the Babylonian Exile

(736–580 B.C.E.)

As the threat of Assyrian attack grew, so too did the struggle within the endangered Kingdom of Judah. The anti-Assyrians tended to look to Egypt for encouragement and aid. On the other hand, those who (like the prophet Isaiah) urged against defying Assyria, opposed any closer ties with Egypt.

The pressures on King Ahaz of Judah were intense. Rezin, King of Damascus, in the effort to punish Judah for not joining the anti-Assyrian alliance, sponsored an uprising in Edom. This deprived Judah of Elath on the Red Sea, for that strategic port was now turned over to Aram, the land of the Arameans. Finally, in desperation, Ahaz offered tribute — in short, a bribe — to Tiglath-pileser. Judah thus became one of the many vassal states of Assyria.

Tiglath-pileser now led his forces south along the Mediterranean coast. They took Ashkelon and Gaza, forging a link to Arab peoples allied with Assyria. Thus, he sealed off against Egyptian attack the southern regions of his vassal, Judah. Then he went on to take terrible vengeance against the northern kingdom, Israel. The Assyrian forces cut through great sections of Israel. North of Israel they seized the city of Damascus itself, slew its king, and carried off its inhabitants, thus ending the Kingdom of Damascus.

These crushing defeats kindled a putsch by the pro-Assyria party in Israel. They killed King Pekah and replaced him by their own man Hoshea.

Archeologists have found an ancient inscription in which Tiglath-pileser boasts, "Since they had deposed their king Pekah, I appointed Hoshea to be king over them."

In Judah, to the south, King Ahaz played the role of an Assyrian supporter. He swore loyalty to Tiglath-pileser and ordered that the Assyrian religion become also that of Judah. However, even irresistible conquerors are mortal, and Tiglath-pileser died in 727 B.C.E. In Israel, King Hoshea undertook a revolt, counting on Egyptian aid. But Shalman-eser V, new ruler of Assyria, defeated Hoshea and forced him to pay tribute.

Later Hoshea tried again. Having made a treaty of aid with the pharaoh of Egypt, he stopped paying tribute to Assyria. Shalman-eser replied by sending men to seize Hoshea, who thus vanished from Israel and from all further records. During three gruesome years the Assyrian forces besieged Samaria, capital of Israel. Shalman-eser himself died, and his commanding general became Sargon II, the new Assyrian ruler. Off at the other end of the Fertile Crescent, in what has come to be called Babylon, another revolt against Assyrian rule flared up, and Sargon II took his army to put it down. While he was away, the leaders of Israel, urged on by Egypt, made a final effort to escape the Assyrian yoke. But Sargon returned to take a terrible vengeance. Israel was crushed and dismembered.

Sargon's own records boast he took more than twenty-seven thousand captives from Israel. They were scattered widely, and thinly, throughout the far-flung Assyrian empire. This was part of Assyrian policy — to scatter leaders and their families in such small groups that there would not be enough in any one place to make trouble. In time they would be absorbed into local populations, losing their former languages, identities, and aims.

This was the event concerned with what later history called "the ten lost tribes of Israel." The deportation of tribal leaders was rounded out by the Assyrian importation into Israel of peoples from far-off regions. They brought different languages, cultures, and religions. The descendants of the interbreeding of these with the remaining Israel residents became known later as "Samaritans," for they lived in the region around the city of Samaria. Because of their mixed heredity and their special customs and manners, they were despised by the more "pure blooded" Jews of Judah. That hostility was still strong some seven hundred years later when Jesus lived and taught in Palestine. His parable of the Good Samaritan showed that humane and loving actions *even* by a despised Samaritan could bring closer the longed-for Kingdom of God on earth.

Israel now ceased to exist, either as a kingdom or as a continuity from the days of David and Solomon. And even Judah had become an Assyrian satellite. Judah's new king was Hezekiah, who began to rule just about the time of the extinction of Israel. He continued to resist the urgings of the anti-Assyrian, pro-Egyptian groups and instead listened mostly to those who, like Isaiah, opposed any alliance with Egypt against Assyria. Isaiah, to dramatize his position, for several years walked in Jerusalem barefoot and unclothed like a captive. This symbolized his prophecy that a pro-Egypt policy would lead into captivity the people of Jerusalem and of all Judah.

In his very first vision, explaining how he had been divinely called to

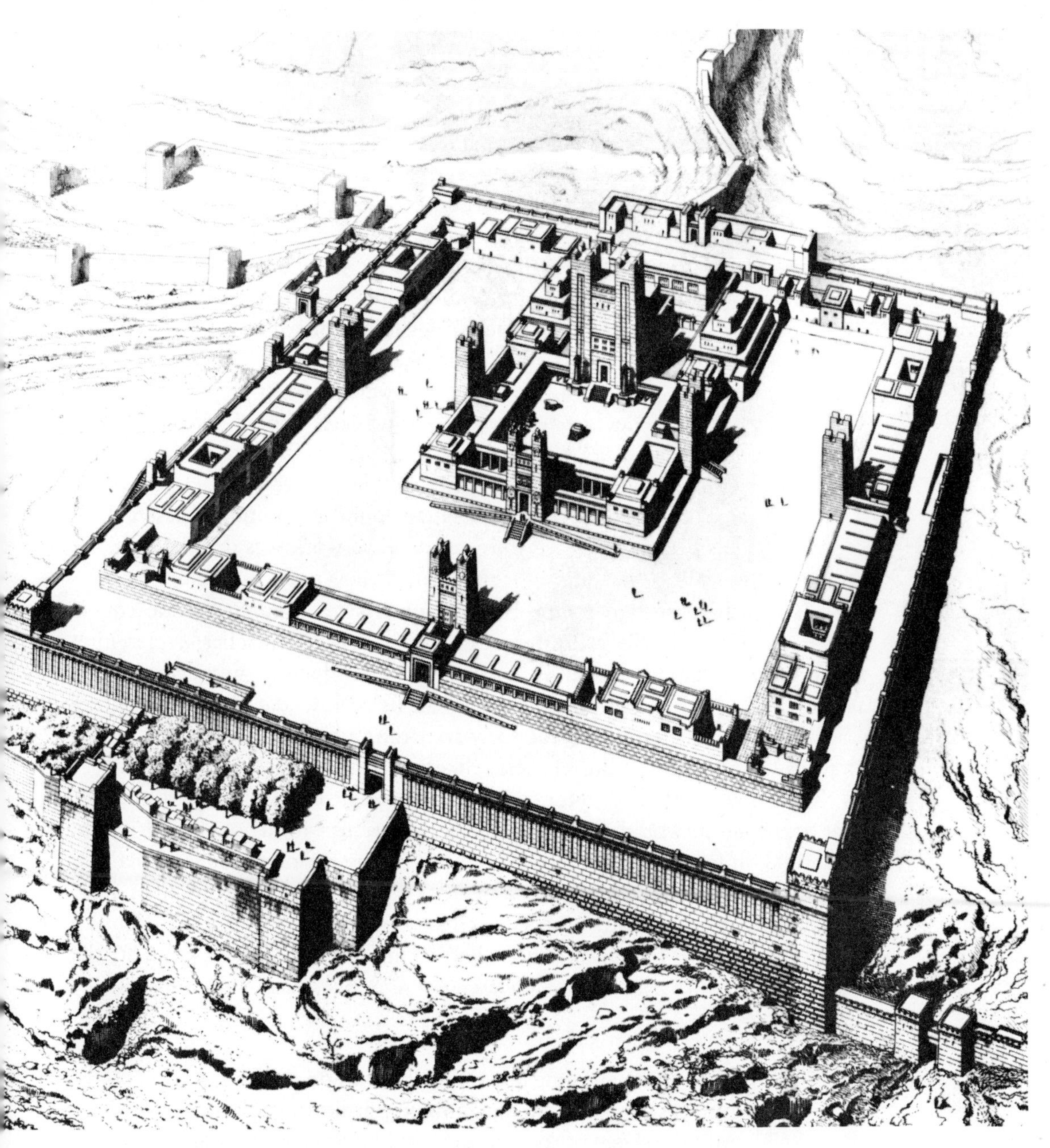

Ezekiel's vision of the ideal Temple was pictured thus grandly by Charles Chipiez, French architect and Bible scholar. Towers are placed to mark various gates and entrances. Worshipers entering the Temple area from the east (nearest us) would mount three different stairways before arriving at the great portal of the Sanctuary itself, into which only priests might pass.

become a prophet, Isaiah told how during the reign of Uzziah a vision of Yahweh, the Lord, had come to him in the Temple. Yahweh appeared surrounded by six-winged *seraphim*, and Isaiah rhapsodized ". . . my eyes have seen the King, the Lord of hosts." Many years later in a time of great stress, Julia Ward Howe began a famous song similarly, "Mine eyes have seen the glory of the coming of the Lord. . . ."

Though born into the aristocratic class, Isaiah realized that rotten social conditions were weakening Judah. The poorer classes were growing poorer as the wealthy oppressed them more and more.

The vassal peoples of the vast Assyrian empire seethed with plans and efforts to break free from the yoke of their conquerors. One vassal state alone could not hope for success. So to Jerusalem came representatives from Merodach-baladan, the native ruler in faraway Babylon. They came supposedly to congratulate King Hezekiah on his recovery from an illness. Actually, they were there to work out if possible a plan for Judah, Babylon, and perhaps some other vassal peoples, to break free from Assyrian rule.

Hezekiah was persuaded. He knew he would have to prepare for siege, and so his engineers devised a new and bold water supply for Jerusalem. They dug a tunnel a third of a mile long through solid rock to bring water into the city from the upper spring of Gihon. The storage basin in Jerusalem was called the Pool of Siloam. An inscription found in the tunnel less than a century ago has been interpreted to mean that the work was done during the reign of Hezekiah. It was indeed a technical achievement.

Hezekiah's effort to escape the rule of Assyria brought in due course that power's formidable army from the north under Sennacherib. Hezekiah found himself alone, his allies in the rebellion having withdrawn. Sennacherib boasted, on an inscription that can be seen in the Oriental Institute of Chicago, that he took by siege forty-six strong places in Judah, and finally shut up Hezekiah, the king himself, "like a bird in a cage" in Jerusalem.

Isaiah was appealed to for counsel. He predicted with strange confidence that Sennacherib would "hear tidings . . . and return to his own land." That leader did, in fact, call off the siege and leave. The reason remains something of a mystery. The Bible hints that a plague or pestilence broke out among the Assyrian forces. Herodotus, the Greek historian, writing in the fifth century B.C.E., spoke of a plague of mice. The romantic poet, Lord Byron, in the nineteenth century penned *The Destruction of Sennacherib* with often-quoted lines such as:

> "The Assyrian came down like the wolf on the fold,
> And his cohorts were gleaming in purple and gold,
> And the sheen of their spears was like stars on the sea,
> When the blue wave rolls nightly on deep Galilee."

Judah did not escape without terrible damage. The Assyrians had devastated much of the land. The common people, workers of the farms and the shops, had been miserable enough before, but now were desperate. Their protests found a voice in another prophet, Micah. He placed blame squarely on the selfishness, greed, and dishonesty of men of power and wealth in Jerusalem.

Perhaps to avoid inner chaos, King Hezekiah now undertook reforms. In that era, every important political policy had its reflections in religious and cult practices. Hence the reforms of Hezekiah extended also to worship and so to the Temple. Assyrian rites and practices were banished from the Temple on the sacred mount. However, it proved but temporary. Manasseh, who became king after Hezekiah's death, made the Assyrian religion official again. There were potent reasons for this change: Esar-hadon, a new Assyrian monarch, had conquered even Egypt. It, too, became a vassal of Assyria.

Revolts followed, and the next Assyrian king, Ashur-banipal, heavily punished the Egyptians, but finally was obliged to let go of Egypt. On the other hand, however, he conquered Phoenicia on the seacoast and sacked its famous port city of Tyre.

King Manasseh of Judah may have attempted some resistance, for once he was hauled off as prisoner of the Assyrian forces. Later permitted to return to his throne in Jerusalem, he appears to have remained an abject supporter of Assyrian rule until the end of his long reign. His son, Amon, also proved pro-Assyrian — and was assassinated by anti-Assyrian partisans, who in their turn were killed by pro-Assyrians!

To the throne in Jerusalem next came Amon's son, a boy only eight years old, Josiah by name. He was in his mid-twenties when he began a series of far-reaching reforms of religion and ritual in the Temple. These reforms linked his name for all time with the Temple, and deeply influenced all later Jewish worship and religious literature.

The Temple itself had fallen into scandalous condition during three-quarters of a century of Assyrian-influenced ritual and idolatry. Repair was important, and Josiah undertook it, aided by the fact that despite the tribute payments to Assyria, the period that had begun with the rule of Manasseh had been relatively prosperous, because peaceful.

More important than the physical repair of the building, however, was a "discovery" that Josiah announced as the work went on. A basic document had been found, he declared, an ancient "book of law" or "book of the covenant." A prophetess named Hulda certified that the document was genuine, and Josiah summoned leaders from throughout his land to a meeting at the Temple. This meeting pledged that the Book would become the basis for the national religion, its rites, and its code of conduct. Later, that discovered document was expanded into an even more comprehensive work known today as Deuteronomy, the fifth book of the Bible (Genesis, Exodus, Leviticus, Numbers, and Deuteronomy making up the fivefold Pentateuch).

Deuteronomy is believed by leading scholars to have been written by a priest or group of priests of the Temple. It does insist on the priority of the Temple in the worship of the one God, and lays down a strict and precise pattern for conducting that worship. It was and remained a work of great importance in reviving and enlarging the religious role of the Temple.

These reforms under King Josiah did not, of course, end the shifting power-struggles within Judah. In that same year Ashur-banipal died, and none of the following Assyrian monarchs was able to maintain the power of that empire. It began to decline. Its many foes lost no time in preparing to attack and take over. Far to the east, the Chaldeans, ruling in their capital Babylon, joined with the newly powerful Medes of Media (in what later became Persia and Iran). Nabo-polassar was the Chaldean monarch who struck at the heart of declining Assyria. Warriors of the Chaldeans and Medians fought their way into Nineveh itself. They took and sacked the city in 612 B.C.E.

After the fall of Nineveh, the Egyptian Pharaoh Necho led his forces through Palestine. Attempting to oppose the Pharaoh's march, King Josiah fought the Egyptians, but was slain in a battle at Megiddo.

Jehoahaz, son of Josiah, now became king of Judah. Again came a summons to appear before Pharaoh Necho. Jehoahaz appeared, kept his life, but was imprisoned and held for a large ransom. Necho called on the people of Judah to pay the sum. Then he appointed over them, as a king more likely to see things his way, another of Josiah's sons, who — again at Necho's order — took the crown name of Jehoiakim.

While showing his strength in Palestine, Necho also was giving aid to a remnant of the Assyrian military and governing group who had made their way from the defeat at Nineveh, and hoped to recoup their losses against the Chaldeans. However, the combined Assyrian-Egyptian forces were decisively defeated at Carchemish in 605 B.C.E., and this disaster obliged Necho to hurry back from Palestine to Egypt.

Now it was the turn of the new Chaldean monarch to move in to become overlord of Judah in place of the former Assyrian and Egyptian potentates. Nebu-chadnezzar, sometimes known as Nebu-chadrezzar, was this conquering ruler from the banks of the Euphrates. He took Judah and added it to his growing domain, called sometimes the Chaldean, sometimes the New Babylonian empire. To him Jehoiakim declared allegiance, but within a few years attempted to rebel.

Again internal conflicts reflected external tensions. Again bold agitators spoke out, in the very shadow of the Jerusalem Temple, against the policies pursued by the King of Judah. Their names this time were Jeremiah and Uriah, both among the prophets. (This Uriah had no connection with the earlier one who had been Bathsheba's husband before David.) The prophet Uriah lost his life because of his blunt criticism, and Jeremiah narrowly escaped execution on similar charges.

To harry rebellious Jerusalem, Nebu-chadnezzar first sent forces of Ammonites, Moabites, Syrians, and Chaldeans. Then he himself arrived with his potent army. During the ensuing siege King Jehoiakim died, and the perilous crown passed to his young son Jehoiachin, who, within a few months, was forced to surrender Jerusalem, its Temple mount, and himself, to avoid total destruction of the sacred city.

The warriors from the New Babylon were systematic in plundering. They seized the national treasure stored at the Temple. They began the mass removal of leading residents of Judah, especially the principal ruling families, craftsmen, and organizers. There were in all four waves of such enforced migrations or banishments. The first wave numbered about twelve thousand. Later waves further depleted the land of important personalities and entire families.

Judah was thus stripped of its "elite," the personalities whose power or prestige might make them able to instigate future resistance. The land did not remain depopulated, however. The obscure farmers, landworkers, propertyless wanderers, and the hewers of wood and drawers of water remained.

A new king was left on the reduced throne in Jerusalem. He was still another son of the late Josiah. His name had been Mattaniah. Now, by order of Nebu-chadnezzar, he assumed the throne-name of Zedekiah, a name that rings like a knell down the echoing halls of history, for he became the final king in the dynasty of Jesse, David, and Solomon: the last of the many kings of Judah.

Zedekiah, supported by the prophet Jeremiah, tried during four years to rule without offending mighty Babylon. Again opposition groups arose in the land: anti-Babylonians who urged revolt and looked once more to Egypt for aid. Zedekiah was called once to Babylon, probably to give an accounting. He went, then was allowed to return to Jerusalem.

After a new Pharaoh in Egypt made overtures to him, Zedekiah, by 588 B.C.E., openly breached his allegiance to Babylon. As swiftly as possible the avenging army set out from there and entered Palestine. Fear afflicted the people of Judah, for against them were massed not only the dreaded Chaldeans but also the Edomites, who had taken advantage of the crisis to invade as well.

One fortified town of Judah after another was taken. The extent of the destruction has been confirmed from recent excavations of ruins. Then came the turn of the sacred city of the Temple, Jerusalem. A great siege was mounted. Finally, in summer of 587 B.C.E. its walls were breached. Chaldeans poured in and celebrated a grisly victory by systematically wrecking and burning the entire city, including its crowning glory, the Temple.

Once more, with smoke straggling into the sky behind them, columns of Judean prisoners were marched off to captivity in Babylon. Five years later, probably in consequence of still another attempt at uprising, still more prisoners followed.

Now Jerusalem ceased to be the center of rule for the subjugated Babylonian province of Judah. It was administered from Mizpeh by Gedaliah, the governor appointed by Babylon. However, the anti-Babylonian patriots, still stubborn and daring, killed Gedaliah. Many militant Jews, fearing even more dreadful vengeance from Babylon, sought refuge in Egypt. There they supplied the nucleus of several military outposts and colonies aiding in the defenses of Egypt.

Amidst widespread devastation in Judah, the remaining farmers and farm workers attempted to manage as best they could. They moved into many an abandoned estate and orchard. Reports of these "squatter" actions reached the banks of the Chebar River of Babylon, along which lived exiled landowners and aristocrats taken from Judah. They were unhappy at the news.

In the central highlands of Judah, however, the "high places" remained tenantless. No replacements had been brought in after the Babylonians had driven out the Jewish farmers. This empty land, like a magnet, drew new settlers from Edom and also Arabs from the desert lands eastward. Thus, beginning some sixty to eighty miles south of the Temple ruins lay a district inhabited by an alien people, the Edomites. It became known later as Idumea, and was distinct from the kingdom of Edom, which lay south and east of the Dead Sea.

7

The Road Back—and a Second Temple

(580–340 B.C.E.)

The Babylonian exile of men and women deported from Judah was not a period of continual weeping and wailing. Most of the exiles seem to have found new lives and even new hope in the small rural communities of southern Mesopotamia to which they were assigned. Some even became prosperous and influential in trade there and helped with the financial operations of the Chaldean empire. Most retained their identities as Jews, however, and avoided complete assimilation. The imprint of the distinctive religious and moral creed crystallized around the Temple at Jerusalem remained strong.

Its strength was most poetically illustrated in the writings of one of the exiles in Babylon, the prophet Ezekiel. He poured out rapturous pages filled with ecstatic visions of return and the rebirth of an ideal community, served by an ennobled Temple in which worship and sacrifice would be perfect. These prophesies of Ezekiel make up one of the books of the Bible. They do not, however, describe facts or even set forth firm expectations on his part. They express dreams, burning desires, and deeply felt aspirations. The ideal state envisioned by Ezekiel would exemplify the best, as he understood the religious heritage of the children of Israel.

Prominent in Ezekiel's vision is his "Temple," which he describes complete with dimensions. He pictured it set in a great square courtyard, each of whose four walls were pierced by three noble gates, twelve gates in all, one for each of the traditional tribes of the nomadic children of Israel. In the center of the northern wall Ezekiel visualized a gate for the tribe of Judah. Then, in succession around the walls, the gates for Reuben, Joseph, Benjamin, Dan, Simeon, Issachar, Zebulon, Gad, Asher, Naphtali, and Levi.

Less than half a century was to go by before the great Chaldean empire, ruled from old Babylon, went down before a new and more formidable power: Persia. That name covers a new combination of peoples, Indo-European in their ancestry, rather than Semitic, such as the Assyrians; or Hamitic, like the Egyptians. The Persians, strictly speaking, came from outside the Fertile Crescent region, and were not direct descendants of ancestors from the Arabian desert south of the Fertile Crescent.

Heading the new Persian power was a dynamic warrior and organizer, Cyrus by name. His rise had been like that of a rocket, sudden, swift, brilliant. He had begun as a little-known chief in the Anshan district of the Kingdom of Media, just south of the Caspian Sea. By 559 B.C.E. he was supreme in Anshan, by 549 in all Media and Persia. His control then stretched from the Persian Gulf in the southeast, to Asia Minor between the Black and Mediterranean Seas. Thus, King Cyrus at this time commanded a crescent of territory lying north of the Fertile Crescent itself.

Inevitably his forces moved south for a final confrontation with the Chaldean-Babylonian empire, whose one-time might had dwindled. Its King Nebu-chadnezzar had died in 562 B.C.E., and for a few years the throne had been held by a less able ruler with the odd name of Evil-Merodach. Then in 556 Nabonidus, sometimes known as Nabonaid, had forced his way to the top. He tried to restrain the influence of the priests of Marduk, the chief Babylonian god. Most of the actual rule he finally turned over to his son, the crown prince Bel-sharuzun, more often known as Bel-shazzar. This was the prince who held a feast one night in 539 B.C.E., famous for the prophetic "handwriting on the wall" — just before the decisive attack by Cyrus and his Persians.

In that battle, Babylonian resistance was swiftly broken, Bel-shazzar was slain, and the Chaldean-Babylonian people became subjects of the new Persian empire. All western Asia was now controlled by Cyrus; and his successors, Cambyses and Darius I, as if by some great momentum, were able to add to their domains Egypt to the west and even India to the east. In that era of extreme imperial expansion, the eastern Mediterranean became, in fact, a Persian lake. In the Bible, the book of Esther thus summarizes the scope of this super-empire: "India to Ethiopia, a hundred and twenty-seven provinces."

They were ruled by *satraps* or governors, and princes appointed by the Persian king. The provinces were grouped into twenty major divisions, the fifth of which was named "*Aba Nahara*," signifying the region west of the Euphrates River. Included in it was Syria and the small land of *Yehud*, better known to us as Judah or by its later Latin name of Judea.

Cyrus' policies were perhaps even more remarkable than his military successes. He allowed his subject peoples to worship their traditional gods in their traditional ways. In Babylon, for example, the priests and worship of the god Marduk again held sway. Furthermore, Cyrus allowed peoples exiled or "scrambled up" by the Assyrians and Babylonian-Chaldean rulers before him, to return to their former homelands if they wished. This privilege he now extended to the Babylonian exiles from Judah.

So it came about that by 537 B.C.E., the first groups of such exiles were gathering from villages and towns along the Euphrates to return to Jerusalem and its sacred Mount Moriah. The number of such "returnees" was not great. Many of the exiles, probably most in fact, had become used to their Babylonian surroundings and felt themselves to be Babylonians of the Jewish faith, not homesick exiles from Jerusalem.

Records of that return are scanty, sometimes contradictory. An organizer of the first group to go back appears to have been Shesh-bazar, a Jewish aristocrat or prince mentioned in the Bible's book of Ezra. He probably was identical with Shen-assar, son of the former King Jehoiachin, and so one of the line of David and Solomon. The returning group set forth, following the winding Euphrates toward the west and north, then turning south near Aleppo, moving down the Mediterranean coast, passing east of such sites as Sumur, Byblos, Sidon, Tyre; passing Samaria, and finally going up to Jerusalem itself. By this time the leaders of those who had returned included a Joshua or Jeshua, serving as chief priest, and another prince of the line of David, Zeru-babbel by name. That name meant "offspring of Babylon." He was a grandson of the one-time King Jehoiachin of Judah, and a nephew of Shesh-bazar.

The name Zeru-babbel is identified today with the project to rebuild the Temple on the same site long ago chosen by Solomon. Many problems stood in the way. Those who had come back were few in number, and they faced much mistrust and actual hostility from those who had remained in Judah during the half century between 587 and 537. There were, no doubt, conflicts over ownership and authority. Jerusalem itself was only a shadow of what it had been. However painfully, progress was made on the project. First an altar was rebuilt among the ruins on Mount Moriah, and sacrifices and festival services resumed there. To the pious of those days a sanctuary was made by the services, not by stones and wooden beams.

A foundation site was selected, and foundation stones were laid. Then friction flared between the newcomers from Babylon and the resident Samaritans. Representatives of the latter wanted their due share in the Temple building, but Zeru-babbel and Joshua rejected their claims, saying, "You have nothing in common with us in building a house to our God . . . we ourselves will together build [it] . . . as King Cyrus . . . has commanded us."

The residents referred to as "the people of the land" in the book of Ezra, thereafter opposed the building project so stubbornly that the new Temple seems not to have been completed until during the reign of Darius II, the sixth monarch following Cyrus the Great. This Darius ruled the Persian empire from 424 to 404 B.C.E. The date of the dedication of the new Temple was very likely about 515 or 516 B.C.E., about seventy years after the first Temple had been destroyed. It was probably small, perhaps even rather in-

Building of the second Temple under Zeru-babbel was thus pictured by Doré. Work went slowly. Human muscle was the sole source of transport; the land and its people were poor. The spear-bearing soldiers drawn by Doré were typical of the era since the Persians ruled the region all during this time.

complete. It was dedicated under the direction of Zeru-babbel and Jeshua. Poverty prevailed among the Jews in Palestine during this part of the so-called "Persian period." Not only had the district called *Yehud* sustained great losses, but as part of the Persian empire it had to pay substantial tribute to the monarch for support of his official machinery and standing army.

Among the Persian monarchs during the two centuries following Cyrus the Great, one finds two named Xerxes and three named Arta-xerxes. An able and energetic young Jew named Nehemiah served in Shushan (also called Susa), the Persian capital, at the court of either the second or third of these Arta-xerxes.

"Cupbearer to the King" was Nehemiah's title, but his position enabled him to do far more than just hand goblets of wine or beer to the powerful ruler. The Bible book of Nehemiah is written as if by Nehemiah himself. It tells how he met a kinsman, Hanani, and some other men from Judah, and asked them how things fared in Jerusalem among those who had returned from Babylon.

"The survivors are in great misery . . ." was the depressing reply; and as for Jerusalem itself, its defensive walls were "broken down, and its gates have been destroyed by fire."

Nehemiah wept to hear this. Then he prayed. When next he served wine to the King, Nehemiah still looked so sad that the King asked why.

"Why should not my face be sad," answered Nehemiah, "when the city, the place of the tombs of my fathers is desolate . . .?" He requested that the king have him sent to Jerusalem, "to the city of my fathers' tombs, that I may rebuild it."

Thus Nehemiah set out, carrying royal letters of safe conduct and authority addressed to Persian officials governing Syria and Palestine. Once there he found, like others before him, suspicion and opposition from those already on hand and in authority. In fact, "it caused them great irritation that a man had come to seek the welfare of the Israelites."

After three days in Jerusalem, Nehemiah set out secretly by night to survey the walls of the city. He found shameful and dangerous decay. He then managed despite opposition to have the walls and defense towers rebuilt. Nehemiah's records indicate the important role of the rebuilt Temple and its staff during these troubled times. The walls of Jerusalem were then pierced by eight gates, five of which gave direct access to various parts of Mount Moriah, on whose summit the Temple stood. Clearly many of those who had entered Jerusalem did so to visit the Temple site.

North of the Temple itself stood the "house of the Temple servants and the merchants." It was they, most certainly, who sold sacrificial animals and incense to worshipers come to the Temple. South of the Temple stood the houses of the priests and in particular of the High Priest Eliashib. They occupied what had once been the original "city of David."

Truly, Jerusalem, including the Temple as Nehemiah found it, was much shrunken compared with the city and sanctuary at the heyday of King Solomon. Besides, "the people were few therein." Nehemiah realized the population was not large enough to provide proper defense for the city and its Temple. Even among those who did live there, a shortage of decent housing existed. Nehemiah then drafted, by a kind of lottery, some 10 percent of the population of the rest of *Yehud* to move to Jerusalem. Housing appears to have been built for them also.

During about a dozen years, Nehemiah served as governor of Jerusalem and its environs. He seems to have met opposition from both within and without the city. The governor of nearby Samaria and the nobility of surrounding regions did not like to see Jerusalem strengthened. They complained, and even threatened to interfere. However, Nehemiah armed his workers and they persisted until the new city walls were completed. Jerusalem and its sanctuary stood strong again.

Nehemiah returned to the Persian court, but later came once more to Jerusalem as a royally approved governor. Again he found conditions that saddened and angered him. The high priest, Eliashib, had given lodgings within the Temple itself to the family of a relative, Tobiah — a family that was not of priestly origin.

"I cast all of Tobiah's household property out of the chamber," Nehemiah reported.

The Levites, who served in the Temple, and the singers who performed its rich musical rituals, had not been paid as they were entitled to be. Nehemiah called to task the responsible officials in Jerusalem. "Why," he demanded, "is the House of God forsaken?"

Nehemiah's reforms were many. They included instructions to merchants to observe the Saturday Sabbath, bans against marriages between Jews and non-Jews, and even orders to dissolve such marriages already in existence. These efforts to purify and purge went to the very top. The High Priest Eliashib's grandson, Manasseh, had married Nicaso, daughter of an official from neighboring Samaria. Manasseh and Nicaso were in effect banished from Jerusalem. They went to Samaria.

Though Nehemiah insisted on such strict pious observances, he was mainly an administrator. The religious reforms were deepened and broadened by Ezra, a priest active about this time in Jerusalem. Ezra was "a scribe skilled in the law of Moses," rather like a rabbi or teacher than a priest in the narrower modern sense. Ezra, too, had come to Jerusalem leading a band of returning Jews. Once there he worked to make "the law of Moses" familiar to the ordinary citizens. He held public readings of sacred writings. In fact, he did much to choose and confirm the content of what was to become the Old Testament, the Bible of the children of Israel.

In that Bible, the book of Nehemiah suggests that Ezra's reforms also were meant to reduce the oppression of the common people by their landlords, aristocrats, and rulers. Ezra for example is quoted as telling his God about "the distress that has come on us. . . . Behold, we are slaves . . . and as for the land that you gave to our fathers . . . we are only slaves in it." Yet that same land Ezra notes, "yields a large income to the kings whom you have set over us . . . they have power over our bodies, and over our cattle . . . and we are in great distress." That "income" of course was the tax taken from the children of Israel to pay tribute to their present overlords, the Persians.

Ezra, however, approved and even demanded from his people a different kind of contribution: to maintain the Temple and its priests. These were the payments or tithes for offerings, services, fixed holy days, festivals, and the seventh-day sabbaths. Ezra called on the people to bring to the Temple "the first produce" of their land, and the "first born" of their flocks and herds. This assured wherewithal for "the priests who minister in the house of our God."

Under Nehemiah and Ezra a new era began in the religious life of the land. Its supreme law became in fact the religious and ritual rules traced back to Moses and later elaborated by Temple priests in Deuteronomy. Marriages outside the family of the "children of Israel" were banned. Rich and poor, high and low, were called on to observe sabbaths and holy days. Greed and desire for gain were somewhat controlled. Even the soil was to be protected against man's excesses, for at fixed intervals it was to be allowed to lie fallow, so as to regain its strength. And at stated intervals mortgaged land was to be restored to its owner in order that creditors might not unduly oppress those in debt. Also, in the Temple, priests and the Levite helpers were assured support — as a right, not a favor.

Thus, in the last half of the fifth century, B.C.E., the Temple, the Torah or Books of Moses, and the Mosaic Law were all assured of basic and continuing importance in the lives of the people of *Yehud.*

A small land it was then, almost insignificant. It had no coastline on the Mediterranean. To its south lay Idumea, peopled by the descendants of non-Hebraic nomads. To its north was Samaria, and Samaria then had a sanctuary and Temple of its own on Mount Gerasim, near Schechem, as a rival to the Temple on Mount Moriah.

The Bible contains no chronicles of events in the land of the Jews between the days of Nehemiah-Ezra and those of Jesus. Highlights of the several centuries following about 400 B.C.E. must be reconstructed from other records, often rather scanty at best. The land remained subject to the Persian rule. Yet Persian interest and interference in its internal affairs seemed to lessen as time passed.

Meanwhile the influence of the high priests of the Temple increased. If there was any one "native ruler" during these decades, the high priest was he. For example, when there were conferences on vital matters of taxes and tributes to be paid the Persian state, the satrap (or governor) for the province of Syria would represent the distant monarch, while the high priest would speak for the people.

8

From Alexander to the Maccabees

(340–142 B.C.E.)

In 332 B.C.E., a conqueror of a new kind led his victorious armies southward through Palestine, along the coastal plain fronting the Mediterranean Sea. He was the youthful Alexander of Macedon, a Greek in culture and outlook, and a military genius who brought doom to the aging Persian empire. He had defeated the Persian king Darius in a great battle at Issus, besieged and taken Tyre and then Gaza, and was on his way to establish control over Egypt. His forces also fanned out and devastated Samaria, then went on to Jericho, nearly 15 miles northeast of Jerusalem.

An oft-told tale asserts that Alexander the Great journeyed to Jerusalem from his encampment at Gaza and there was received in ceremonial splendor at the Temple itself. Josephus, the noted Jewish historian, writing about four hundred years later, pictured the high priest, Jaddua, greeting the meteoric young world conqueror, who was friendly, and favorably impressed by what he found at the Temple. The Talmud, that rich repository of Jewish commentary and legend, tells also of such a visit, but names the high priest as Simon the Just. Trustworthy evidence for such a visit, however, appears to be lacking.

Far more important, though, are several facts that are safely beyond doubt. Alexander's defeat of the Persians and his conquest of Palestine ended one great era and began another for the land of the Temple. Ended was rule by conquerors based in the East: the Assyrians, Babylonians, Persians, and even the Egyptians (commonly considered part of the East, though their land lies well west of Jerusalem). The new era brought rule by conquerors based in the West, the Greeks, or Hellenes as they called themselves. They initiated the Hellenistic period in the Middle East. Greek culture, Greek commercial practices, and Greek political ideas penetrated ever more deeply, even though the rulers themselves did not reside in palaces located in Greece itself. Then finally they were to be followed by a force from still further west—the Romans.

Alexander's brief career of conquest continued less than a dozen years after his supposed reception at the Temple. He had become master of almost all the known and wanted world when he died aged only thirty-two. More important, his conquests had not been mere marauding or plundering expeditions; they had been followed by the Hellenization or Grecianizing of the regions he won. Cities arose on the Hellenistic pattern, a blend between the Hellenic of Greece itself and the Oriental with which it was mixed. Commerce, trade, and transport expanded. The Persian control of the eastern Mediterranean was broken.

In the cities and towns of Palestine, the simpler, sterner Hebraic ways now were influenced and infiltrated by Hellenistic games, spectacles, cabarets, distractions, discussions, and sophistications. Hebraic and Hellenistic attitudes clashed at many levels and over a long period. The Hellenistic way of life was alluring, full of pastimes and luxuries for the wealthy. Slaves did most of the tough, dirty work. Manual or even craft labor was held in contempt. Worship was idolatrous, indifferent, cut off largely from questions of daily conduct. The rulers and aristocrats of the Hellenistic world placed first pursuit of pleasure rather than righteousness or piety. All this was a long time at work, and its interactions were complex, rather than simple. One fact stands out: new ways of life and attitudes of mind impinged on Palestine following the new era inaugurated by Alexander the Great.

Great numbers of Jews became residents of the new city of Alexandria near the mouth of the Nile, a fully Hellenistic community, not an "Egyptian" one. Increasing numbers of Jews lived, traveled, and traded outside Palestine. Greek became the international language of all this empire. It was the language of the wealthy and sophisticated also in Jerusalem and all Judah. The common people had long spoken not Hebrew, but Aramaic, a related tongue.

Alexander died in 323 B.C.E. No single competent heir took over his vast empire. Instead, his principal generals and administrators now struggled for shares. Ptolemy retained Egypt and managed also to get Palestine, though it was wanted and claimed by Seleucus, who kept control of a huge segment of the empire centered around Syria.

Thus began two great Hellenistic dynasties that lasted long in history: the Ptolemies of Egypt, and the Seleucids of Syria. It is important to recall that in origin the Ptolemies were not "Egyptians" any more than the Seleucids were "Syrians."

Jewish Palestine remained part of the empire of the Ptolemies between 300 and 200 B.C.E., though that interval was bloodied by four separate cycles of wars involving the rival dynasties. During the peaceful intervals, the people of Jerusalem and Judah fared not too badly, for the Ptolemies allowed freedom of worship and traditional usages, so long as taxes were paid and the rival Seleucids were not supported.

The back-and-forth struggles between the rivals, however, were felt more than once in the sacred city and on its Temple mount. Thus, in 217 B.C.E., Ptolemy IV, having defeated the Seleucid monarch Antiochus III near Gaza, marched triumphantly through Palestine and visited Jerusalem and the Temple site along the way. His Egyptian cavalry, numbered by the thousands, and his hundred war elephants apparently did not make the visit to Mount Moriah, however.

Antiochus III attacked Palestine again in 201 B.C.E., but was driven back by Ptolemaic forces whose commander, Scopas, then marched into Jerusalem and occupied it — probably to crush pro-Seleucid support that had appeared there. A short time later, Scopas' warriors were defeated by those of Antiochus, who now marched triumphantly through Palestine, and to Jerusalem. There the Seleucid supporters helped Antiochus' Syrian-Greek soldiers to find and dispose of the Egyptian garrison that had held the city.

Antiochus, now overlord of the region, showed some gratitude. He supplied approved materials for sacrifices and rituals in the Temple: cattle, wheat, spices, salt, oil, and wine. Exemptions from the oppressive head tax and salt tax were granted to the Temple priests and scribes. Other citizens were given a three year pause in such taxes. The Seleucid monarch also pledged to respect the Temple and to protect the freedom of his Jewish subjects to worship according to their traditions and laws.

During more than thirty years following, relative peace prevailed in Jerusalem and Judah under Seleucid rule. The new monarchs, however, pushed harder than the Ptolemies had, to reshape the life of the people along Hellenistic lines. The reason for this push was the threat of far away Rome, the conquering city-state-empire in the boot-shaped Italian peninsula. The cycles of empire were still under way: the Greeks had broken Persian control over the eastern Mediterranean lands; now the Romans were breaking the Hellenistic powers, one by one. In 197 B.C.E., they had dealt a crushing blow to Macedonia, motherland of Alexander the Great. By 192, the Roman leaders felt able to take on the Seleucid monarch, Antiochus III himself. The next year they drove his forces from Greece, and the year after that from Asia Minor. Antiochus was forced to destroy his war fleet, to pledge payment of a huge tribute to Rome, and to see his own son taken to Rome as hostage or pledge for payment.

Antiochus, desperate for funds, sought to take them from temple treasuries in his realm. He was removing treasure from a pagan temple in Elimaid,

Mesopotamia, when the people there, furious at the sacrilege, rose up and killed him and his men.

Seleucus IV was the next to occupy the endangered Seleucid throne. During his reign, the Jewish high priest in Jerusalem was Onias III, member of an aristocratic family, the Oniads, from which had come a number of high priests during the period of Ptolemaic rule. This Onias supported the traditional Jewish rites and observances. Ranged against him, in growing opposition, were priests from other families supporting the Hellenistic policies of the Seleucid rulers.

Simon, one of these Hellenizers among the priests, determined to unseat Onias, told Apollonius, the Seleucid governor, that the Temple treasury stood "full of infinite sums of money" not needed for the services. What followed is part of a miraculous folktale, related in II Maccabees, in the Apocrypha, the collection of writings that were considered but excluded when the present Bible was finally compiled.

> Seleucus IV, avid for money as his father had been, sent Heliodorus, his treasurer, to bring wealth from the Temple on Mount Moriah. Onias stood helplessly aghast when he found what Heliodorus intended. However, divine protectors appeared and thwarted the theft. One was in the form of "a horse with a terrible rider," the other two were handsome young men. They whipped Heliodorus till his body showed "many sore stripes." He would have been killed, had not Onias hastily offered sacrifice for his health, and thus saved him.

Next on the Seleucid throne was Antiochus IV who had spent some fifteen years living as royal hostage in Rome. He is described as combining the worst characteristics of both the Greeks and the Romans: on the one hand a craving for luxury and splendor, on the other a craving for violence and cruelty. He added to his name *Epiphanes*, meaning that he was a divine being. His detractors, however, secretly lampooned him with a Greek pun: *Epimanes*, meaning crazy or wild.

Mad he may have seemed sometimes, but with a method. Rome threatened to bite off and swallow his remaining empire. He was determined to unify his subjects to resist this growing danger. Religion was to become the strong cement to hold them together: a single, identical religion for all, with himself Epiphanes, worshiped along with the assorted Olympian gods, headed by Zeus. Such enforced paganism violated the pledge Antiochus III had given the leaders in Jerusalem: to respect their religious rights and rites.

Another priest of the Temple staff encouraged Epiphanes to forget that pledge. He was, in fact, a brother of Onias, and had been named Joshua, but chose rather the Hellenistic name of Jason. To King Epiphanes, Jason now offered a bribe: "Make me high priest and I'll see that you get much more tribute than you now do from Jerusalem."

Thus Onias was ousted and banished in 174 B.C.E. As new high priest,

How Heliodorus was foiled in his attempt to steal the Temple treasure, as pictured by Gustave Doré in his *Bible Gallery*. In an interior like an Egyptian Temple, three winged avengers have felled Heliodorus and four of his men at arms. These angels carry as weapons bundles of branches to use as lashes, rather than swords to pierce.

Jason tried to Hellenize Jerusalem and all Judea. A typical Hellenistic *gymnasium* was built near the Temple. It combined Greek games and dances with pagan worship. Young Jewish men, unclothed in defiance of their traditions, appeared there. Even young priests from the Temple sometimes took part in these fashionable rites. Jason sent a delegation of young men with money to pay for a sacrifice to the Phoenician god Heracles, in honor of an appearance that King Epiphanes was to make at a Greek games festival at Tyre. The young Jews could not bring themselves, finally, to be parties to such idolatry, and instead contributed the money to the royal treasury, to use for building ships.

Epiphanes himself visiting Jerusalem was received with torchlight processions and flattering attentions. Jason was rewarded with authority to issue decrees changing the basic law — the constitution, so to speak — of the land of *Yehud*, now known as Judea.

Another Temple priest, also with a Hellenistic name — Menelaus — belonged to the family of Tobiads, long rivals of the Oniads. Menelaus, being sent to take "pay off" money from Jason to Epiphanes, delivered it — and also the suggestion that if *he* were made high priest he would make these payments larger still.

Jason fled for his life across the Jordan, and the high priest in the Temple was now Menelaus, who (according to II Maccabees) possessed "The fury of a cruel tyrant and the rage of a savage beast," but "nothing worthy of the high priesthood." Menelaus soon was in trouble. Unable to make the promised payments to the monarch, he was called to the capital, Antioch. He left the Temple in charge of his brother Lysimachus, and took along some of the Temple's sacred vessels of precious metal, with which to bribe the King's men.

In Antioch, the former Jewish high priest, Onias III, appeared, and raised charges of Temple looting against Menelaus, who responded by having Onias murdered. The murderer was later convicted and executed, but Menelaus managed to retain his position as high priest. Further Temple plundering by Menelaus' brother Lysimachus roused a storm of popular protest. People marched on the Temple, routed the guarding soldiers with paving stones and crude clubs, and then, finding Lysimachus in the Sanctuary's treasury, killed him there.

A delegation of Jewish representatives was sent to tell the king of the crimes committed against the Temple and to beg him to rid them of Menelaus. Epiphanes, however, rejected their plea and had three of them executed.

This Seleucid monarch had concerns greater than little Palestine. Believing Rome to be preoccupied elsewhere, he invaded Egypt in 170 B.C.E. Rumors reached Jerusalem that he had been killed, and the former high priest Jason, returning to Jerusalem with a small army, was apparently welcomed as a far lesser evil than Menelaus. The latter took refuge with the Seleucid soldiers who garrisoned the city, while the people, headed by Jason, celebrated the overthrow of Syrian tyranny. This was premature, for Epiphanes hurried back, still much alive and bent on vengeance. Aided by Menelaus, his men seized the most precious remaining treasures of the Temple and carried them off to Antioch. Menelaus, depending more than ever on the swords of the Syrian garrison, stayed on as high priest.

Again in 168 B.C.E., Epiphanes sought to invade Egypt, but within a few miles of Alexandria was halted by a Roman commander and ordered, in a most insulting way, to leave Egypt at once. He withdrew, seething with rage, and vented it on his stubborn subjects in Jerusalem. His army of Syrian and Greek mercenaries ran amok there on a Jewish Sabbath, plundering, kidnapping, murdering. Thousands died, other thousands fled.

Now the city was transformed by orders of Epiphanes. A lofty Hellenistic fortress, the "Acra," was erected, dominating the Temple itself, and garrisoned by Syrian soldiery. In Jerusalem's western hills was built a Hellenistic section that came to be known as "Antiochia in Jerusalem." In it were lodged the Seleucid soldiers, officials, their families, and servitors.

Crushing decrees were issued against observance of the Jewish Sabbath, of Jewish dietary laws, of the rite of circumcision, and of Jewish traditional worship of the one God. Only the pagan gods of Olympus were to be worshiped henceforth, and to enforce this, an altar to Zeus was erected on top of the famous Temple altar to Yahweh. The date of that infamy became a Jewish tradition: 168 B.C.E., on the 15th day of the third lunar month, *Kislev* (equivalent to January). Ten days later, on the 25th, the first burnt offering to pagan gods was made at the Temple. Within its walls and courts now stood statues of those alien dieties, Zeus, Hera, Dionysius (Bacchus), Aphrodite (Venus), Ares (Mars), and others. Pagan priests walked its corridors.

Compulsory paganizing went even further. Pious Jews were forced to eat pork, or to wear vine and grape leaves in honor of Bacchus. Some found reason to save their lives or families by swearing allegiance to pagan creeds. Others refused and died as martyrs. Still others declined either to comply or die. They found ways to resist, to fight back.

One such was a Jewish priest named Mattathias, of the family of the Hasmoneans. His great gesture took place not in Jerusalem where he had lived, but at a small village, Modiin, where he had sought refuge. An agent of the new tyrannical regime had come to Modiin to see that pagan sacrifices were conducted as decreed. Mattathias refused to take part. When another Jew stepped up ready to do so, Mattathias killed him, and the royal agent also. Then, with his five stalwart sons, Mattathias fled to the mountains. They were joined there by other resisting Jews, called the *Hasidim* or "pious ones." Soon, out of those forbidding hills came commando bands destroying the pagan altars, summoning farmers and workers to resist with them. In their mountain hideaways they practiced their traditional worship and planned new forays against the infidels.

Mattathias died but his sons carried on, led by Judas, who struck so hard in his raids that he came to be called the *Maccabee*, or Hammerer.

In 167 B.C.E., the Seleucid general, Apollonius, who had commanded during the massacre in Jerusalem, led troops to find and destroy these impudent rebels. Judas' raiders, however, struck first; the soldiers were wiped out, Apollonius died, and his sword was taken and used from then on by Judas. During the next years, this Hammerer and his armed "Hasidim" won one victory after another against the Seleucid forces. Finally, they achieved their first great goal — they liberated Jerusalem, regained and cleansed the Temple, after its three years of pagan desecration, and rekindled the traditional lights in the Menorah or seven-branched candelabrum.

That day, the 25th of *Kislev*, 164 B.C.E., has been celebrated ever since by observing Jews as the Festival of Lights or *Hanukkah.* Tradition tells that though there was ritually pure oil for the lamps to burn only a single day, they nevertheless shone on during eight days of great thanksgiving. Thus the Hanukkah lights always hold eight candles, as well as one more from which the others are lit, in increasing numbers, night after night.

The Maccabee, or Hasmonean, rulers lived at Jerusalem in a colonnaded palace like this model, today standing on the grounds of the Holyland Hotel of that city. This is part of a remarkable scale reconstruction of old Jerusalem, based on research by an eminent art historian and archeologist, Dr. Michael Avi-Yonah; built by architect Rolf Brontzen; and sponsored by Hans Kroch, proprietor of the Holyland Hotel.

The victory in Jerusalem was not yet complete, however. Though the Sanctuary was secure, the Acra fortress overlooking it remained in the hands of Seleucid troops. Jerusalem was cut into hostile sectors — as it was to be again more than once in the following centuries, down to our own twentieth century. To counterbalance the Acra, the Maccabee forces built counter-fortifications on the Temple mount, and also south of it.

Under command of Judas and of Simon Maccabee, the patriots went on to win a series of scattered and improbable victories. Finally, a huge Seleucid army marched into Palestine, headed by a new king, Antiochus V. (Epiphanes having died while warring in Persia far to the east.) These forces did retake the Temple, but, guided by past lessons, did not interfere with its traditional sacrifices and services.

A complex series of events led finally, by 141 B.C.E., to the gaining of power over all Jerusalem and environs by the forces under the surviving Maccabee. The hated Acra was pulled down, leaving no fortress to dominate the Temple. A new building arose, however — the residence of the Maccabee leader, who now became both high priest for the Temple and political head, prince, or "ethnarch," of the Jewish commonwealth. This dual role was filled by Simon, last of the five sons of Mattathias. The other brothers had all died in battles.

For the first time in many bloody centuries, the land of the Temple and of the children of Israel was free of a foreign yoke. Yet many of its citizens, traditional in their attitudes, looked with doubt or disfavor on the new situation in which one leader was both high priest and also head of the state and its armed forces.

9

Rome and King Herod in Judea

(142–22 B.C.E.)

The era of the native Maccabee or Hasmonean rulers brought increases in territory, through conquests of neighboring regions. It brought also marked increase of population and growing awareness among the Judean people of their diverse aims and interests. Two principal parties or pressure-groups came to the fore: the Sadducees and the Pharisees.

The Sadducees were in general wealthy aristocrats. From their ranks came the priests who staffed the Temple under the high priest, who was now also the ruler or king of the nation. The Sadducees supported formal Temple rites and traditions, though in their private lives they leaned toward Greek culture and sophistication. They believed in a kind of national "church," with themselves in authority; in a strong aristocracy; and in expansion by military conquest. They stressed the rigid written Law of their religion.

The Pharisees, on the other hand, represented the educated "middle class," the scholars, teachers, early rabbis, and moral leaders. They favored general schooling, urged popular participation and control in the national religion, stressed the oral and traditional rather than the written Law, supported the new synagogues that were springing up, and opposed both the Temple monopoly of the priests and the militaristic adventures of their monarchs.

Differences on these broader issues were sometimes hidden behind clashes over small details of ritual or observance. This was illustrated during the reign of one especially warlike Maccabee, King Alexander Yannai or

Janneus (103–76 B.C.E.), who held the throne and also the position of high priest. When not leading his armies of mercenaries and other troops in costly wars, he actually presided as high priest in some important Temple services. On one memorable day, the final one of the Festival of Tabernacles, or *Succoth*, this king-priest approached the altar in the presence of worshipers, who were carrying traditional palm branches and citrons. On this special holiday ordinary worshipers, though not of priesthood, might enter the sacred enclosure around the altar. There, according to the ritual code of the Pharisees, the high priest should make a "libation" by pouring water on the altar. The Sadducees, however, opposed this ritual. The short-tempered king-priest, sharing this opposition, suddenly dashed to the ground the water he was holding. An uproar of protest followed this outrage. The worshipers, mostly Pharisee in their convictions, even dared pelt the monarch with the citrons they carried, accusing him of being unfit to serve at the great altar.

The king then ordered his soldiers against the congregation, many of whom were killed. This Temple episode served as prelude to an outright civil war (94–88 B.C.E.). So desperate became the people's hatred against this king, that leaders of the Pharisee uprising even called in the aid of a foreign monarch, one of the last of the waning Seleucid dynasty. The opposing forces met in battle at the historic site of Schechem in 88 B.C.E. On each of the two sides were both Jews and Greeks. King Yannai and his Sadducee supporters lost the battle, and he took refuge in the hills of Ephraim. This might have become the end of Maccabee rule, had not many of the Jews on the victorious side had a change of heart. They found they feared more the presence of the Seleucid monarch and his troops than they disliked their native-born king. They went over to Yannai's side, and the Seleucid left the land. Only then was Yannai able to quell the revolt and resume his kingship.

His death in 76 B.C.E. brought his widow, Queen Alexandra Salome, to the throne. She was as friendly to the Pharisees as her husband had been hostile. Her reign brought peace, internal improvements, and marked the beginning of schooling provided for children. A queen was not permitted to serve as high priest, but Alexandra did lead her land during an interim of recovery and hope.

Unfortunately her two sons were deadly rivals. Hyrcanus, the elder, preferred peace and leaned on Pharisee support, but lacked firmness and magnetism. Aristobolus, the younger, was an ambitious fire-eater, who led a coup against the crown by army officers and other Sadducee partisans. Just after his mother's death, he arrived with his warriors to enter Jerusalem, while the legal king, his brother Hyrcanus, sought refuge in the citadel beside the Temple.

Complex moves and countermoves followed. By 66 B.C.E., the positions had been reversed. Now Aristobolus and his men were holed up in the Temple citadel, and under siege by an army from the southern kingdom of the Nabateans, who were backing Hyrcanus — for a price. It was a desperate situation. Among other resulting evils, the people were deprived of the Temple and its rites. The Passover festival approached, and some Jews even traveled as far as Egypt seeking a Jewish temple where they could celebrate their great feast of liberation.

Aristobolus and the priests remaining on the Temple mount tried to maintain the daily rites, but had no animals to sacrifice. They worked out a curious deal with their besiegers. Each day they would lower a basket containing agreed sums of money from the Temple treasury, and when the basket was drawn up it would contain some expensive animal, such as a ram, for sacrifice.

The wars of brother against brother, neighbor against neighbor, were wasting past gains and preparing for future enslavement. At that very time, the greatest imperial enslaver of them all was in action in Syria to the north. There, Roman legions, under command of Pompey, were completing their conquest of what had been the heart of the Seleucid empire. The two rival Maccabee brothers inevitably each sought to buy Pompey's aid. Thus, from Syria, Pompey began in 65 and 64 B.C.E. to take a hand in the power struggles in Judea, and having completed his Syrian operations he was ready by 63 B.C.E. to make a personal appearance. Heading his seasoned legionnaires, he marched into the land of the Maccabees — and demanded the surrender of all concerned.

One faction opened to him the gates of Jerusalem, but another, composed of supporters of Aristobolus, held the Temple mount and refused to give way. Again, as so often before and afterward, the sacred city was the scene of a stubborn siege. Roman military engineers proceeded with customary thoroughness. First they flung an oblong dike entirely around the Temple mount like a great noose, to prevent escapers from leaving or helpers from entering. Then they erected runways or ramps at strategic points both north and west of the courtyard on which the Temple stood. They did this work purposely on Jewish Sabbaths, knowing that the Temple defenders were forbidden by their religious laws to fight on the Sabbath except in actual defense of their lives. From the ramps huge Roman catapults began to fling rounded boulders as missiles at the Temple. Yet its services were continued, and each morning burnt offerings were made.

After preparations lasting three months, Pompey mounted his attack, selecting again a Sabbath while the priests were conducting Temple services. Roman battering rams breached gates and walls, and the tough legionnaires swarmed through, their short swords naked in the autumn air. Those swords spilled the blood of priests beside the altars where they had neither paused nor sought refuge from their ritual tasks.

Rome, in the persons of Pompey and his captains, now strode over dead defenders and priests, into the Temple itself. Like tourists they walked from room to room, staring and commenting. Pompey entered even the westernmost sacred chamber, the forbidden Holy of Holies. A strange temple this, in the eyes of pagan Romans! Not one idol. Not one worshiped statue or picture. Only sacred vessels and utensils for ordained rites in honor of one invisible Lord of heaven and earth.

Pompey did not compound his desecration by plunder. He looked at but did not remove the Temple treasure. Nor did he cause the destruction of the building.

Under the new Roman overlords, life in Judea was rapidly changed and restricted. Great sections of territory gained under Maccabee leaders were cut loose and added to the Roman colonial province of Syria. Pompey named Hyrcanus to serve as high priest and also as "ethnarch," a title that was not that of a king, but rather merely of a spokesman or ceremonial figurehead for his people. The real "general manager" proved to be a subtle, sinister figure, Antipater of Idumea, a region distrusted and feared by the Judeans. Antipater may well have felt resentment and contempt for the Judeans. He ensnared their leaders with devious and usually successful schemes, and step by step connived his way upward, flattering and serving the Romans until he had become the real ruler.

Pompey meantime had returned to Rome to enjoy a traditional "triumph" such as was granted to returning victors and bringers of booty. He had this time well answered the crass question asked later by the Roman Tribune Marullus, a character in Shakespeare's drama, *Julius Caesar*:

> What conquests brings he home?
> What tributaries follow him to Rome
> To grace in captive bonds his chariot wheels?

Aristobolus, once high priest and king in Jerusalem, was among the captives as Pompey's chariot pounded along the Roman pavements. With Aristobolus were three of his children and many lesser captives, as well as much plunder from Jerusalem and Judea. The joy which greeted such evidences of Roman gains abroad was indicated by that same Marullus in Shakespeare's *Julius Caesar*:

> . . . To see great Pompey pass the streets of Rome.
> And when you saw his chariot but appear
> Have you not made a universal shout . . . ?

The Romans from the start met with resistance and trouble in their rule of the new Judean colony. Descendants of the Maccabee kings led uprisings in 57 B.C.E. At one period, in the effort to disunite Judea, the Romans ordered it divided into five governing districts, each with its own Sanhedrin or high council, instead of just the one centered in Jerusalem at the Temple. Yet even during that period the Temple retained for the people its preeminence as sanctuary and symbol.

In Rome itself a ceaseless struggle for power led to the formation of the first triumvirate or three-way rule, headed by Pompey, Julius Caesar, and Crassus, a corrupt financier. Crassus visited Judea and headed for the Temple, not to gaze on its treasures but to steal them. He took away about ten thousand "talents," equal to nine or ten million dollars today! Still another rebellion flared in Judea. Its leader, Pithalus, was executed, and some thirty thousand Jews sold as slaves.

This first triumvirate broke up, and in a decisive battle at Pharsalia, Greece, in 48 B.C.E., Caesar defeated the more numerous forces of Pompey, who fled to Egypt where he was slain. Caesar, in pursuit, reached Egypt. As the sole surviving member of the triumvirate he was now virtual dictator of Rome. While in Egypt Caesar fell under the spell of Cleopatra, one of the most fascinating and poisonous of the long line of the Ptolemaic dynasty.

Caesar, however, was not too preoccupied to extend his attentions also to Judea to the east and north of the Nile valley. He abolished the offensive five-way division of the land of Judea, and re-established old Hyrcanus, the Maccabee, as high priest, with Antipater, the Idumean, as procurator or governor in the name of Rome. Caesar also allowed restoration of Jerusalem's protective walls which had been destroyed by Pompey. Caesar indeed sought, and to a large degree won, the gratitude and loyalty of the people of Judea.

After Caesar was assassinated in Rome in 44 B.C.E., Cassius, one of the conspirators against him, solicited and received support from the Roman legions stationed in the East, including Judea. However, the conspirators were defeated at Philippi by a new or second triumvirate, including Mark Antony and Caesar's nephew Octavian, later to be known as Augustus. Mark Antony then became ruler of Roman Asia, Cleopatra's new lover, and the deciding voice for the time in the affairs of Judea.

In 40 B.C.E., during one of history's strange interludes, the Parthians from Persia invaded Syria and Asia Minor. Antigonus, son of Aristobolus the Maccabee, persuaded these new conquerors to make him both high priest and king in Jerusalem. His uncle Hyrcanus became a Parthian captive, after his ears had been cut off so that he might never again be a priest. (Jewish religious law required priests of the Temple to be free from major bodily blemishes.)

Antigonus became the last of the line of Maccabees to bear both the titles of king and of high priest of the Temple. He remained there until 37 B.C.E. when a Roman army sent by Mark Antony besieged Jerusalem. Again the Temple became a refuge, again the Romans broke through after a three months siege, and again Temple defenders and their families were slaughtered. Antigonus himself was dragged off and beheaded, a punishment unusual among monarchs captured by the Romans.

Now Mark Antony's good friend and helper, Herod, Antipater's son, rose to the top. His name is one of the most despised and denounced in history. He was truly in many ways a monster. He was also one of the most resourceful, ruthless, and successful royal schemers of his own or any other era. (Perhaps only a monster could have secured and retained the subjugated throne of Judea under the iron heel of Rome!)

From 37 to about 25 B.C.E., his first dozen years as king of Judea, Herod intrigued, schemed, battled, and betrayed to strengthen his rule. His Roman masters found he had one ability they prized most highly: he was efficient in exacting taxes from his people and forwarding the proceeds to Rome. This made him, in Roman eyes, a statesman, a pillar of law and order, and a ruler deserving of still larger territories to administer and exploit. Herod weathered many a storm, including the defeat, downfall, and death of his great friend and sponsor, Mark Antony. In fact, Herod managed before long to ingratiate himself also with the very man who had defeated Antony and was now Rome's first real Emperor — Augustus.

With the last serious opposition dead or paralyzed in Judea, King Herod turned to less strenuous and more congenial tasks. He loved large, imposing structures — especially when they bore his name as builder. Also, he was determined to establish his image as that of a loyal, up-to-date, civilized Roman. He tried to make Jerusalem resemble other fine cities of the Roman empire. Within the city he built a Roman theater, and an amphitheater on its outskirts. He staged Roman-style games to glorify his current patron and friend — the great, the "divine," Augustus. These pagan displays in old Jerusalem included the usual gymnastic and athletic contests and exciting "specials" — gladiatorial combats between humans, or between humans and beasts, usually wild from fear and hunger.

Many, perhaps most, of Herod's Jewish subjects resented, despised, or even denounced these brutal shows, so alien to Jewish customs and principles. There were complaints, too, against the "advertisements" for the spectacles — dummies in military garb, looking far too much like pagan idols. A plot to assassinate Herod was uncovered, but the people showed more sympathy for the plotters than for the king. Herod was not so stupid as to forget that to most of his Judean subjects he was still an inferior outsider, an alien Idumean, a Roman puppet, and also a pagan profaner of the ancient law of Moses. Even his marriage to Mariamne, the beautiful Jewish princess of the Maccabee line, did not make Herod himself "one of ours" in the eyes of large numbers of his subjects. His suspicious and hostile treatment of members of his family, which led finally to his orders to execute Mariamne, was known widely. Herod, acutely sensitive to opposition, did not dare go too far in risking greater hatred from the Jews, even to win greater approval from his Roman masters.

His building projects proved heavy burdens to the people. Worse, a famine struck the land in 24 B.C.E. Herod bent before this tempest, that it might not break him. He brought food from Egypt to feed some of the hungry. Also he sought for a project or gesture to win him good will in Judea — and also add to his chosen image of splendor and achievement.

He found his answer at last in Jerusalem itself, not far from his own costly palace of marble and gold, so different from the earlier modest quarters of the Maccabee rulers.

The Temple! The Sacred Sanctuary itself! King Herod would rebuild it — larger, more impressive, and more resplendent than ever before.

The palace of King Herod in Jerusalem combined luxury in the Roman fashion with fortress-like walls and towers. Herod, a cruel and clever tyrant, lived in fear of his subjects. This reconstruction is in the grounds of the Holyland Hotel in modern Jerusalem.

10

The Great Temple Rises

(22–4 B.C.E.)

The Temple had been repaired and rebuilt to some extent in the era of the Maccabee priest-kings. The ravages of the centuries, plus earthquakes now and then, made such renovations essential. But in size and plan it remained, inside and out, basically the same modest building begun under Zeru-babbel more than five hundred years before. It was not even so grand as the first Temple of Solomon.

Herod began to plan and arrange for this, his greatest building project, about 22 or 23 B.C.E. From the start, he tried to show himself as pious or observant of religious tradition as any among his Jewish subjects. This new Temple must be not only bigger and more beautiful, but also free from any sacrilege in its construction. Herod decreed that it should be erected in accord with rules laid down by priests and scholars learned in the laws of Moses.

The core of the construction crew was a staff of a thousand priests trained in stone masonry. Laboring under their direction were nearly nine thousand men. Actual work began about 19 B.C.E. Because continuity of sacrifice and ritual was maintained during the construction period, some scholars apply the term "second Temple" to the sanctuary of Herod as well as to that of Zeru-babbel which preceded it.

First came the clearing, upbuilding, and surfacing of a vastly larger stone platform or great court on which the new Temple was to rise. This platform when finally finished seemed enormous, almost overpowering, to those who remembered the old so well. It was a trapezoid, rather than a strict rectangle. Its total perimeter measured about 4600 feet. The longest side was the western, close to 1600 feet. The northern was about 900 feet, while the eastern side was somewhat shorter than the western and the southern shorter than the northern.

This platform enclosed within its surrounding walls a total area about as great as that of a square a quarter of a mile on each edge. This almost doubled the area of the previous Temple court. Today in Jerusalem one may still see the extent of this great platform, known now as the Haram esh-Sherif. Its dimensions have been increased, but only a little, since it was first built under Herod. The enlargement of level top surface at that time was achieved partly by cutting into the natural rock outcropping in one direction (the northwest), and partly by piling up vast quantities of dirt and rubble as "fill" in other directions (the southwest, and also the southeast).

All this filling for the top platform was retained within massive walls. History had shown, later would show again, the need for such brute strength. Not only were destructive forces of weather to be resisted, but also periodic military sieges and civil disturbances.

The extreme height of platform above foundation rock was 155 feet, at the southeast corner. The southwest stood about two-thirds as high. The southern summit's average elevation above its foundation was well over 100 feet. These man-made cliffs were walled with huge Herodian masonry, still recognizable today. Sheer size and exactness of finish are the outstanding characteristics of these enormous blocks. They are arranged in great parallel layers or courses, like bricks in a wall, and measure between 3 1/3 and 6 feet from bottom to top. Some are as much as 30 to 40 feet from end to end. They are correspondingly large from front to back. A single Herodian stone block may contain from 600 to more than 1200 cubic feet of stone, and weigh 50 to 100 tons. Typical of Herodian blocks is the double flat border or rim around the side of the stone that faces outward. Within this framelike rim lies the slightly projecting central portion called "the boss." Great technical skill went into the building of enduring walls from such giant blocks, in an age when muscle power had to do all heavy work.

Along the western wall, which became and remains the most famous, twenty-five layers or courses were laid, the average depth of a layer being between 3½ and 4 feet. By autumn of 1968, eleven of those great Herodian stone courses were still visible above ground, and many more, buried beneath the rubble of nearly two thousand years, remained to be excavated and exposed. Sieges and destructions at that sacred and bloody site have greatly raised former ground levels. The floor of the Kidron Valley, to the east of the Temple platform, stands in fact in some places fully 90 feet higher than it did when Herod's engineers and architects made their plans.

The great platform of the Temple mount must have loomed even more boldly above the small buildings of ancient Jerusalem than it does over today's busy city. This Temple mount was the sacred citadel of Jerusalem, its *acropolis*, as the Greeks called it. And the platform prepared for the Temple of Herod provided about five times as much flat space as that on which stood the famous temple of Athena, the Parthenon, overlooking Athens, Greece.

Shrewd financier that he was, Herod knew that the grander the new Temple, the greater would be the influx of pilgrims from Palestine itself and from the many other Jewish communities all over the Roman world. The space atop the great platform was divided so as to shelter and serve large numbers of visitors, whether they came to worship, to sightsee, or simply to trade. "The Temple" before and after this time did not mean simply a central building or inner sanctuary. It was a complex of rites and functions, many of which, such as animal sacrifices, necessarily took place outside that building.

First, for privacy, but most of all for protection, the summit of the platform was ringed round with a great top wall or barrier. Each of the four rather unequal sides of this uppermost wall was pierced by one or more gates, leading to the less sacred world outside. Since the greatest number of visitors would come from Jerusalem's upper city, toward the west, four gates were provided in the upper wall facing in that direction. On that same side, the upper Tyropeon valley had been spanned by a single viaduct from upper city to Temple mount. Now a second viaduct was added. The first is called today "Wilson's Arch," for the archeologist who identified its ruins. The second has similarly come to be called "Robinson's Arch." Two gates faced south, one north, and but one to the east, where lay the Mount of Olives, and beyond it the Judean wilderness. Thus the wall facing west had as many gates as the other three together.

High walls and strong gates were not the only protections for the huge new Temple platform. At its northwest corner stood a strong fortress named the *Antonia*, for Herod's late friend, Mark Antony. Herod, in fact, was a prolific builder of fortifications, for like many a tyrant he was constantly afraid. His own splendid palace in the upper city was partly a costly mansion, partly a powerful citadel. And many miles south of Jerusalem, just west of the midpoint of the Dead Sea, atop a steeply sheer cliff, stood his private fortress-palace of Masada, complete with royal apartments, baths, granaries, and guard quarters.

Around the margins of the Temple platform, just inside the upper walls, stood great covered arcades or porches. Their broad, shady roofs rested on huge carved beams, in turn supported by many hundreds of fine columns in Greco-Roman style. The most elaborate was the so-called "royal porch" along the south wall. Its roofs were supported by about one hundred and sixty pillars arranged in four rows. The row closest to the wall was actually sunk part way into it. The three other rows formed three long passageways or aisles under the roof. These colonnades resembled a great hall or "basilica," though they were open toward the north, allowing easy access to the unroofed courtyard beyond.

The porches along the other three sides were supported on double rows of pillars. Even these supported roofs were said to be some 50 feet wide. The two aisles thus formed also opened freely on the inner, unroofed courtyard. A visitor to the platform could use these porchlike arcades to walk to almost any point on the outer margin of the platform without facing the burning sun in summer or blasts of wind in winter.

Such was the foundation and the outside "frame" for the Temple and its associated structures. These occupied a raised rectangular area measuring about 500 feet from east to west and a little more than half that from north to south. This interior rectangle stood almost entirely in the northern half of the great platform and was surrounded by a stone balustrade or fence about 5 feet high. All the platform outside this fence was a court or area of "the gentiles," meaning that it could be used by people of whatever faith or ancestry. But no gentile, or non-Jew, might pass within. Warnings were inscribed on the stone fence in Greek and Latin, the languages of most gentiles then. "Strangers may not pass here to enter the sanctuary," these notices read. "Anyone found doing so will bring down on himself the penalty — death."

Within the fenced area were three additional courts. If one entered from the east, bound for the Temple itself, one first mounted several steps, passed through a fine gate in an outer wall, and reached the women's court. Jewish women might enter it, but not go beyond, for the Temple rites were restricted to men by ancient religious laws. There were also gates to the women's court on its northern and southern sides.

If one left the women's court, still headed westward, one passed an imposing gate, climbed some fifteen steps, and entered "the court of Israel," also called "the men's court," measuring about 22 feet by 116 feet. Beyond it was a larger court reserved for the priests themselves, and set about 18 inches higher than the men's court. Only on a few special holiday occasions might non-priests, the laymen of the religion, enter the priestly court.

The "court of Israel" was small indeed compared with the number of worshipers who crowded into it on high occasions. A legend arose that at certain points in the service when they all bowed in reverence, the court area miraculously expanded, allowing them to bow without hindrance.

Near the eastern end of the priests' court loomed the great Rock supporting the altar of burnt offerings. A ramp on its southern side led to the sacrificial summit. This was probably the same large outcropping that had served as the threshing floor of the Jebusite Ornan in the days of King David. And about 20 feet west of the altar stood the front of the radiant new Sanctuary itself: the Temple of Herod, as he loved to hear it called.

Indeed, the new Temple was a striking and dazzling structure, all white marble set off by gleaming gold. Its façade rose some 150 feet high and it was equally wide. Along a glistening front were spaced four great columns about 60 feet high, with capitals in Greco-Roman style. In the center stood its lofty and imposing gate.

This resplendent mansion of the one God could be seen from a long way off. Its fame soon spread through the imperial Roman world, especially among Jewish communities and colonies widely scattered outside Palestine and including between four and seven million people. The saying arose, preserved in the *Talmud*, "Whoever has not seen the Temple of Herod has never seen a beautiful building!"

If viewed from above, the new Temple appeared like a great block letter T, covering some 18,000 square feet of area. About a quarter of this was in the crossbar section which lay to the east and was fronted by the façade and entrance gate. The other three quarters were in the broad stem, extending westward. This stem section was some 105 feet wide, or about 45 feet narrower than the front crossbar section. From front to back the full building extended about 130 feet, of which 30 was in the front crossbar section, and the final 100 feet in the stem behind it.

The authors of this book incline to the view that this new Temple's imposing exterior was in fact a sort of shell or jacket for an inner structure whose dimensions were about the same as those inside the old Temple. The Temple of Solomon had been but 50 feet high, 115 feet from front to back, and 65 to 70 feet in total width, including the belt of storerooms that surrounded the innermost holy places.

Priests entering this new Temple of Herod first climbed a dozen impressive steps, then passed through the entrance portal into the *ulam* or porch chamber, about 100 feet from side to side and 20 feet from front to back. A smaller doorway led from there into the *hekal* or Holy Place, which was but 30 to 35 feet from side to side and 65 feet from front to back. At that back wall hung a marvelous large veil or curtain, which partitioned off the final section — the *debir*, or Holy of Holies, still no more than 30 to 35 feet square. The Temple of Solomon had a wall between *hekal* and *debir*; now only this famous veil supplied the separation. It was a substantial double curtain.

These two innermost holy chambers were relatively tall — 60 to 65 feet from ceiling to floor. There seems also to have been a "second story" above them in the Herodian temple, providing an upstairs chamber also 60 or 65 feet in height and measuring as much as 100 feet from east to west.

It appears that surrounding small cells or chambers for storage and safe-keeping were provided also in this new Temple. Between thirty-five and forty separate chambers apparently were arranged in three tiers as before, and used to hold garments, equipment, supplies, records, and all other necessaries.

The essential structure of the Temple stood in all its glory by about 9 B.C.E., ten years after the work first began. However, various details were not then finally finished, and, indeed, during the following seventy-five years, work still continued. Herod never lived to see it fully completed. He died, of a painful disease, in the year 4 B.C.E.

The Temple itself revealed the clash between Herod's two great purposes in building it — namely, to prove to his subjects that he was basically a pious and observing supporter of the Jewish faith; and also to prove to his Roman overlords that he was a thoroughgoing supporter of their Empire.

This clash was embodied in a huge golden eagle with outstretched wings displayed above the doorway of the Temple, a bird of prey, symbolic of the power of Rome. This winged predator offended the pious of Judea. They resented Rome, and besides, it seemed a flagrant breach of the ancient Mosaic ban against the worship of graven images, whether of men or beasts.

The high priest and his staff priests did not call for removal of the eagle. They were in general docile supporters of Herod. He could not himself hold the high-priesthood as had the Maccabee kings before him. However, he could decide, with the consent and backing of Rome, who should hold that high office, and for how long.

When one day Herod, aged 70, lay desperately ill and clearly growing worse, a rumor raced through Jerusalem and out into the rest of Judea: Herod was already as good as dead! Up flared the fierce resistance that his terror had forced underground. Two pious Pharisee teachers called on their students to make a great gesture of faith and patriotism: destroy the detested eagle! A crowd gathered at the Temple, pulled down the golden bird, and hacked it to bits. Herod's police arrested forty persons, including the teachers, Matthias ben Margolith and Judah ben Tsarifah. The sick old tyrant Herod raised himself to look at the prisoners brought to his bedside. The prospect of a new punishment always seemed to stimulate him. "Did you do this?" he demanded. "Yes," answered the prisoners calmly. "Who told you to?" Herod asked next. "The laws of our fathers," they replied.

Herod's last question did not concern their guilt or punishment, which he had already decided. It reflected rather his own preoccupation. "How can you be so joyful when you know you must die?" Their answer, "Because we know that after death the supreme reward will be ours."

The executions took place in March of 4 B.C.E. The two teachers of the law were burnt alive, the others beheaded. Herod's revenge went still further. He removed the high priest of the Temple, since the eagle had been destroyed during his tenancy in that office. A certain Joezer of the Baethus family was then installed as the new high priest. Not much later, after having ordered the execution of his son Antipater (named for Herod's own father) Herod himself died.

The winter before, in 5 B.C.E., a son was born to Mary, the espoused wife of Joseph, a good carpenter of Nazareth in Judea. (This is the most probable date in the opinion of leading Bible scholars.) The boy was given the common Jewish name of Jesus or Jesua, a form of the ancient name of Joshua. This Jesus of Nazareth and Herod's Temple at Jerusalem were to be linked unforgettably in the religious annals of the world.

11

The Temple of Jerusalem and Jesus of Nazareth

(4 B.C.E.–29 C.E.)

Archelaus was the name of the son to whom Herod, in his final will, tried to leave Jerusalem and most of Judea. Archelaus began by securing a pledge of support from the mercenary army that Herod had maintained; then he observed the traditional Jewish week of mourning for his dead father, after which he appeared at the Temple to speak to the waiting people.

Their reply was a demand for relief from tyrannical rule, for reduced taxes, for greater freedoms, and for release of political prisoners who had been incarcerated under Herod. Archelaus promised to do what he could, but pointed out that first he had to wait for approval from the Roman Emperor, Augustus.

Many in Judea wanted changes far more basic than these reforms. Among the most discontented and nationalistic, a party called "the Zealots" had formed. After the end of the official period of mourning for Herod they declared their own period of mourning — for Herod's victims, and especially for the executed teachers, Matthias and Judah. During that period they called for punishment of Herod's henchmen and advisors, and insisted on assurances that from now on only *worthy* men would be appointed as High Priests of the Temple. Archelaus again urged patience and delay, but in vain.

The great Passover festival came in the spring of the year 3 B.C.E. As customary, numbers of pilgrims went up to Jerusalem, and to its Temple area. In the broad Temple court a great political demonstration took place on the Passover eve. Against it, Archelaus sent both foot and cavalry soldiers, who killed almost three thousand civilians. Then Archelaus ordered the Passover pilgrims to leave Jerusalem.

By now Archelaus was hated much as his father Herod had been. Hurrying to Rome, Archelaus pleaded with Emperor Augustus to confirm him as King of Judea. Meanwhile, Roman commanders and their legions moved into the land to suppress the outbreaks, which clearly carried threats to Roman domination. To Jerusalem came Sabinus, a Roman procurator (or governor), who installed himself in the fine palace of Herod, confiscated its treasures, and proceeded to oppress the people. All too clearly, naked and brutal Roman rule was replacing the partial independence that had been allowed under King Herod.

The holiday of *Shavuoth*, or first fruits, that year again brought crowds of pilgrims up to Jerusalem and its Temple. Once again demonstrations flared out, this time openly anti-Roman. One crowd threatened the Procurator, Sabinus, in the royal palace, another took over the royal hippodrome (circus), and a third gathered around the Temple on the sacred mount. It was there that the clash came. When Roman soldiers blocked off the inner Temple area, the protestors climbed to the roofs of the great arcades or porticos surrounding it and pelted the soldiers with stones and missiles. The Romans countered by setting fire to the supports of those roofs. As these collapsed in flames, many demonstrators were killed, and others were slaughtered by the soldiers.

Then the troops broke into the Temple itself and began to plunder it. They were joined in this by their chief, Sabinus, who arrived from his palace in time to seize some 400 talents, a tidy sum, from the Temple treasury. That did not end the struggle, for protestors surrounded the palace, threatening to burn or wreck it. They were joined by some of Herod's former soldiers. Soon the general revolt spread from Jerusalem into surrounding Judea.

Finally, Quintilius Varius himself, the Roman imperial regent for the colony of Syria, arrived with a force of both Roman and Arab troops. They occupied Jerusalem and scoured the country roundabout, seeking Jewish partisans. Of those they were able to capture, some two thousand were executed by means of that peculiarly Roman and brutal torture called crucifixion.

The year 4 B.C.E. remained dark and accursed in Jewish tradition and legend. The invasion under Varius may well have been even crueler than the earlier invasions under the Seleucid king, Antiochus Epiphanes, or the first Roman conqueror, Pompey.

Soon the Emperor in Rome handed down his august decision: Archelaus should receive Jerusalem and Judea around it. However, the title of King, once held by Herod, should not be his. Instead he was to be merely an "ethnarch." Nevertheless, Rome had returned the land of the Temple to a regime hated by most of its people, and their urgent calls for relief had been rejected amidst bloodshed and violence. A miserable period followed. Arche-

A multisided Dome of the Rock appears here in the place of the Temple that stood before Jesus' birth. This is *Lo Sposalizio,* "The Espousal," the first signed painting by the great Raphael of Perugia, Italy, 1504. Joseph (right) places a ring on the finger of Mary, while the High Priest (presumably) looks on—as does young Raphael himself, facing us near the far right. His name and date appear on the façade of this "Temple."

laus seemed to have Herod's worst qualities, without his father's formidable skills in intriguing and maneuvering.

The Temple became a pawn. In swift succession high priests were appointed and unseated, three of them within the nine years that Archelaus was ethnarch. Finally, delegations of discontented Judeans dared go directly to Emperor Augustus with their complaints. Archelaus was called to Rome to make answer, but was unable to placate Augustus, and in 6 C.E. (Common, or Christian, Era) was ordered out of Judea. Henceforth, it was to be ruled by officials directly appointed in Rome, and in fact, together with Samaria and Idumea, was treated as a sort of southern annex of the Roman colony of Syria.

"Procurators" became Rome's local rulers for this unruly "annex." They made their headquarters in Caesaria on the Mediterranean coast, rather than in Jerusalem, so full of traditions and site of the troublemaking Temple! Thus, after seventy years of Roman overlordship, came the naked reality of rule as a Roman colony. It was to endure about sixty years, till a desperate and catastrophic finale in 70 C.E.

Within that period, a segment of barely two years is especially vital in the annals of the Temple and of all Christian creeds. It began during the fifteenth year of the reign of the Roman Emperor Tiberius — that is, in 27 or 28 C.E. — and it climaxed in springtime, the period of the Jewish Passover, at the edge of Jerusalem, with the crucifixion of a troublesome Jewish "agitator," Jesus of Nazareth.

The Temple at Jerusalem is linked intimately with important events in the life of Jesus of Nazareth. Some of these occur in books of Matthew, Mark, Luke, and John, the four New Testament "gospels" — or chronicles of good tidings — all set down in writing long after Jesus died. Other links are found in folklore and legend outside these gospel narratives.

Luke tells how, following the birth of Jesus, Mary and Joseph had him circumcized in accord with the Jewish religious law. As soon as possible afterward, they brought the infant to the Temple at Jerusalem, to be "presented," or consecrated. This again was an observance of Jewish religious tradition, for every first-born child who was male was to be "consecrated to the Lord." Mary and Joseph brought to the Temple also the required pair of turtle-doves, or two young pigeons, to offer in sacrifice.

A pious man named Simeon, then in Jerusalem, longed for the deliverance of the people of Israel through the promised redeemer or "Messiah." Simeon had been told by God that he would survive until he had seen that Messiah with his own eyes. When Jesus was brought to the Temple, Simeon took the infant into his arms, praised the Lord, and asked that now he might die in peace for he had seen "a light that will be a revelation to the heathens, and a glory to your people, Israel."

Simeon blessed the parents and predicted that this child would "become a sign that men reject . . . many in Israel will stand or fall because of him . . .

you too shall be cleft by doubts; and so the inmost thoughts of many will be revealed."

Luke also contains the next link uniting Jesus and the Temple. Joseph and Mary, as observant Jews, each year journeyed from Nazareth up to the Temple for the Passover festival. They went also in the year when Jesus was twelve years old. Jesus, while in Jerusalem, strayed away from his parents, and was later found discussing religious law with teachers and learned scholars.

Most Bible translations speak of the boy Jesus as having sat among the teachers "in the Temple." This, however, did not mean the interior of the Sanctuary itself. Religious teaching and discussion were carried on in the porches or porticoes lining the inside of the walls around the great Temple court. These porches served as a kind of "free speech" zone where the so-called "doctors of the law" debated matters of religion, ritual, morality, and even major political issues of the time. Meanwhile, they no doubt took care

This vigorous etching, by Rembrandt, suggests great vaulted ceiling and massive pillars inside the Temple. At upper right are the turbaned figures of priests and officials, who watch with obvious displeasure and concern as Jesus drives the moneychangers from the Temple.

to offend no Roman soldiers or agents who might be about in the area, to which gentiles as well as Jews were admitted.

The gospel of John mentions several visits of Jesus to the Temple prior to the final week of his life on earth, including one Passover when, with his mother, brothers, and disciples, Jesus went first to Capernaum, then to Jerusalem. There in the Temple area came a confrontation that the other gospels place in the final few days before his crucifixion. Resenting the trading and commerce he found in the Temple court, Jesus used a rough whip or lash to drive merchants and moneychangers out of the sacred area.

Though the gospels differ on details, all agree that it was at a Passover time that Jesus thus confronted the profit-seekers and tried to purge the Temple precincts of their presence. The picture is a vivid one. Jesus entering the great Temple courtyard, watching the worldly hubbub and business

The Temple Mount loomed powerfully in the background as Jesus prayed in the Garden of Gethsemane on the Mount of Olives in this painting by Andrea Mantegna (1431-1506.) As the disciples sleep, the arresting Roman soldiers approach, led by Judas. Jerusalem looks like a hillside town of the Italian Renaissance, and many of its towers bear Moslem crescents, suggesting the rule of the holy city at the time Mantegna worked.

bustle: moneychangers with coins and scales, vendors of birds and animals for sacrifice; hawkers offering for sale foods, spices, and other goods. And across the open spaces, porters jogging along, bearing burdens, just as if this were any ordinary market place.

Indignantly, Jesus turned to the use of force. He overturned tables of the moneychangers and stalls of the bird-sellers. He halted the bearers of burdens. He denounced them, recalling from the writings sacred to the Jews that the Temple ("my house") should be known as "a house of prayer for all the nations."

"But you," Jesus charged, "have made of it a den of thieves."

Thus in the Temple itself Jesus showed a most active concern for the purity and sanctity of the place, in deed as well as in words. His emphasis is on the spirit that prevailed; not on the stones and timbers of which it was built.

According to the version in the book of John, when asked to justify his forceful protest, Jesus returned a baffling answer: "Destroy this Temple, and in three days I will restore it." His listeners were unbelieving: the Temple had taken forty-six years to build. How could it be restored in three days?

That same gospel of John, written later than the other three, placed in the Temple area the famous incident when Jesus expressed his gentle judgment concerning the woman who had been caught commiting the sin of adultery.

The gospel incidents connecting Jesus as an observant Jew, with the Jerusalem Temple are varied and sometimes contradictory. Their spirit, however, is consistent with that of the lowly teacher and reformer who declared that a camel could more easily pass through the eye of a needle than a rich man could enter the kingdom of heaven.

12

The Great Revolt in Judea—and Destruction of the Temple

(29–75 C.E.)

The strains and stresses among the people of Judea grew greater under the direct rule of Rome. It was a time of powerful and endless ferments. Prophecies, fantasies, visions, and mystical hopes flickered like wildfire.

Jesus and the prophet John the Baptist were by no means the only reformers and foes of the "Establishment" in that agitated era. In many directions rang out the calls for repentance and radical changes in the ways men lived and worshiped.

Strangest and most fascinating among the dissenting and resisting groups were those who called themselves "the Pious Ones." They withdrew into the harsh Judean desert, living apart, sharing their scant property in common, and living a monastic kind of life. Only in recent years has knowledge been gained of their way of life and thought, through discovery and decipherment of the so-called "Dead Sea Scrolls," which they wrote and hid in caves before Roman soldiers finally overran and destroyed their religious "fortresses."

These communities of Pious Ones, at Qumran in particular, were closely related to a radical sect, the Essenes, of whom John the Baptist may have been one, and — some hold — Jesus himself. These "far out" sects shared one burning conviction: they rejected the official Temple as it existed at Jerusalem. It was not the building or its utensils that they repudiated, for they held a true Temple not only acceptable but essential to their living religion. They insisted, however, that the Jerusalem Temple had been corrupted and tainted by false priests and improper practices. In this they resembled some of the most radical protestants during the early days of the Reformation in Europe and Britain, who demanded nothing less than total purity in their houses of worship and in the lives of those who served there.

Much of the thinking of these Pious Ones of the desert was concerned with describing what a true and acceptable Temple should be. As recently as 1967 a new hidden document came to light which has already been given the name of "the Temple Scroll" because of its intense concern with these subjects. The well-known Israeli archeologist, Yigael Yadin, believes the author of this Temple Scroll was both an Essene and a member of the Khirbet Qumran community of Pious Ones near the Dead Sea. This scroll offers a detailed description of how a true and holy Temple *should* be built, to replace the actual Temple then existing at Jerusalem. In much the same way, the fifth chapter of the book of Exodus describes how a true or acceptable tabernacle was to be built.

The scroll calls for a Temple differing significantly from the Temple descriptions in the six principal sources previously known to scholars. These include the Bible books of I Kings, II Chronicles, and Ezekiel; as well as writings of the Jewish-Roman historian Josephus; the so-called Letter of Aristeas; and the Mishnah, which is the section of the Talmud concerned with the oral, or word-of-mouth religious law.

This Temple Scroll is much concerned with physical cleanliness as well as ritual purity. Thus, it calls for construction of public toilets more than a quarter of a mile from the Temple building on Mount Moriah, and invisible from it.

Doubtless additional light will be cast on the Temple as it existed, and as these desert radicals desired it to become, when this new Temple Scroll is fully studied by scholars. Still other precious scrolls may yet be discovered in desert hideaways, adding to the world's tantalizingly meager knowledge of these Pious Ones, of the Essenes, as well as of the tensions surrounding the Temple and its role in the religious and national life of the people of Judea.

Resistance to the yoke of Rome never died out among the Jews of Judea, yet for many years it smoldered rather than flared widely or wildly. The notorious Roman Emperor Caligula (37–41 C.E.) aroused opposition by attempting to have his statue placed in the Jerusalem Temple, a proposal regarded by both pious Pharisees and radical Zealots as an intolerable desecration. After Caligula was assassinated, the next Emperor, Claudius (41–54 C.E.), chose a new ruler over Judea. He was Agrippa I, a grandson of the first Herod and of Mariamne. Under Agrippa, Jewish traditions were observed in the Temple and elsewhere, and resentments relaxed somewhat.

However, after Agrippa's death in 44 C.E., Claudius again sent Roman procurators to rule Judea. A series of these alien fortune-hunters held office, shuttling between their headquarters in Caesarea on the coast and Jerusalem in the hill country. They were, by and large, both brutal and greedy, seeking to amass quick wealth, not above stooping to graft or other misuse of their powers.

The lives of the masses of citizens in Judea went from bad to worse. Finally, the Pharisees, who had been a relatively moderate pious group, saw but one course open: they made common cause with the Zealots, long-time foes of Roman rule. A first sharp clash occurred at Caesarea, then demonstrations against Rome burst forth in Jerusalem. A bold and sensational act of defiance took place in the Temple where, during years of Roman rule, sacrifices had been offered on behalf of the Emperor, as well as in the traditional Jewish rites. Eleazar, son of the captain of the Temple, ordered an end to such imperial sacrifice, following which Jewish partisans went into action and stormed one Roman strong point after another.

Jerusalem was entirely in Jewish hands by late summer of 66 C.E. Then Menahem, a leader of the revolt, was assassinated by conservative Saduccees among the Jews. The ranks of the Jews were deeply and tragically divided. This hindered the resistance to Rome, but did not halt it. Even when Cestus Gallus, Roman governor of Syria, arrived with the formidable Tenth Legion, he was unable to take the Temple mount, and the Romans lost much equipment to the Jewish defenders.

News of this defeat of "invincible" Rome crystallized into a full-scale rebellion what had been previously only local outbreaks. Rome had never before faced so stubborn and desperate a revolt. Jerusalem became the seat of the new Jewish revolutionary government. It coined its own money, collected taxes when it could, and divided Judea into seven defense districts, to each of which a commander was assigned. (One of these appointments proved unfortunate, though famous: he was a young priest, Joseph by name, who later under stress of danger went over to Rome and afterward wrote extensive histories under his Romanized name of Flavius Josephus.)

Shaken by the success of this Jewish revolt, Emperor Nero (54–68 C.E.) sent Rome's best commander, Vespasian, with picked legions to crush it at all costs. Massive and bloody actions followed in Judea during the years 67 and early 68. Rome's veteran fighters struggled and strained to make headway. When they did, it was largely because of the terrible factional strife within Jewish ranks.

One of Vespasian's crushing campaigns invaded the valley of the Jordan river. There, Roman legionnaires took Jericho, wiped out the monastic sect that had lived apart at Khirbet Qumran, and cut Jerusalem off from the rest of the land. By the summer of 69 C.E., the Judean patriots held only Jerusalem with its Temple, plus a south-pointing wedge of territory whose apex included Masada, one-time fortress hideaway of Herod. It had been used as a Roman outpost, until in 66 C.E. a desperate and devoted band of Zealots had stormed and taken it.

Vespasian, backed by the Roman legions stationed at Caesarea and Alexandria, Egypt, was chosen Emperor of Rome and began his rule there

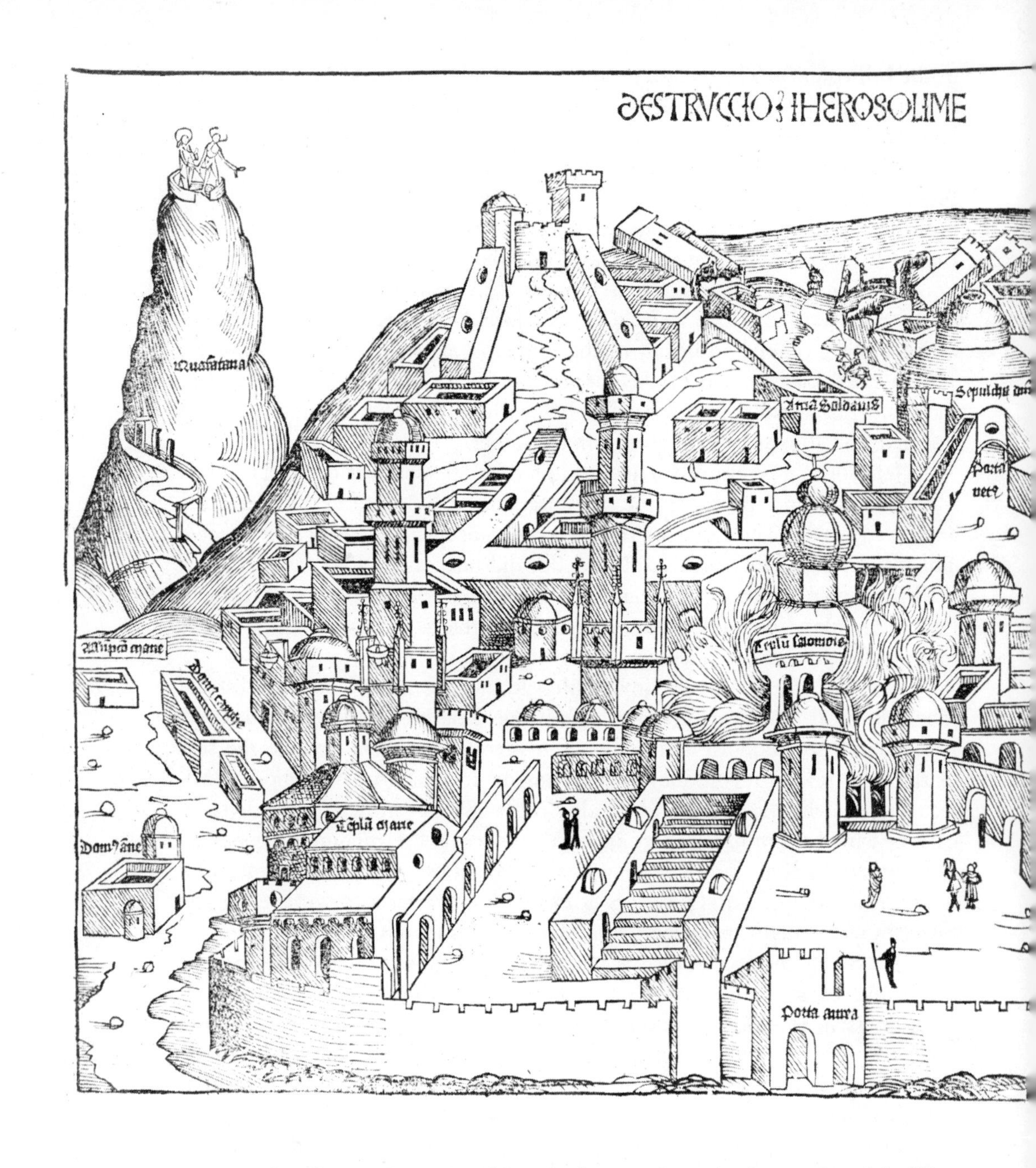

Destruccio Iheroslime — "Destruction of Jerusalem" — was shown thus in a woodcut of the *Nürnberg Chronicle* of 1492. Atop the hill at far left appear two figures, probably weeping as the Romans ravage the sacred city. Flames envelope a "Temple of Solomon" clearly derived from the far later Dome of the Rock. A river, presumably of blood, is shown flowing through the city. In the far background lie shattered towers.

early in 70 C.E. He left his son, Titus, in command of the campaign in Judea. During that same year began the drawn-out, desperate, and cruel siege of Jerusalem by eighty thousand veteran Roman warriors under Titus. The defenders of the sacred city were outnumbered more than three to one. Divisions

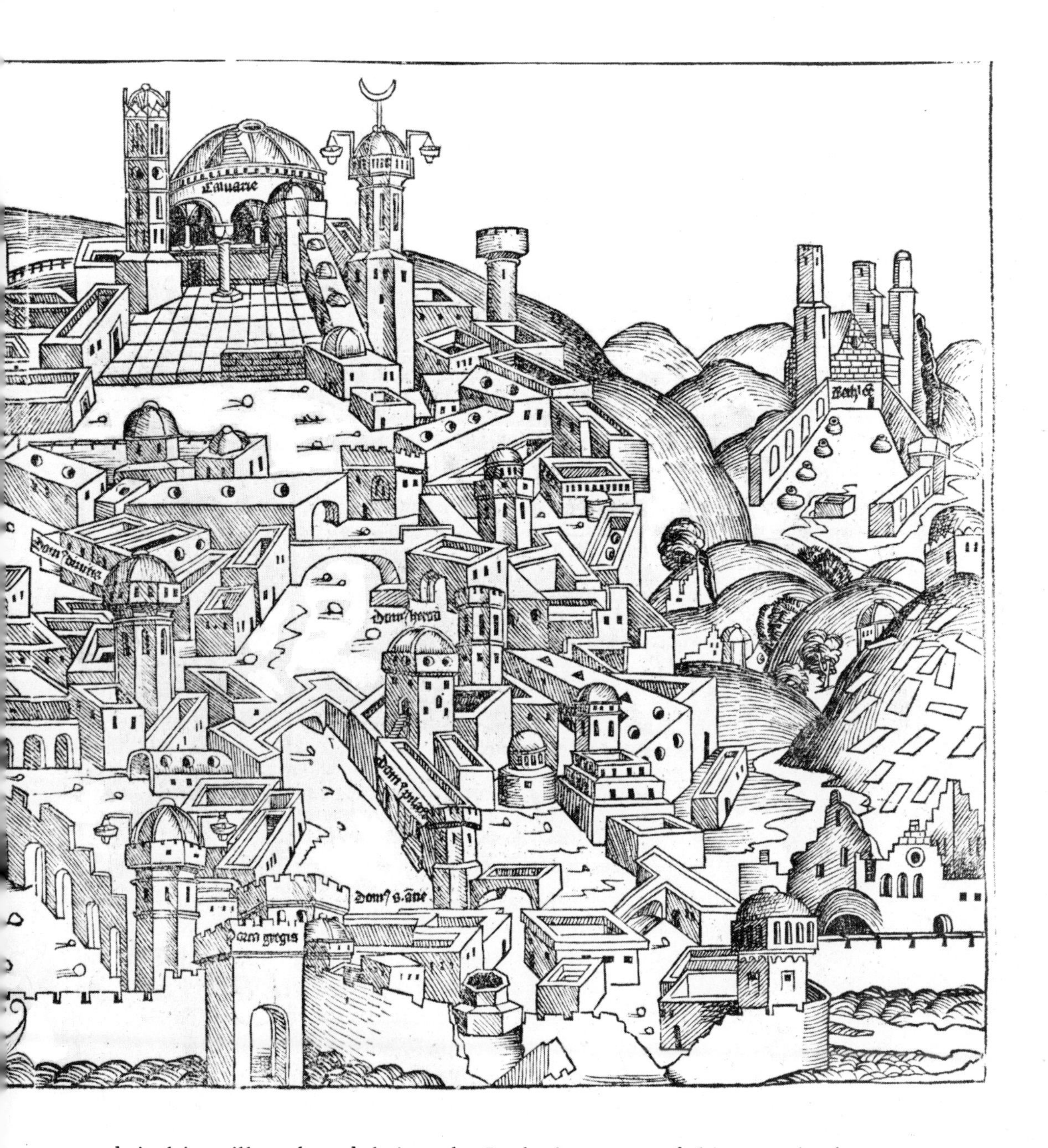

and rivalries still weakened their ranks. In the last stages of this struggle, the upper city (then called the "new") was defended by forces under Simon bar Giora; while east of it, the Temple mount was held by men under John of Gischala.

Many supplies had been wasted in the fatal inner struggles. Now the Roman blockade cut off all food and other essentials. Shortage and outright starvation raged within. Yet even then the Romans outside made headway only slowly and at great cost. By late July, they managed to storm and destroy the fortress of Antonia that Herod had erected at the northwest corner of the Temple platform. But the defenders built a new defense wall and continued, famished and hollow-eyed, to hold the courtyard and the Temple within.

By early August, shortages of both animals and priests forced a halt in the daily sacrifices at the Temple. From the Roman ranks outside the walls, the renegade Josephus shouted appeals to the defenders — surrender, to save the Temple, he urged! Desertions to the Roman side were few, however, and those chiefly aristocratic priestly families who crossed the lines in secret. The Zealots, die-hards of heroic mold, fought on. They used the great roofed porticoes around the Temple courtyard as platforms from which to fling down on the besiegers stones, arrows, and fiery brands. They even succeeded by means of clever ruses to entrap some Roman soldiers.

Finally, Titus told his men to set fire to the wooden roofs and porches of the Temple platform. When these were consumed, the Romans moved into the outer courtyard, the "court of the gentiles," but the defenders fought on from the inner courts, those of the women, the men of Israel, and the priests, around the Sanctuary itself. That became the next victim of the Romans' fire. Flaming faggots were flung at the Temple; a blazing torch entered a window and set the structure afire.

As the Temple burned, frenzy gripped both attackers and defenders. Roman shock troops burst through, and Titus was able to dash into the Temple just long enough for a brief look; then the heat forced him out. His soldiers continued burning whatever could be kindled, and killing all they could reach, whether combatants, women, or children. Many Jews flung themselves into the fire and perished with their Temple. Others, hiding in corners, were burned to death as Roman torches set new fires.

Later, safe in his residence in Rome, Josephus described in Greek the fate of the Sanctuary where once he had served: "The whole Temple mount appeared to flame, from foundation to top, but the blood streams were greater than the fire streams. Piles of corpses covered the ground, and over the heaped-up dead the soldiers ran to catch those yet alive." Several priests of the Temple, pleading for mercy, were dragged captive before Titus. "It is proper for priests to die with the Temple," he sneered, and they were dispatched. Somehow, John of Gischala, commander of the Temple area, managed to penetrate the Roman ranks and reach the upper city where the forces of Simon bar Giora still held out.

Titus gave his men leave to plunder all parts of Jerusalem now under their control. This done, they burned and destroyed the municipal buildings and all the lower city. Not until the next month, September, were they able to take the upper city and fly their banner from the former palace of Herod. Now, masters of all that was left of Jerusalem, they continued plundering and burning.

Jerusalem was reduced to rubble, save only the triple towers of the palace of Herod where now the Tenth Legion was stationed to guard what had once been a city of world renown. The legionnaires on duty among the ruins could still see the remaining walls, massive and grim, which had supported the Temple platform or esplanade. Among these great stone constructions one sector, that along the western edge of the platform, was destined to gain a great and enduring fame. The Hebrew name for this western bastion of Herodian stone was and still is the *Kotel Maarabi*, meaning Western

The surviving segment of the Western Wall, or *Kotel Maarabi*, as it looked nearly nineteen hundred years after the Roman destruction. The typical flat borders of Herodian building blocks can be seen clearly in several layers and courses of stone.

Wall. During most of the next nineteen centuries, Jewish pilgrims from all over the western world and eventually from the New World across the seas, would come there when they could to mourn for their vanished Temple, of which the Wall became the immortal symbol. Their laments, as heard by non-Jews, led to a name that Jews themselves did not use or even approve: "the Wailing Wall."

Prayers at that Western Wall became common about 700 C.E. They continued unbroken, except when Jews were physically prevented from approaching that great wall, until the day when these lines are written. Each passing century added to the weight of tears and tragic supplication associated with that one segment of the ancient wall.

From deep longings and desperate hopes, legends are born. Folktales and myths about the Temple and the Wall accumulated among Jews, who now were scattered more widely outside Judea than ever before.

> Why had only this one particular segment of the western wall survived? It was divine justice, said one tale. Herod, to build the Temple, had done as Solomon before him: assigned different building tasks to different groups among his subjects. The poorest had been ordered to erect that western wall. The Romans would have destroyed it with all the rest, but angels appeared and halted them. "This wall," the angels declared, "was built by labor of the poor, and must not go!"
>
> A Roman officer, another Jewish tale relates, tried to pull down that wall, but at once fell dead. Titus, the supreme commander, raised a hammer to destroy it, but as he did so, his right hand withered.
>
> Half a dozen angels remained seated on the wall, weeping for the lost Temple. Their tears soaked into the very stones, and so toughened the mortar that the wall stands firm forever, beyond time.

Every night, legend says, Heaven itself weeps for the Temple, and those tears can be seen on the wall. (Skeptics would say it is the dew that collects there at night.)

The ninth of *Ab*, day of the Temple's destruction, became a date accursed, an occasion for mourning and grief. The earlier date of the seventeenth of *Tammuz* when sacrifices had to be halted in the Temple, was observed also as an anniversary of disaster. For each of the ten or eleven Sabbaths after it, Jewish services commonly included discussions of the meaning of the great catastrophe. On the eve and day of the Fast of Ab, discourses were given based on a great collection of commentaries called the *Midrash of Lamentations.* (*Midrash* stands for explanation.)

> The three week period between the seventeenth of *Tammuz* and the ninth of *Ab* is a time of heat and oppressive weather. In our common calendar this period may run from early July to late July, or even begin as late as mid-August, depending on the shifting relationships between

the Jewish lunar calendar and the common solar calendar. Sages pronounced this period a pernicious one of plagues and afflictions, during which a demon of pestilence walked the earth, threatening men.

Grief greater than words could express afflicted the faithful as they recalled what had been the fate of their Temple and its defenders. Some rabbis were said to have suffered permanent facial wounds, so furrowed were their cheeks by tears shed for the Temple. Others were said to undergo a kind of mental paralysis and loss of memory when they thought of those events. A sorrow that seemed to grow with passing generations became part of the memorial of the vanished Temple beyond time.

After leaving the ruins of Jerusalem, Titus traveled a roundabout route to Rome, pausing in Caesarea and Berytus for victory festivals with gladiatorial games in which Jewish captives had to fight each other or become victims of wild animals. In this way Titus journeyed also through Syria and then Egypt, for it was important to prove to other subject peoples that revolt against Rome would inevitably be drowned in blood and flame.

He arrived at last in Rome itself with some seven hundred Jewish captives. In 71 C.E. he, his father the Emperor Vespasian, and his brother Domitian, all rode in a great procession of triumph, accompanied by the Roman elite and acclaimed by plebian and proletarian onlookers.

Carried ahead of Titus were famous golden trophies from the Temple: the *menorah* or candelabrum with its seven branches; a great table for the rites of worship; and a scroll of the law, or Torah.

The procession paused at a very different temple, that of the Capitoline Jupiter. There a noose was cast around the neck of Simon bar Giora, and he was executed next to the Roman Forum. John of Gischala, also a captive, was thrown into prison for life.

Later Titus and Vespasian built another temple in Rome. They dedicated it to the Goddess of Peace. Perhaps this reflected their realization that Romans were sick of the costly wars in Judea and elsewhere. In that new temple, as trophies, were placed the Menorah, the golden table, and the scroll of the law, from the vanished Temple of Jerusalem.

Jewish captives were sold in the slave markets of the Empire. Many lingered on to labor in Rome itself. Roman coins were struck to advertise the outcome of the Judean rebellion. They showed on one side a dejected woman with bound hands, and below Latin words meaning "Judea vanquished; Judea captive."

13

Romans, Byzantines, and Persians in Jerusalem

(75–633 C.E.)

Despite the Roman decrees barring Jews from setting foot in devastated Jerusalem, some apparently managed to live in or near the city — and to mourn and pray at the ruined Temple mount.

About 113 C.E., while the Roman emperor Trajan was occupied by war against the Parthians of Persia (now Iran), Jews rebelled again, this time in Egypt, Libya, and Cyprus. They fought three years before lack of arms and men forced their surrender. It was called the "War of Quietus" after a Roman official who had proved especially able in massacring Jews in Babylon and Mesopotamia. His reward was appointment as governor of Palestine with unlimited power over Jews there. Suppression of the rebels in the War of Quietus further drained Roman strength.

In 117 C.E., after Trajan's death, Hadrian became Emperor. In order to gain some stability for the Empire, he attempted to establish a period of peace. It has been said — but again denied by respected authorities on history — that Hadrian promised the Jews that they could rebuild the Temple in Jerusalem on condition that they would lay down their arms and cease to trouble Rome.

There is firmer ground for believing that Hadrian made a gesture of reconciliation toward the Jews by recalling to Rome and executing the cruel Quietus.

In any case, whatever Jewish hopes may have been raised by Hadrian's words or actions, were soon enough dashed. The historical evidence suggests strongly that Hadrian came to believe he had Judea well under his control. He informed the Roman Senate that all was placid in Rome's relation with the Jewish subjects. Coins struck at this period show Emperor Hadrian, clad in his toga, raising a kneeling Jew; meanwhile three boys hand Hadrian palm branches. They probably represented Judea, Samaria, and Galilee — the three divisions of the region we know as Palestine.

Hadrian moved to paganize this region. He drew up a plan: to rebuild what had been Jerusalem as a city in the Roman style, dedicated to the many-god worship of the Roman state. As its name he chose "Colonia Aelia Capitolina." This honored himself (Publius Aelius Hadrianus was his full name). It also honored the Capitoline Triad, or trinity of pagan gods: Jupiter Capitolinus, Juno (his wife), and Venus-Aphrodite.

On the site of the one-time Temple of Solomon, Hadrian planned to place a Temple dedicated to Jupiter. Work on this new pagan city advanced far — far enough to give rise to another, and even more desperate Jewish revolt. It is famous under the name of its colorful and vigorous leader "Bar Kochba."

The people of Judea had causes for bitterness besides Hadrian's pagan temples and sanctuaries. He had issued an edict against "mutilation," the effect of which was to ban the required rites of circumcision, so deeply rooted in Judaism. Resentment mounted. Preparations for armed uprising got under way. The mountains of Judea became honeycombed with stores of weapons and hideaways for rebels. Jewish smiths, ordered to supply weapons for Roman legions in Judea, managed to make them weak or defective enough so that they would be returned for repair — and thus fall into hands ready to use them against Rome!

Meanwhile, efforts were made to mediate between Rome and the rebellious Jews. A wise and gentle patriarch, Joshua ben Chananya or Hanania by name, tried to persuade both sides to find a middle ground. He had known the glories of the Temple in his youth, and had even sung in its choir. He tried to restrain militant Jews by urging the hopelessness of another uprising against Rome. And, though very old, he traveled all the way to Egypt to talk to Hadrian in the effort to persuade him against building the pagan Aelia Capitolina on the sacred site of Jerusalem. Instead of attention, however, he met ridicule and mockery. Not long after this journey he died — some said from grief as well as age.

Leader of the rebellion that followed was Simon bar Kosiba, or ben Koseba, better known in history as Bar Kochba. This name means "Son of the Star;" it was given to him by Rabbi Akiba ben Joseph, a revered scholar and teacher and also a forceful leader in the new Jewish revolt. Akiba was deeply impressed by Bar Kochba, a man of outstanding strength and magnetism. "Koseba has arisen as a star (Koseba) in Jacob," declared Akiba, and attributed messianic qualities to him.

The star of Bar Kochba rose high for a time. He united the Jews and filled them with hope. His influence radiated far. From many countries outside Judea recruits flocked to join his forces. Even Samaritans and gentiles, eager to resist the Roman yoke, swelled his ranks.

His forces grew to four hundred thousand. His personality inspired fear among the hardened Roman warriors. Legends about him sprang up on both sides. Romans told that he blew burning tow from his mouth, so as to seem to be spitting fire. Jewish stories stressed his tremendous strength. They said he was able to hurl back with his knees alone the heavy stone missiles flung by Roman machines against the Jewish fighters.

It was near the end of 131 C.E. that the Bar Kochba revolt burst into the open. The Romans were not prepared for Jewish determination and stubborn will to win. Fighting was fierce and furious.

Battle followed battle. The Romans were driven out of Judea and part of Samaria. Once more Jerusalem was ruled by Jews. A Bar Kochba government came into being. Between 132 and 134 C.E. it minted its own bronze and silver coins, known today as "Bar Kochba coins" or "coins of the revolt." They were old Roman coins, reminted. One carried the slogan, "For the Freedom of Jerusalem." Sacrifices very likely were resumed at the historic site of Mount Moriah. However, the government, harassed and burdened as it was, found no time to attempt a rebuilding of the Temple.

Hadrian feared the effect of this Jewish revolt on his weakening Roman Empire. He summoned from Britain his most successful general, Julius Severus. With an army of one hundred thousand veterans, in at least five legions, Severus arrived in Palestine. They swept through the land from north to south, slaughtering men, women, children, and livestock, destroying and burning all that lay in their path. One by one, 985 towns and villages and fifty fortifications fell to them. By 134 C.E. they regained Jerusalem itself, and by 135 C.E. the Jews of Judea had been forced to surrender.

Bar Kochba, tough to the last, held out for about a year in his final fortress of Beit Ter in the mountains just southwest of Jerusalem. He was finally captured and killed.

Legend says that his death was caused by a scorpion, for no mere Roman soldier could have killed him. The story was told that when the Romans finally entered Beit Ter, their horses waded up to their bellies in a river of blood which swept corpses along with it to the sea. Beit Ter fell on the ninth of Ab, the very date on which the Temple of Jerusalem had twice been destroyed.

Losses of life on both sides were enormous — about half a million each. In addition to these, many Jews had died of hunger and from fire. Roman losses so damaged the Empire's prestige and "face" that Hadrian did not send the customary message of a victor to the Roman Senate: "I and my army are well." Nevertheless, the Senate saw fit to strike coins at this time with the inscription: *Exercitus Judaicus.* (Thanks to the army victorious over the Jews.)

Letters and documents of this period recently discovered in both Jordan and Israel shed light on the character of the magnetic, fearsome warrior Bar Kochba, and his relations with his officers and followers. They vividly reveal the day-to-day routines and concerns during the course of this long, stubborn revolt.

The victorious Romans were furious and ruthless. Rabbi Akiba, among others, was executed after untold tortures, including, legend says, having the skin stripped from his body. Jews who had not been massacred or escaped to Asia, Africa, or Parthia, were sold as slaves or exchanged for horses. Thousands died of disease and hunger.

To intimidate the survivors, burial of corpses was forbidden, and heaps of dead bodies were allowed to pile up and rot in the sun, their stench and sight a powerful, heartbreaking warning.

Hadrian was determined to make further revolt impossible. Tinaeus Rufus, Roman governor of Judea, was ordered to convert Jerusalem into a pagan city. He began with a symbolic act. Some historians say that it was on the first anniversary of the fall of Bar Kochba's fortress of Beit Ter, on the ninth of Ab, that the Romans plowed Moriah, the Temple mount, as well as the city of Jerusalem itself. Then, as was Roman custom, with the same plow they marked the outlines that were to form the boundaries of the future city.

Hadrian's Aelia Capitolina was erected north of the original City of David and exactly where the present Old City of Jerusalem now stands within its walls. It had four sides, like a Roman camp. Its two main roads crossed each other at right angles, one running north and south, the other east and west. Its style was Grecian with two market places, a theater, a circus or enclosure for public games, baths, and various public buildings. It was divided into seven sections.

A Forum and a temple to Aphrodite arose on the approximate site of today's Church of the Holy Sepulcher, west of the Temple mount. Statues of Roman, Greek, and Phoenician gods decorated the city, whose population consisted at this time only of Roman soldiers.

No walls enclosed this pagan city, but it had huge elaborate gates. The Bethlehem, or western, gate carried the emblem of the Roman Tenth Legion, a wild boar or swine. Before the north gate, on the site of the present Damascus Gate, appeared a tall column dedicated to a Roman emperor. It is pictured in the famous Madaba mosaic map dating back to approximately the middle of the sixth century. Statues of Hadrian and other notables also stood on the former Temple platform, renamed the Quadra (square). Saint Jerome is said to have seen them there in the fourth century.

Information is meager and authorities do not agree as to just what stood on the actual Temple site at this time. Some say a heathen temple to Jupiter Capitolinus was built there; others, that the sacred Rock which has so captured imaginations for centuries, was bare, but that a small temple to pagan gods might have been erected on the site of the present Dome of the Chain, just slightly east of today's Dome of the Rock.

Under punishment of death, Jews, as well as Christians of Jewish origin were forbidden to enter the new city and the site of the former Temple. Severe punishments were meted out to those who kept the Jewish Sabbath, read or taught the Torah, practiced circumcision, and followed Jewish laws. Though Hadrian persecuted both Christians and Jews, he did not, however, force them to worship pagan gods.

The name of Judea was changed to Syria Palestine, and Caesarea became its capital. Jerusalem, or Aelia as it was called in all official communications, was relegated to an unimportant role. Over the years, its population of Roman garrison soldiers slowly grew by addition of their family members, traders, and foreign travelers. So forgotten was the name of Jerusalem, as one historian relates, that when a century later a governor of Palestine was informed that a group of Coptic Christians had come from Jerusalem, the governor had to inquire where the town was located.

Hadrian's successor, his adopted son, known as the Emperor Antoninus Pius, ushered in a somewhat favorable period for the Jews. In 139–140 C.E., some of the anti-Jewish decrees of Hadrian were revoked, including the ban on circumcision. Burial was at last permitted for the remains of the Jewish warriors slain at the end of the Bar Kochba war years before, but living Jews were still denied entry to Jerusalem on pain of death.

Even the "best" of the Roman Emperors, Marcus Aurelius, who visited Judea in 175 C.E., did not issue a single law in favor of the Jews. He was followed by a succession of Emperors whose laws still kept the Jews out of Jerusalem and the Temple site. The Emperor Caracalla, however, in 212 C.E., did grant Jews throughout the Roman Empire equality and citizenship.

Between 135 and 299 C.E., soldiers of the Roman Legion stationed in Jerusalem worshiped various Oriental gods including Serapis, an Egyptian deity. Also at this time, a Christian community, probably composed mostly of foreigners, was beginning to grow. It actually had its origins even before 135 C.E., for the Roman edicts forbidding Jews access to Jerusalem did not apply to Christians, except those of Jewish origin, as stated earlier. Jerusalem's first Christian church was, in fact, built on Mount Zion, southwest of the Temple site. Many others followed it. Soon after 200 C.E., the first pilgrimages of Christians began to the "Holy Places" in Jerusalem. Such pilgrimages gained great significance in the later history of Jerusalem and its Temple site.

Under the Emperor Constantine the Great (288?–337), the Christian faith became a permitted religion. Toward the Jews Constantine showed a brief period of tolerance, but in 325 C.E. he revived the edict which prohibited them from living in Jerusalem (Aelia). Jews had to pay in order to enter the city to mourn at the Temple ruins on the ninth of Ab, anniversary of its destruction. Under Constantine, however, Jews did retain the Roman citizenships which had been granted to them by the earlier Emperor, Caracalla.

Important changes on and near the Temple mount appear to have been launched at this time. Constantine was "undisputed master of Rome and the West." He created a new capital in the eastern city of Byzantium, which was renamed Constantinople in his honor. This shift of the seat of his government from pagan Rome to a site central to his Eastern empire is linked closely with his decision to permit Christianity as an accepted religion for the state he ruled.

Increasing Roman acceptance of Christianity now made Jerusalem the religious center of the Empire, and interest was reawakened in its holy places. Macarius, the Christian bishop of Aelia (Jerusalem), was given the support of Constantine in excavating and preserving sites sacred to Christendom. The emperor also sent his own mother, Helena, to Jerusalem — with instructions to rebuild and glorify spots linked with the life of Jesus and his associates. Helena ordered the destruction of the pagan Temple of Aphrodite at Jerusalem, whereupon — so it was declared — she "discovered" under it the very sepulcher where the body of Jesus had been entombed between the crucifixion and the resurrection. Also, under the guidance of local bishops, Helena conveniently "found" in a crypt below these ruins the supposed True Cross used in the crucifixion of Jesus more than three centuries earlier. On this same site, about a half mile west of the Temple mount, the Church of the Holy Sepulcher was built in the year 335.

These and other discoveries of relics of Jesus brought about a real building "boom" and an increase of pilgrimages to Jerusalem. Constantine encouraged and aided these constructions. Churches, monasteries, and hospices for pilgrims continued to rise. Jerusalem became once more a religious center as it had been before the destruction of the Temple.

Constantine, and the emperors who followed him as rulers of the Christianized Byzantine empire, did some altering and rebuilding on and around the Temple mount. The extent and appearance of their changes, however, remain uncertain.

Paganism was revived briefly with the advent of Emperor Julian in 361. Julian befriended the Jews and respected their religion. He freed them from their heavy taxes and restored their civil rights. In the history of the Christian Church, this emperor became known as Julian the Apostate. He hated the ruling church and its endless inner quarrels and sought to protect the oppressed of all nations and religions. He did not persecute the Christians but restricted their influence.

Julian admired the custom of sacrifice, but discovered that Jews no longer practiced it, because, as they told him, they no longer had a Temple. He then authorized the rebuilding of the Temple. So interested was he in the reestablishment of the Temple at Jerusalem that he appointed his best friend, Alypius of Antioch, as building overseer, and urged him to spare no expense. The courtyard of the Temple had been left in ruins, the Christians having taken the stones remaining from Herod's Temple to build their own churches.

The governors of Syria and Palestine were ordered to assist Alypius in every way. Great numbers of workmen were assembled to clear away the heaped-up ruins which had lain there almost three hundred years since the destruction of the Temple. Building materials were prepared, and work was begun in the spring of 363.

Historians differ as to the attitude of the Jews toward the restoration of the Temple at this time. Some say they were overjoyed, that they gave their labor and their savings, that communities in far-off lands collected money, that women sold or brought their jewelry as contributions, even though Julian's provision of workmen and materials made this unnecessary. Will Durant in his *Age of Faith* says: "We can imagine the happiness of a people that for three centuries had prayed for this day!"

However, among others, the historian Heinrich Graetz, in his *History of the Jews* says the Jews did not support the rebuilding of the Temple at this time. It may be that the uprisings and subsequent brutal suppression by the Romans, which had claimed many victims over the years, had extinguished any hope for the re-creation of the former magnificent Temple. On the other hand, Graetz states that, according to ideas prevalent among Jews at this time, a Temple would have been unthinkable without a Messiah, and they were still waiting for his appearance. (At the time of the uprising in 132 C.E., many Jews influenced by Rabbi Akiba, had believed Bar Kochba to be that Messiah.)

In reality there were probably mixtures of reactions, with only the literal-minded fanatics holding out for the coming of the Messiah. (Much the same attitude was held by a small sect of twentieth century Jews in Jerusalem at the time of the establishment of the State of Israel in 1948. They refused to recognize the new state on the grounds that the Messiah had not yet arrived.)

Many obstacles impeded the rebuilding of the Temple. Even while the ruins were being cleared away and the foundations excavated, underground fires broke out, claiming the lives of several workmen. These repeated fires and explosions in the passages below the former Temple were caused possibly by kindling of the natural gases trapped beneath the surface as they were exposed to the air — or perhaps by an earthquake which took place on May 27, 363 C.E. At any rate, the discouraged workmen gradually ceased their labors.

Christians had been resentful of efforts to rebuild the Temple, and Julian appears to have blamed them for the repeated fires. One of the unfounded Christian stories of this period charges that Julian threatened to build a prison for the Christians using materials from the ruins of the Temple. Many Christian tales arose, explaining by means of miracles, the various troubles that beset Julian's building plans — tales designed to blacken Julian's reputation, to serve as a warning to the Jews, and to glorify Christianity.

Julian's friend, the overseer Alypius, also became discouraged and halted the building to await the absent Emperor's commands. But Julian died in 363 from an arrow wound received in the war against the Persians. It was the final blow. State funds were withdrawn, and the rebuilding of the Temple was finally abandoned.

Judaism, the Church Fathers explained, was punished by loss of its Temple for failing to accept Jesus as the Christ or Messiah. The abandoned and neglected Temple courtyard, they said, was a result of this continuing and stubborn refusal.

The Emperor Theodosius I, sometimes called "the Great," during his period of rule (379–95 C.E.) made Christianity the official state religion of the Roman Empire, rather than merely a "licit" or allowed religion as it had been during all but a few years since the reign of Emperor Constantine, about a century before.

As 400 C.E. approached, Jerusalem was once more a Christian city. To it came refugees fleeing from the Huns who at that time were overrunning the East. They even threatened Jerusalem. Additional convents and churches arose, and the city became again the center of religious life of the Christian world. By 450, it was a recognized patriarchal administrative center of the Church.

From about 440 to 460 C.E. Palestine had a strange distinction. The Roman Empress Eudocia made it her residence, having been exiled there by her estranged husband, the Byzantine Emperor Theodosius II. During the period of Eudocia's presence, Jews were once again permitted to live in Jerusalem, or Aelia as the Romans tended still to call it.

Eudocia's "exile" resulted in important changes in Jerusalem. She had wealth at her command, and brought about the construction of many religious buildings. She lavished about 20,480 pounds of gold on the city, and is said to have completed the restoration and extension of the city's walls begun by her husband in 413. She is also credited, along with Herod, Hadrian, Constantine, Justinian, and others, with the building of the Golden Gate which stands today, though sealed with blocks of stone, on the eastern side of, and below, the present level of the Temple platform. Many legends, Hebrew, Christian, and Moslem, are told about this gate and its connection with the Temple.

During the sixth century, Jerusalem reached a high level of commercial and spiritual development. It had many splendid new and beautiful buildings. Justinian (483–565), who ruled from Constantinople, had a passion for architecture. He was, in fact, the builder of that city's beautiful Church of Hagia Sophia (also known as "Santa Sophia"). Today under Moslem control, it remains a world-famous work of art and a travel attraction. So powerful had been the impression made upon Justinian by the renown of the vanished Temple in Jerusalem that, at the dedication of the Church of Santa Sophia in Constantinople, he is said to have raised his arms to heaven and exclaimed: "Glory be to God who has thought me worthy to accomplish so great a work! O Solomon! I have vanquished you!"

Like Constantine before him, Justinian gave his permission for the erection in Jerusalem of new churches, monastic foundations, and other religious edifices. The city at this period contained more churches than it would ever have again.

As Christianity became more entrenched, the search for sacred "relics" grew. A new idea was added to the drive to collect "memories of Jesus" (tombs, relics, sites, etc.) It was believed that if some part of a saint or martyr could be found — some bone of an arm, a leg, a finger or toe — it could be used to consecrate an altar, or any sacred building. Jerusalem, and Palestine as a whole, became the hunting grounds of these searches. They laid the foundations for future pilgrimages and quests, and prepared the way for the coming of the Crusades.

After Justinian, Jerusalem suffered an economic decline. Prices rose, wages fell, and the inhabitants grew disgruntled with Byzantine rule. In the early seventh century the Persians swept through Syria and Palestine. They received the support of the Jews and Samaritans as they advanced against the Byzantine or Eastern Empire centered at Constantinople.

In 614 C.E., Jerusalem was besieged by the Persians under King Chosroe II. He had made peaceful overtures in vain to the Patriarch Zachariah, the Christian administrator. Many exiled Jews flocked to the aid of the Persians in an attempt to regain the city of their Temple. With the aid of the battering rams and huge fires, the Persians were able to force a hole in the walls and pour through into the city to massacre and burn. Many thousands are said to have lost their lives, while monasteries and churches, including the Church of the Holy Sepulcher, disappeared in the flames.

Once more, throngs of captives were led out of Jerusalem, the Patriarch Zacharias among them. The relic of the True Cross was taken in triumph to Persia.

The Old City of Jerusalem, spread out in the sunshine. Clearly visible is the eastern wall with its crenellated top, and behind it the platform of the Haram esh-Sherif, topped by the Dome of the Rock.

The Persians remained in control until 629. Then Heraclius, the Byzantine Emperor (610–641), invaded Persia, won back his provinces, released the prisoners, and regained the relic of the Holy Cross. He brought it back to Jerusalem on March 23, 630, pausing at the Golden Gate, eastern entrance to the Temple area. Then he carried the relic of the Cross on foot to the ruins of the Church of the Holy Sepulcher, west of Mount Moriah.

Hundreds of years later, when the Turks were in control of Jerusalem, it was their fear that a Christian Messiah would enter the Haram area on a Friday through the Golden Gate. They therefore sealed up this historic gate and it has remained blocked to this day.

One of the many legends about Heraclius relates that astrologers told him Byzantium would be overthrown by a circumcized people. The emperor, taking it for granted this must mean the Jews, renewed the ban against anyone of Jewish faith living in Jerusalem. He also permitted massacres and various persecutions of the Jews. It did not occur to him that the victors would be another circumcized people — those of the Islamic faith.

Many Christian religious edifices were restored or reconstructed after 633 under the Patriarch Sophronius, but on a simpler scale, and the city did not attain the churchly splendor it had before 614.

Increasing tensions and rivalries had begun to split Christendom into

Smaller cupola (left) is that of the el Aksa Mosque. The sealed double-arch gateway (right) in the wall is the Golden Gate.

western and eastern factions. Christian Jerusalem itself was part of the eastern faction. Its Christian organizations belonged to the Byzantine or Eastern Church, rather than to the Church centered at Rome. These struggles limited the influence of Jerusalem in the Christian world as a whole. Also, Byzantium and Persia, having fought each other for almost two centuries, were by now utterly exhausted. The stage was thus set for the arrival of a new power.

It came, in the form of Islam, a religion which arose out of the desert. Jerusalem was to be ruled by Islam for more than twelve and a half centuries, with the exception of only eighty-eight years. Still greater changes were ahead for the site of the Temple beyond time.

14

"...and Mohammed is his Prophet"

(570–638 C.E.)

Millions of people of the Moslem world believe that one night their prophet Mohammed appeared miraculously on the Temple mount in Jerusalem and from its sacred Rock, the "Stone of Foundation," ascended to heaven.

Mohammed's "night flight" has been recorded in Sura (section) XVII of the Koran and called "The Nocturnal Journey" or "The Sons of Israel." This record has, however, been embellished by his followers over the years and the results added to the tradition of Islam, the religion he founded.

Here is a synthesis of many versions of the tale:

> That "night of the journey," as he lay asleep in his bed in Mecca, Mohammed, escorted by the Archangel Gabriel, and at God's summons, was whisked instantly on the back of a horse to the Western ("Wailing") Wall of the Jewish Temple in Jerusalem. The horse, named al Burak ("Lightning"), had the face of a woman with the tail of a peacock. Alighting at the Western Wall, Gabriel fastened al Burak to a ring in a gate which afterward became known to Moslems as the Gate of the Prophet. The ancient Jewish prophets were said to have tethered their mounts there also. (It is said the Western Wall is still called "al Burak" by some Arabs.) This gate, located immediately south of today's Western Wall, has been closed for centuries. It is sometimes called Barclay's Gate after the American missionary who discovered it in the nineteenth century.

Mohammed then went to the sacred Rock, still standing on the Temple mount as it had beneath the Holy Ark in the center of the Tem-

The Ascent of Mohammed from the sacred Rock atop Mount Moriah, as depicted by Siyar-I Nabi in a seventeenth century Turkish manuscript. The Prophet, his face veiled as customary, is flying toward the seven heavens on his remarkable steed *al Burak,* with the face of a woman, body of a horse, and tail of peacock. Convoys of angels led by Archangel Gabriel accompany and glorify Mohammed.

ple of Solomon. Assembled here were other major prophets including Abraham, Moses, and Jesus. With these he performed his prayers. Then from the sacred Rock he climbed via a ladder of light through the seven heavens of Paradise to stand finally in the presence of Allah from whom he received instructions for the prayers of his followers. Afterwards, the Prophet descended to earth by the same ladder and stood again upon the sacred Rock in Jerusalem. He returned to Mecca the way he had come — on the back of al Burak, and reached his bed before the night was over.

Another version tells that as he started to climb to Paradise the sacred Rock tried to follow him, but Mohammed commanded it to stay and put his hand upon it to force it down. It is said the Rock, however, remained suspended in air, forever marked by the pressure of Mohammed's fingers, and the ground beneath it became a cave.

The cave beneath the Rock seems to have stimulated the imaginations of both Moslem and Hebrew folklorists. Actually, through early Jewish converts, many Talmudic stories found their way into Moslem lore and many similar Arabic and Jewish legends find a common source in the Old Testament and the Talmud. These stories are numberless. Even Abu-Bekr, Mohammed's successor, the Caliph who preceded the famous Omar, claims or pretends to have seen the Rock floating in air without support.

It is said those who saw the hovering Rock were filled with fear and wonder. So the people built a fence on the ground below it, creating the cave which reached from the floating Rock to the earth. The story says that a guard of seventy thousand angels surrounds it, and that all the prophets, kings, and angels since the creation of the world still come here to pray. On this spot, the prayers of men are most pleasing to God. At one time, the legends say, those men who prayed on the site were given a certificate by the Moslem guardians testifying to this fact. When buried with the dead, this testament could be shown to the doorkeeper of Paradise as a ticket of admission.

The cave can be visited today. A small hole in the Rock seen from below is said to have been used as a run-off for the blood of ancient sacrifices.

Beneath this cave, it is told, is another cave now blocked with a round slab where the souls of the dead come to pray. This second cave is like a bottomless well and is reported to be called by the Arabs *Bir al-Arwah*, the Well of Souls. Here it was believed the vessels of the Temple and the treasures of the Kings of Judah were hidden when the Temple was destroyed. And a very recent folk tale tells of people gaining access to the lower, closed cave in 1911 and carrying off the crown of David, the sword of Solomon, the Holy Ark, the Tables of the Law, as well as large quantities of gold.

The "miracle" of Mohammed's night flight made Jerusalem the third most important city of Islam, after Mecca and Medina, and the Temple mount and the "glorious stone" became a very holy place for the people of the Koran.

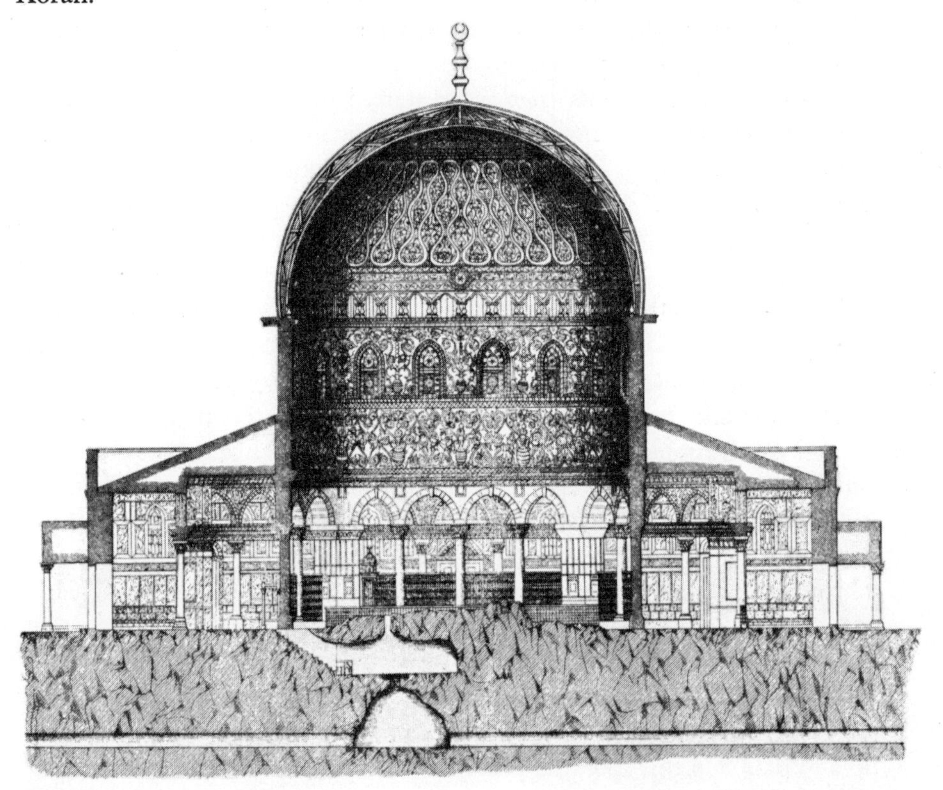

The great cupola and foundation of the Dome of the Rock, in cross-section. Though often rebuilt, its basic plan is still that of the first structure of 691 C.E. Under the Dome is the Rock itself, and within it two caves are shown, one under the other. A stairway today leads down to the upper cave. A hole runs from the top of the Rock into the upper cave. Through it may once have flowed blood from animals sacrificed in Temple rites.

In fact, early in the history of their religion, the Moslems used to face toward Jerusalem and the site of the Temple when they prayed, just as the Jews were instructed to do several times a day. After the Jews angered Mohammed by rejecting him and his new religion, this direction (*Kibleh*) was changed to Mecca, Mohammed's birthplace, where stands the sacred *Kaaba* (a square building whose name means "cube") containing a black meteorite worshiped as a sacred stone.

The new religion that was to dominate the Temple mount and the Arabian and Mediterranean world for hundreds of years is called Islam, which means "submission" (to the will of God). The name "Islam" is said to derive from the biblical story of Abraham "submitting" his son for sacrifice to God, on what is believed to be the same sacred Rock over which the Temple of Solomon was built. From the verb which means *aslama*, "submit," Mohammed took the name — Islam. Abraham, who substituted the one God for the worship of many idols, is designated by both Hebrews and Moslems as the ancestor of their peoples. Mohammed claimed to be the true prophet of Abraham, and Islamic tradition says it was Ishmael (son of Abraham and Hagar), called the ancestor of the Arab peoples, who was being sacrificed — and not Isaac as the Bible states.

Followers of Islam are known as Moslems, or Muslims (from *Muslimin*: "The surrendering ones," "those who have made their peace with God").

Mohammed, whose name means "highly praised," has been called the most important figure in medieval history. He was born in Mecca about 570 C.E., in what is now western Saudi Arabia near the Red Sea. It was a country three-fourths desert, with a population of nomad Bedouin tribes and poverty-stricken people.

He was orphaned early and cared for by a grandfather, later by an uncle. No one bothered to teach him to read or write. When he was twelve, he began to work with his uncle in camel caravans carrying merchandise between Mecca and Syria.

In the days of Mohammed, the majority of the people of the Arabian Peninsula, including Mohammed's clan, the Zoraishites, worshiped a variety of idols. On camel caravan journeys to far places, Mohammed became acquainted with Christians and Jews and held long discussions with them. Both these religions influenced him, but the one-God faith of the Hebrews made the most profound impression and he was to borrow heavily from their traditions, their religious laws, their Talmud, and their prophets. In fact, the Koran, which means "recitation," a compilation of his sayings, decisions, and maxims, is adapted largely from Hebrew doctrine and its Talmud, and is peopled with Judaic prophets and sages, including the David and Solomon concerned with in this book. Abraham, Joseph, Moses, Aaron, and Job appear time and again. Elements of Jewish ritual law, such as that of circumcision, fasting, and the prohibition of the eating of pork, still remain in Islam.

It was Mohammed's claim that his "new" religion came to him in a series of revelations from Allah, through Gabriel, the angel messenger. He then went among his own people, preaching the religion of the one God — Allah, the delights of Paradise, and the horrors of Hell. He was ridiculed and called a heretic by many, especially the powerful Quraish tribe whose best economic interest it was to see that pilgrimages continued to the Kaaba in Mecca which they controlled.

Mohammed preached at Mecca for some twelve years. Finally, about 620, he was invited to make his headquarters in Medina. His move to Medina in 632, or "flight," as some have called it, is known as the "*Hejira*," and the

Moslem era was designated seventeen years later by the Caliph Omar as starting from that year beginning on July 16.

Since much of his new religion was based on the ideas of Judaism, Mohammed hoped the large Jewish population of Medina would join him in his battles against the pagans. When they refused, rejecting his warlike doctrines, he broke with them as well as with Christianity, changing many of the laws and customs of his new faith. It was at this period that the "*Kibleh*," the direction to be faced in prayer, was changed from Jerusalem to Mecca; Friday, instead of Saturday became the new Sabbath day, and the month of Ramadan was designated for fasting instead of the Hebrew fast days.

Mohammed's remarkable political and organizational skill and his great success as a statesman and religious leader enabled him in the ten short years before his sudden death on June 8, 632, to build an empire out of nothing. All of Arabia fell to him, and his armies were poised for further conquest. Less than a hundred years later, Islam had triumphed over half the then known world. The leaders or Caliphs (from *Kalifah*: successor) who came after him continued the expansion of the Islamic state, until by 700 it included not only Syria, Egypt, and Iran, but had reached Spain and threatened Constantinople (unsuccessfully however.)

The Moslems were now known as "Arabs" which had come to mean those who followed Islam and spoke and wrote the Arabic language, regardless of whether they had come from Arabia itself or Persia, Syria, or Egypt.

Their solid empire was to last until the year 1000. Then the incessant rivalries among the caliphates of their various conquered lands led to a breakup. They were further devastated by the invasion of Genghis Khan and his Mongols in the thirteenth century, and by 1500 the great Islamic Empire was at an end.

However, even today, most of the area originally conquered by Mohammed's followers in their period of "blitzkrieg" remains Islamic in faith.

They number today almost a half billion, about one-seventh of the world's population. Sometimes the word "Islam" is used to denote the whole of the Moslem world, its states, social, political, and cultural institutions, and its lands.

Today in Jerusalem, city of the Temple mount, three Sabbath days each week are kept by three religious groups: Fridays by the Moslems, Saturdays by the Jews, and Sundays by the Christians.

15

Islam on the Temple Mount

(638–763 C.E.)

In 638, Jerusalem, after a siege of four months, was ready to surrender to soldiers of Mohammed's second successor, the Caliph Omar (Umar Abu ibn el-Khattab, 582–644).

The Christian administrator of Jerusalem, Patriarch Sophronius, had become sole authority there after the defeat of Byzantium in 636. He remembered well the fearful massacre when Persians had conquered the city in 614. Accordingly he sought to surrender to Omar himself in order to avoid bloodshed.

Omar, a wise, austere, and simple man, though a fanatical follower of the teachings of Mohammed, was also eager to avoid such evils. He feared the influence on his troops of a sudden acquisition of riches through plunder. He therefore agreed to Sophronius' request that Omar come in person to negotiate the surrender. It is said he traveled in utmost simplicity on camelback, all the way from Medina in Arabia to Jerusalem. Dressed in rags, he carried "a sack of corn, a bag of dates, a gourd of water, and a wooden dish." The leaders of his army came out to meet him, they and their steeds clad in finery. Omar, disgusted, pelted them with gravel. He himself is said to have had only one set of garments, heavily patched.

It was February, 638, when Sophronius met Omar on the Mount of Olives where the Moslem army was encamped and which overlooks the Temple area.

Omar granted generous terms. Christians were allowed to keep their shrines and their freedom of worship. Their tax payments were to go to the Moslems instead of the Byzantines. Omar's treatment of Jerusalem contrasts sharply with the bloody massacres when the Christian Crusaders took possession of that city in 1099.

Omar was less generous to the Jews. He instituted many restrictive laws against them. At the instigation of Sophronius, he barred them from living in Jerusalem. However, many of these laws were not enforced, and Jews actually did re-enter the city. In fact, not long after, the body of supreme Jewish authority, the *Gaonim*, was moved from Tiberius to Jerusalem and remained there until the eleventh century. Jews were actually freer under Islam — especially in Asia, Egypt, and Spain — than in Christian countries.

The period of the Islamic Empire has been called "the Jewish Golden Age." Great Jews appeared, accomplished in science, mathematics, medicine, philosophy, and languages. When the Islamic Empire ended in 1500, that Jewish Golden Age ended also.

Names of rich poetry were given by the Moslems to the site and buildings of the Temple mount. The entire great platform on Mount Moriah they called "Haram esh-Sherif," meaning noble or venerable sanctuary. This name, often shortened to Haram, is still used for the whole complex of buildings.

Another name was applied to the Temple area during the early period of Moslem control there. It was called the "faraway sanctuary" — in Arabic, the Mosque el Aksa — in memory of Mohammed's night flight to this "further" sacred site of the Rock and of Solomon's one-time Temple. Later, when a large and important mosque was erected at the southern end of the Haram platform, the name el Aksa Mosque was transferred to it, and thus it is named today.

As these words are written, the noble Haram platform contains both the central Dome of the Rock and, to the south, the imposing el Aksa Mosque. The Haram is the framework or setting; the Dome and the el Aksa are the principal jewels within it. Through the long centuries, a name may have shifted somewhat, but not the veneration for the site or its importance to those of Islamic faith, a veneration that reaches back beyond Mohammed to that earlier "prophet" Solomon, who caused there to be erected the Temple beyond time.

When Omar first entered Jerusalem, his great desire was to visit the spot from which Mohammed had ascended to the seventh heaven. Islam already regarded it as a sacred place to which angels had made pilgrimages long before the time of Adam. It was the direction toward which Moses prayed, and even (said some Moslems) the spot where he had received the Ark of the Covenant. It was also, as stated earlier, the first *kibleh*, meaning direction toward which Moslems face for ritual prayer.

Sophronius feared that Omar would build a house of worship on the Temple site, or perhaps even turn it back to the Jews. Hence, the Patriarch tried to hide its location from Omar, showing him instead various Christian churches. Omar, however, refused to pray in them.

Vivid and earthy tales are told how Omar at last did reach the sacred Temple site. Accompanied by several thousand of his men he came there, and was shocked to find it heaped high with rubbish, dung, and filth — tossed there by Romans and Christians to insult the Jews. Omar and his men were forced to crawl on hands and knees over garbage to get through a ruined archway.

Omar, in a great gesture of indignation picked up a handful of rubbish and tossed it into the valley below. Those with him understood this signal to start cleaning the site. They followed his example. Omar then took off his own cloak and used it as a bag for carrying away the filth. Again his followers did likewise.

Then he and they went to the southern end of the Temple area, faced Mecca, and began to pray, while Sophronius looked on in horror. Islam had taken over the Temple site.

> A Moslem tale says that Omar first dug down to the great Rock, then delayed prayers until three rain showers had fallen. It is likely that the stench of the filth and dung of this "garbage dump" made it impossible to linger for prayers.

With Moslems in control, a thorough cleaning of the Temple mount was carried through.

> Later legends varied these details. In 1333, a Jewish rabbi from Spain wrote his family about an "Arab king" (Omar) who had sworn that if he could conquer Jerusalem he would restore the ruined Temple. However, said this version, Omar was unable to find Temple remains under the piles of rubbish until at last he secured the aid of an old Jewish man who agreed to show where the Temple had stood, if Omar promised to leave the Western Wall to the Jews. When Omar had thus found the site of the Temple itself, he ordered it cleared, built there a fine mosque, and did leave the Western Wall for praying, mourning Jews.
>
> Another rabbi, about 1540, wrote an interesting tale, though it confuses dates. That story says the Temple site was sought by "Sultan Suleiman," who actually ruled some seventy-seven years after Omar's famous visit to Jerusalem, and is not to be confused with the sixteenth century Suleiman the Magnificent. Having vainly searched all Jerusalem for traces of the Temple, the Sultan's representative one day saw a woman carrying on her head a basket full of garbage and filth. He learned she had come all the way from Bethlehem to a certain dump site in Jerusalem.
>
> "Our tradition tells us," she explained, "that it is a good deed to dump garbage in that place."
>
> It was there that Suleiman's men dug and indeed did discover the sacred Temple site. Overjoyed, the Sultan ordered it cleaned, and the Western Wall sprinkled with rosewater.

Though Sophronius died a year after Omar's visit to Jerusalem, and no new Christian Patriarch was appointed during the next sixty-seven years, the city remained under Byzantine Christian administration. Christian pilgrims continued to come there, and the city continued much as before, though Moslem control tightened as the years went by. The Moslems gave the city several new names: sometimes Iliya (based on Hadrian's Aelia); sometimes it was poetically called al Balat (the palace), often Beit al-Maqdis (resembling the Hebrew name for the Temple). Mostly, however, the Moslems called it al-Quds (sanctity, or holiness).

An Armenian manuscript, copied in 1693, reviews all history from the Creation to Jerusalem and says that this city was called by nine names: Shalem, Luz, Bet El, Erusalma, Jebus, Aelia, the Holy City, Salim, and Jerusalem. Somehow, none of the many names bestowed from time to time on that city and site survived in men's memories and imaginations, save only Jerusalem.

In Jerusalem new changes appeared. Religious activities of its Christians became more restricted. Jews now lived in their own section, had their own synagogues, and prayed constantly at the Western Wall. To Moslems, Jerusalem remained the third holiest of cities, even though Ramleh (meaning "sand"), a purely Moslem town, had been set up on the coastal plain as seat of government for the region in place of Jerusalem.

Moslems now worshiped at their own buildings in Jerusalem. Soon after Omar's visit, a simple temporary mosque was built in the southern part of the Temple platform where Solomon's palace had once stood, apparently just south of the old Temple site. Arculf, a French bishop, described it about thirty years later as a "square house of prayer, roughly built of vertical boards and of large beams . . ." This sounds like the simple structure Omar would have approved.

Then nearly sixty years after his death, a stone building called the Mosque of el Aksa is said to have been built, also at the southern end of the Haram. Its builder was al-Walid, the Caliph of the Ommayad dynasty, son of the Abd al-Malik who built the Dome of the Rock near by. (Some writers have credited Abd al-Malik with building this first el Aksa mosque, and the authors deem it likely he did make some start in that direction, whether or not it was completed during his reign.)

Often enough the title "Mosque of Omar" has been given to the Dome of the Rock, which today stands on the site of the Temple of Solomon and Herod. Omar, however, had nothing to do with it. Indeed, he would doubtless have denounced this imposing octagonal structure, for he held luxury and splendor in disdain and believed a building should be small and simple, with three rooms at most.

The Ommayad caliph, Abd al-Malik (685–705 C.E.) was a man of decision and ability. Rival factions had for some time disrupted Islam. He ruthlessly suppressed them and governed wisely and justly. He is said to have kept eight wives, fathered fifteen sons of whom four ruled after him — justifying his name, which means "father of kings" — and to have written poetry.

There may have been reasons other than religious ones that moved him to build on the Temple mount the Dome of the Rock, or, in Arabic, Qubbat al-Sakrah. Ruling from Damascus, he had lost the holy cities of Mecca and Medina to his Moslem rival, Caliph Abdallah ibn-Zobeir. Abd al-Malik doubtless wished to attract pilgrims from Mecca to Jerusalem. Income from pilgrims has long been an active factor in the life of the Holy Land. It has been said, too, that Abd al-Malik wished to build a beautiful house of worship lest Moslems be led astray by the beauty of Christian churches.

The Dome was begun in 687 and completed four years later. Two men oversaw the construction, one a former slave whom the Caliph had freed. Some of the craftsmen who made the great structure beautiful were Jerusalem residents, descended from the Byzantines. Most of the workers, as well as most of the building materials, were foreign in origin. Yet fragments and columns of Byzantine churches destroyed in 614 by the Persians were used here, as well as later on in Jerusalem.

Abd al-Malik during several years poured into this project the revenues from his Egyptian domain, for he was eager to surpass the splendor of the Church of the Holy Sepulcher restored after the Persian invasion of 614. If he hoped also that the Dome of the Rock would replace the Kaaba of Mecca as the principal shrine of Moslem worship, he was doomed to be disappointed.

The Dome of the Rock was built eight-sided on a square base reached by six stairways. It was not primarily a mosque, but also a shrine for the sacred Rock beneath. Some have called it the most beautiful Islamic monument in all the Middle East. It ranks third among the four "wonders" of the world of

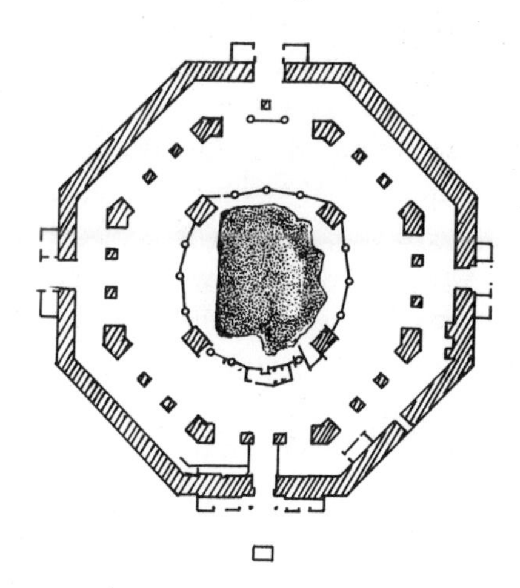

An octagon around a circle around a great Rock — such is the plan of the Dome of Rock, first completed in 691 C.E. The Rock is at the very center, under the midpoint of the cupola above. Around it is a protective screen. Still further from the center is the ring of columns and pillars supporting the roof. Finally are the walls, shaped in a perfect octagon, with doors facing east, north, west, and south.

Islam. The other three are the mosques at Mecca, Medina, and Damascus.

A Moslem writer tells of the proclamation spread by criers after the Dome of the Rock stood completed: "Verily, the Sakrah is open. He who would pray therein, let him come."

We learn from the early Arab historian Ya'qubi, writing less than two hundred years after the Dome of the Rock was completed, ". . . Abd al-Malik . . . hung [the Rock] round with curtains of brocade, and he instituted door-keepers . . . and the people began the custom of walking around the Rock even as they had paced around the Kaaba [in Mecca], and the usage continued all the days of the dynasty of the Omayyads."

Such circling around sacred objects has been traced to ancient pagan as well as Hebrew rituals. It had been done earlier on this same site around the altar of the Jewish Temple.

Time and earthquakes took their toll of the Dome of the Rock. It has been many times renewed and altered. Yet its shape today is basically what it was when it first stood resplendent in 691 C.E. Its internal decorations are also largely those of the time of Abd al-Malik — especially the arches and various interior mosaics made by Byzantine craftsmen in the forms of flowers, vases, and scrolls. These can still be seen over corner stones between the arches and the barrel of the dome above. The Dome of the Rock, as a prime example of the best Islamic architecture of the early years of the Omayyad and Abbasid dynasties, blends elements that came from the finest of earlier Grecian, Persian, and Byzantine styles.

Fabulous details recorded about the original Dome of the Rock show that it, like the temples there before it, kindled men's imaginations. Its new cupola was said to have been totally gilded, thanks to the melting of vast quantities of gold coins from Abd al-Malik's treasury, plus jewelry given by pious women. So dazzling was it, says a fifteenth century Moslem writer, that no one dared look at it by day. To protect it skins were spread over it in winter.

Inside — the heart of the Dome of the Rock, then as now — rested the great sacred Rock, some two hundred feet in perimeter. Screens of ebony and curtains of brocade surrounded it. Mixed scents prepared by scores of people, working day and night, were spread upon it: saffron, musk, ambergris, and rosewater. The faithful who prayed there were afterwards recognized by the odor of fine incense clinging to them. Candelabras hung above the Rock on more than 150 chains.

> At first, says one tale, from a central chain hung a matchless pearl, two horns of the ram that Abraham once had sacrificed on this same Mount Moriah, plus a fine crown. Later, it is said, these treasures were taken to the Kaaba at Mecca.
>
> Legends relate that the Rock once loomed twelve miles high, its shadow reaching over distant Jericho. Above the Rock, the night sky was lit by a great ruby, destined on Judgment Day to be transformed into a white coral throne for God.

A slab of green jasper, known as the Stone of Eden, had been inserted in the floor of the Dome of the Rock, says another tale. This slab covered King Solomon's grave and one of the gates to Paradise.

Another story relates that Mohammed, when he reached this Temple site on his memorable night ride, had placed nineteen golden nails in the Stone of Eden as mementoes. He assigned the Angel Gabriel as guard, warning that if all these nails were removed, the world would return to nothingness. Bent on destruction, Satan began pulling out the nails one by one. He intended to enter Eden from under the Stone. But Gabriel drove him off after "all but three and one-half nails" were removed. Over this remnant Gabriel still stands guard. So close is the world to destruction!

Not only the building but also the upkeep of the Dome of the Rock was costly. It involved much incense, and three hundred maintenance workers, all exempted from paying taxes. They included Christians in charge of the carpets, with Jews working as sweepers and glassmakers creating glass plates and vessels for lamps.

Still standing slightly east of the Dome of the Rock is the graceful little Qubbat as-Silsila, or "Dome of the Chain." Its construction is also attributed to Abd al-Malik, and it does look almost like a model erected to test a hexagonal design for the far larger Dome of the Rock. The tales tell that it was once the Treasury for the el Aksa Mosque.

Moslem legends refer to it also as "the Tribunal of the Prophet David." Its chain served as an early "lie-detector." The Angel Gabriel had given a silver chain to King David, who hung it from this small dome. Witnesses about to testify in lawsuits were made to take hold of this chain. If they told a lie, a link would drop off.

One day, as the stories go, a man was accused of stealing coins. He cleverly concealed them in a walking stick, which he handed to his accuser to hold for him. Then when he was asked, "Did you take the coins?" he replied, "I have already returned them to the plaintiff." No link fell then from the chain, but from heaven a voice rang out, "From this day forth, the chain shall be hid, so that justice may not falter because of human deceit." Since then the wonderful chain has never been seen.

In 705 C.E., Abd al-Malik was followed by his son al-Walid I, called the greatest builder in the Omayyad dynasty. During a ten-year reign marked by peace and plenty, he erected schools, hospitals, houses of worship, enlarged the Mecca mosque, and rebuilt that of Medina. He has been called the first medieval ruler who provided hospitals for the blind, the crippled, the leprous, and victims of chronic diseases. Like his father, he wrote poetry. Also he played the lute and composed. Arts of peace were dearer to him than those of war.

Such was the ruler who erected or completed the first great el Aksa Mosque where the present el Aksa stands, at the southern end of the Haram platform. Still visible at the far end of its lovely interior are old Byzantine columns said by some scholars to have come from the ruins of Justinian's Church of Saint Mary, erected in the period 530–60 C.E. just west of where the el Aksa now stands, but destroyed in 614 when the Persians overran Jerusalem.

In the opinion of one Jerusalem resident, al Mukaddasi, writing in the latter part of the tenth century, the el Aksa was far more beautiful even than the Great Mosque of Damascus, also erected under al-Walid.

These two Omayyad rulers, Abd al-Malik and al-Walid, glorified the Temple mount once again with buildings of noble style and scope. Moslem commentators say that in the Dome of the Rock and el Aksa together, six thousand beams were used in the ceilings, beside many great wooden pillars, and sixty marble pillars. Seven *minrabs* (pulpits) were provided. Light was supplied by two thousand candles and five thousand lamps, many of them suspended on nearly three hundred chains in the two buildings.

The last of the Omayyad line was Merwan II, slain 749 C.E. in battle with Abu al-Abbas, an Abbasid monarch and direct descendant of an uncle of the Prophet Mohammed. This Abu named himself "al-Saffah" (the Bloodthirsty One). He ordered that all remaining Omayyad princes be hunted down and slain. Thus perished the dynasty under which the original Dome of the Rock and el Aksa had arisen on the Temple mount.

In 746 C.E. a great earthquake had damaged the el Aksa. Some six hundred years later an Arab writer recorded the accumulated oral tradition. Both eastern and western parts of the el Aksa lay fallen during the reign of Caliph al-Mansur (754–75), he wrote. Since that ruler lacked funds for rebuilding, he ordered the silver and gold plates stripped from the mosque's doors. The precious metal was cast into dinars and dirhans, coins of the time, which were spent on restoration work.

Hardly did the el Aksa stand complete again, when another earthquake occurred "and the building . . . fell to the ground." Trouble was never long absent from the site of the Temple!

16

From Caliphs to Sultans on Mount Moriah

(763–1095 C.E.)

In the last half of the eighth century C.E. the Christian Byzantine empire was involved with internal religious conflicts, and was not at this time a threat to Islam. The leading Islamic ruler was now al-Mansur, half-brother of the cruel, bloody al-Saffah.

Al-Mansur appears to have rebuilt the el Aksa around 771. After it was destroyed once more by earthquake, his successor, al-Mahdi, rebuilt it again, and this time its shape was changed to one broader and shorter.

Harun al-Rashid, made famous by the *Thousand and One Nights* tales, ruled the Islamic empire 786–809 C.E. During the latter part of his reign, Omar's old law against the Christians was revived and enlarged to include Jews. Christians had to wear blue badges, Jews yellow ones.

However, in distant lands near the Rhine River a memorable Christian monarch was building strength — Charlemagne (742–814), king of the Franco-German empire, sometimes called the greatest of medieval rulers. Trying to find eastern allies against the Byzantines, he wooed the favor of Islam. Embassies and gifts were exchanged. A mission from Charlemagne to the court of Harun al-Rashid in 797 received permission to bring back religious relics from the Christian patriarch in Jerusalem. The Islamic caliph sent to Charlemagne keys to sacred places in Jerusalem, including the Church of the Holy Sepulcher. Grateful, Charlemagne sent alms to the Holy City. Such funds allowed a number of Christian churches, monasteries and the like to be built and staffed in Jerusalem. Thus the Franks, or Latins as they were sometimes called, gained a foothold there, and a base was laid for the later great movements known as the Crusades.

Pilgrims to Jerusalem and environs had previously come largely from the Byzantine Empire, with its eastern creed of Orthodox Christianity. Now more and more pilgrims began to come from western Roman Catholic lands, including what is now France, Germany, Italy, and even Britain.

Such visitors were impressed by the beauty of the Dome of the Rock. It became even more lovely, for in the eighth century were added unusual mosaics adorning its aisles: palm trees, grapes, fruits, flowers, and foliage of many kinds glowed in intricately-assembled decorations.

Al-Mamun, son of al-Rashid, ruled 813–33. He committed artistic plagiarism by ordering his name to be substituted for that of al-Malik in the Dome of the Rock inscriptions (made in Kufic script). However, since by oversight the date was not changed, they still revealed their real origin.

A translation of this stolen inscription declared: "Hath built this dome the servant of God Abdullah al-Imam al-Mamun, commander of the believers, in the year two and seventy. May God accept of him and favor him. Amen." That "two and seventy" is the number of the Islamic year which reckons from the date of Mohammed's "flight" from Mecca to Medina.

Tolerance of other religions continued during al-Mamun's reign. Throughout the Islamic empire thousands of Christian churches, monasteries, and convents operated, and hundreds of Jewish synagogues. The prevailing freedom of exchange of ideas and commerce won converts to Islam from among the non-Moslem populations. Such converts adopted the language and dress as well as the religion of the Arabs.

Though Palestine and Jerusalem in particular continued to attract Christian pilgrims, the ninth century brought to Europe conflict and disruption in place of the unity that had been maintained under Charlemagne and his followers. Jerusalem, in consequence, once again came to be neglected by the Christian west.

Jews were permitted, during about 350 years from 637 to 1009 C.E., to enter the Haram area and to pray at what had been the Temple gates. In return they were expected to clean up rubble and refuse there. An added privilege was granted them during about 150 years prior to the Crusades. On their religious holidays they were allowed to worship within the sacred area itself, "To make the rounds of the Temple gates and pray beside them in a loud voice." At this time they were also able to build a synagogue near the Western Wall.

During the tenth century, Moslem resentment increased in Jerusalem and survival of the Christian holy places was threatened. The Moslems in 935 C.E. built a mosque in the courtyard of the Church of the Holy Sepulcher itself. About thirty-two years later, fanatic Moslems burned that church, also known as the Anastasis, and John, the Christian Patriarch, perished in the flames. To Constantinople went a Christian appeal for aid, and the Byzantine armies began moving victoriously toward Jerusalem, but as they were in sight of it, the sudden death of the Byzantine Emperor cut short the campaign.

The Moslem dynasty of Fatimid caliphs, then governing Jerusalem, realized the city needed stronger defenses. They bolstered and shortened the city walls, and in so doing placed outside those walls the old section that had formed the "City of David." But the Temple mount, with the Dome of the Rock and el Aksa, remained within.

About the year 903 one of the earliest detailed descriptions of the Haram area and the Dome of the Rock was written by the Persian Ibn al Fakih. According to him, the Dome of the Rock stood in the midst of the Haram on a paved platform reached by six stairways. The building's four

The stairway to the southern entrance to the Dome of the Rock.

gates were roofed over with porticos of marble, and each gate or archway had four doors. Each night, within the Dome of the Rock, three hundred lamps burned. Beneath the Rock itself, he said, was a cave in which more than sixty people could pray. The Dome, he said, was covered on the outside with "red gold," its interior with white marble, while fifty-six stained glass windows pierced the supporting walls and drum of the Dome. The cupola, above, was supported by twelve piers and thirty-six pillars.

Al Fakih described also the small Dome of the Chain nearby, and counted twenty marble columns supporting its leaden roof. A later Moslem traveler said that this small Chain building measured sixty paces round.

Still later Moslems paid tribute to the beauty of these buildings: "At dawn, when the light of the sun first strikes on the cupola . . . then is this edifice a marvellous sight," wrote al Mukaddasi of Jerusalem, a travel writer and geographer of the late tenth century, ". . . in all Islam I have never seen the equal, neither have I heard aught built in pagan times that rivals in grace this Dome of the Rock."

He described also the building's four gates, one facing each of the four stairways which then led up to the platform of the Dome of the Rock from the surrounding court. To the south was the Kibleh Gate; to the east the Gate of the Angel Israfel; to the north the Gate of the Trumpet; and to the west the Women's Gate. Each gate was gold-trimmed and closed by cedar-wood doors.

"From afar off," wrote al Mukaddasi, "you may perceive on the summit of the Dome the beautiful pinnacle . . ." Today the gold-plated cupola is surmounted by a knobbed staff topped by a closed crescent. When seen by al Mukaddasi, the cupola was covered with brass plates to which gilt had been applied.

He described, too, the el Aksa, which by his day had been rebuilt several times. He mentioned its twenty-eight doors or gates, 280 columns, and the coffers roundabout into which were placed contributions from various cities in Syria and Iraq. Inside to the south was an enclosure for important personages. Behind its pulpit stood an inscription intended to ward off the bites of serpents. Though magnificent in its dome and mosaics, the el Aksa, al Mukaddasi thought, did not quite equal the Mosque of Cordoba, (Spain) which had 850 columns, often compared to a forest.

The main el Aksa door, facing north toward the Dome of the Rock, was of brass so heavily plated with gilt that it was, he said, hard to move on its hinges. Rich carpets were spread on the floors of both el Aksa and the Dome of the Rock. Then as now they were gifts of wealthy Moslems.

Al Mukaddasi, though a Jerusalem citizen, was aware of his city's shortcomings as well as its merits. He found its inns costly, its water scarce, its baths dirty as well as expensive. School attendance was bad, and justice poor. Nevertheless, he praised the city's beauty, its hills, climate, and food, the virtues of its citizens, and the pleasures of life there. All in all, "People find themselves drawn here — people from all over the world — drawn here as if by some irresistible, intangible force." This sentiment is often echoed today.

A strange, cruel caliph, Hakim of the Egyptian Fatimids, governed Palestine from Cairo between 996 and 1021. Rich, tyrannical, he persecuted all who doubted that he was godlike, whether Christians, Jews, or Moslems.

He broke with the long tradition of religious tolerance, when in 1009 he decreed the elimination of Christian and Jewish religious buildings in his domain. At his command, the Church of the Holy Sepulcher was wiped out again. This, plus destruction of many other Christian relics, helped kindle the Crusades.

Mass slaughter threatened Christians and Jews. Thousands, to save their lives, embraced Islam. In that black year of 1010, it is said, Hakim commanded Jews to wear six-pound wooden blocks around their necks and bells on their clothing, so they could be spotted as unbelievers from a distance. Finally, in 1014 he ordered that both Jews and Christians be banished from his realm.

Hakim's end is described differently by various historians. Some say he disappeared mysteriously, others that Moslems, in disgust at his actions and by order of his own sister, assassinated him.

After his death arose a strange cult worshiping Hakim, despite the tenets of Islam. Called the Druze for their leader Darazi, the sect still exists and its followers are said to number about 150,000, some living in modern Israel, others in Syria and Lebanon. During the Six Day War of June, 1967, some Druze fought on the Israeli side. Others in Syria and Lebanon were opposed to Israel.

Earthquakes continued to take their toll on the Temple mount. In 1016 the cupola of the Dome of the Rock was shattered and had to be replaced. In 1034 an earthquake devastated even the remains of the Church of the Holy Sepulcher, a structure so important in the later Crusades. Its history has been closely tied to that of the Temple mount somewhat east of it. The Church of the Holy Sepulcher and other Christian churches were finally rebuilt by means of funds from Byzantium. During a period of some forty years of peace, additional religious structures were erected and pilgrimages by Christians increased again. Wounds inflicted by the mad Hakim seemed to be healing.

Nasir-i-Khusrau, a Persian traveler in Jerusalem of 1047, gave a picturesque description of the great Rock within the Dome of the Rock. He noted that it dipped on one side toward the south, the *kibleh* or sacred direction of prayer toward Mecca. Also that it had foot or toe marks as though imprinted at some time long past when the stone had the consistency of clay. He mentioned seven such marks. "I heard it stated that Abraham — peace be upon him! — was once here with Isaac — upon him be peace! — when he was a boy and that he walked over this place and that the footmarks were his." He also mentioned Moses and said that King Solomon had once built a "Mosque" around the sacred Rock.

The respect shown to the Dome of the Rock was suggested by the fact that over the Rock, on a silver chain from the inside of the cupola, was hung a silver lamp. It and many other lamps in the building were gifts of the Sultan or Caliph of Egypt.

In 1351, Jamal ad Din Ahmad of Jerusalem told how the Dome of the Rock's "Great Lantern" containing five hundred lamps, had fallen in the year 1060 C.E. Moslems then said to each other that this accident boded some ill, and indeed, thirty-nine years later in 1099 C.E., Jerusalem itself fell to the Crusaders.

During the eleventh century, the ruling dynasties of the Islamic empire had begun to depend more and more on hired Turkish troops and guards. These were called *Seljuks* after a Turkish chief who had adopted Islam. His grandson, Toghrul Beg, in 1055 was named regent of the orthodox Moslem world. From then on, the Seljuk rulers, calling themselves *sultan* (master), gained full control. The caliphs were reduced to dealing with merely religious matters.

The Seljuk Turks, known as tough, fierce, and cruel warriors, extended their power greatly throughout the East. They did not conduct campaigns of total destruction. Rather they managed to borrow the best of the civilizations and cultures they conquered. Thus they replaced the dissolute and dying Moslem dynasties by a strong, unified new empire.

They went on to administer a defeat in Armenia to the Christian Byzantine Emperor himself, and to threaten his capital city, Constantinople. The Byzantines urgently appealed for aid to the Western Christian nations and to the Roman Catholic pope.

The Seljuks demanded heavy tolls from Christian pilgrims to Jerusalem. In Europe, hatred grew against the Turks and fear for the safety of the holy places in Palestine. Between 1009 and 1012, Pope Sergius IV had issued a "bull" calling for Christian retaliation. Later, in 1070, as the Seljuks took the control of Jerusalem from the Fatimids, tales of their cruelty reached Europe. Gregory VII, who was Pope from 1073 to 1085, called for a holy expedition or "Crusade" against the Turks. He hoped himself to lead it, but it was Pope Urban II who whipped the movement into action. In November, 1095, at an historic gathering of clergy in France, Urban issued his call for Christians to lay all else aside and march to deliver Jerusalem from the "infidels." All who set out under the banners of this Crusade, he promised, would be granted full forgiveness for their sins.

Thus was laid the foundation for a long, bitter struggle between Christianity and Islam.

17

Crusaders and Crusader-Kings in Jerusalem

(1095–1171 C.E.)

Jerusalem, its Temple mount and adjoining sacred relics, were the proclaimed goals, the focal points, for the strangest, most dramatic, and often most shocking mass movements in the history of Europe and the East — The Crusades. In all, there were eight different crusades, plus a ghastly children's venture. Together they covered almost two centuries: from 1095 to 1291.

Underlying causes of the Crusades were not purely religious. Economic and political forces also played enormous roles. Yet the accumulated weight of religious influence was great. Even naked greed for gain disguised itself as piety. In this sense, the Crusades were hypocritical or deceitful. Yet the masses of Crusaders were often as self-deceived as they were deceiving of others who watched them in admiration, wonder, or dread and hate, as the case might be.

Those two centuries still fascinate modern man, for the Crusades merged devout faith with ambition, greed, opportunism, violence, and bestial cruelty.

Between Europe and Asia, or the East, had long stood the old Byzantine Empire, the Christian survival of the one-time world power, Rome. Now, however, that Empire was split, weakened by religious sectarian strife and political feuds. Moreover, since 1054 this Byzantine buffer had been increasingly cut off from the dominant powers in Europe. That was the year of a great split in organized Christianity which left the Roman Catholic Church supreme in the West (Europe), while the Greek Orthodox Church held sway in the East (Byzantium).

Further, while isolated as never before from Europe, Byzantium was attacked from all sides. The Turks, in particular, overran its Asiatic provinces. Finally, Alexius I, emperor of Byzantium, made his appeal for help to Pope Urban II in Rome. Better to fight the Turks in Asia, Alexius urged, than to wait for them to reach the capitals of Europe.

Europe, however, was not united. Far from it. Its feudal princes, dukes, and barons conspired and warred against each other. Pope Urban knew that a great common cause could distract them from fighting among themselves. Their aggressions might be focused on the Middle East.

In Italy, the merchant princes of the powerful port cities — especially Pisa, Genoa, Amalfi, and Venice — were impatient to end Moslem control of the harbors and markets of the rich Middle East. They thirsted for the lucrative trade of the eastern Mediterranean. They, too, pressed hard, if less openly, for military action that would bring them the free hand they wanted.

How Pope Urban and his aides proclaimed, preached, and promoted the First Crusade is beyond the scope of this book. The outcome was a vast and motley army of "soldiers of Christ." They included nobles, footloose knights, freed serfs or criminals, adventurers, merchants, propertyless vagrants, monks, militant priests. All swore to fight until Jerusalem and its holy places were freed from the infidel Turk.

August of 1096 was the official starting date. But many groups headed toward Jerusalem still earlier, led by a strange fanatic, Peter the Hermit. Bloodshed marked their path even in Europe. Especially in the Rhineland, the rich region linked with Charlemagne's efforts toward unity, they ran berserk. In a frenzy of religious fury they attacked, burned, and slaughtered thousands of local "infidels" — Jews, many of whose families had lived there five hundred or even a thousand years.

In the great city of Prague alone, the Jewish community was nearly wiped out. Many Jews, forewarned, committed suicide at the approach of this uncontrolled rabble headed for Jerusalem. The end of an era of stable Jewish communal life in Europe has been traced to this period. It led into centuries of "race hatred" and anti-Semitic persecutions.

Jews were not the only sufferers in the Crusaders' pathway across Europe. Often, when short of funds, the Crusaders plundered homes and fields that lay at hand, safe in the assurance of Pope Urban that taking part in the Crusade to save Jerusalem would win them forgiveness of all sins. Arrived outside Constantinople, and thinking they were not fed well enough by Emperor Alexius, they plundered and wrecked the suburbs of that Byzantine capital. To protect the city itself, Alexius bought them off with food and ships to take them across the Bosphorus on their way to the Holy City. As the first of the wild band approached Nicaea across from Constantinople, the Turks attacked and almost wiped them out.

The next "wave" of Crusaders, mostly nobles and knights, were received by Alexius with supplies and bribes. In return he obtained their pledge of allegiance and the promise that the lands they won, they would turn over to him.

These "Franks" — most of whom came from what later became France — did take the city of Nicaea in June, 1097. Then they moved on and besieged Antioch, in northern Syria. It fell after eight months. By this time great numbers of Crusaders had died of hunger, thirst, and exposure. The survivors, however, pressed on toward the south, kindled to fresh efforts by "discovery" of a lance said to have been the one with which a Roman soldier pierced the side of Jesus as he hung on the cross.

At last on June 7, 1099, the Crusaders finally stood before the gates and walls of Jerusalem. They had been under way three years — years filled with marching, fighting, suffering. Their reaction was described, some ninety years afterward, by the Archbishop William of Tyre, then engaged in preaching a Third Crusade: "... they raised their hands to heaven ... unshod themselves ... bent and kissed the soil. Whosoever beheld this sight, however hard of heart, could not fail to be moved by it."

Their foes on the walls of Jerusalem were now not the Seljuk Turks, who had been ousted in 1098. They were troops of the Fatimid dynasty, and they had greatly strengthened the city's defenses. But they numbered only a thousand, and the Crusader force still had about twelve times as many. The Fatimid caliph tried to negotiate for peace, offering to assure the safety of pilgrims and other Christians in Jerusalem. The Crusaders, however, demanded unconditional surrender.

Again, as in the days of the Romans, Jerusalem was besieged, and the Crusaders took the same northern positions that Titus' men had held in 70 C.E. For more than four weeks, the thousand Fatimid soldiers resisted stoutly. Finally, Peter the Hermit announced he had received a message from the spirit of a dead Crusader. Stop quarreling among yourselves, it said. Instead, send your people marching around the walls of Jerusalem daily for nine days, and it will fall.

Indeed, while some of them distracted the Moslem guards by such marching and chanting, others used their new siege machinery, towers, and ladders. They fought their way over a northern section of the walls, near where Herod's Gate now stands. Once inside, they forced open the doors to admit their companions, and so, on July 15, 1099, the Crusaders stood within the Holy City. Their nominal leaders, Godfrey de Bouillion and Tancred of Hauteville, did not prevent the horrible aftermath to this success — a vast massacre of Jerusalem's inhabitants, both soldiers and civilians, Moslems and Jews. It has been described by various eyewitnesses. A priest told how "numbers of the Saracens were beheaded ... shot with arrows ... forced to jump from towers. Others were tortured for days, then burned ... In the streets were seen piles of heads and hands and feet. One rode about everywhere amidst corpses ..."

The slaughter went on also in the holy sites. The Crusaders believed that the Dome of the Rock was the actual Temple of Solomon, and eyewitnesses among them told how "Saracens," driven into that structure, resisted there one whole day until "their blood flowed throughout the whole Temple . . ."

Not only were Moslem soldiers slain. Women, children, and old people were brutally slaughtered. Babies were thrown from high walls or dashed against stones. The Jews remaining in Jerusalem, who were said to have aided the Moslems in defending the city against the Crusaders, were herded into a synagogue and burned alive. Crusaders ran through all Jerusalem, wading in blood, plundering, burning, killing — and then "rejoicing and weeping our men went to worship at the Sepulcher of our Saviour Jesus and thus fulfill our pledge to Him . . ."

Modern historians have estimated that when the Crusaders took Jerusalem they killed nearly forty thousand people, mostly civilians — nearly three times as many victims as there were Crusaders. The Moslem world never forgot the horror of this massacre.

Jerusalem now became a Christian stronghold, and was called a "Latin Kingdom" to stress its allegiance to the Roman Church and papacy. Installed as ruler in Jerusalem was Godfrey of Bouillion, said by some historians to have instigated the massacre. His title was "Defender of the Holy Sepulcher."

The Byzantines in Constantinople now discovered the worth of the Crusaders' oaths of allegiance. Not only did the Crusaders turn over no land or power to the Byzantine Emperor who had called them to his aid, but they even expelled from Jerusalem his form of Christianity — the Greek Orthodox Church. The Catholicism of the Pope of Rome dominated the Holy City.

Jerusalem and its surroundings were now forced into the feudal patterns that the Franks had brought from Europe. The land was divided among barons. They elected their king. Two codes of laws were set up: one for the landed nobility; the other for the common city citizens, or bourgeois.

Christians were encouraged to come to Jerusalem from Europe and Syria. Moslem mosques were converted to Catholic churches and chapels. The previous landowners, whether Moslem or Greek Orthodox Christians, became serfs to the new Frankish overlords. The system of serfdom in the Kingdom of Jerusalem was said to be even more rigid and repressive than in Europe at the same time.

The Franks were generally hated by Moslems and by native-born Christians. Both looked on them as aliens and intruders. Yet, as the years went on, the Frankish nobles seem to have been more and more fascinated by the customs and culture of the land they ruled. Many adopted Arab dress and habits.

Jerusalem's first Frankish ruler, Godfrey, died only a year after the conquest and massacre. His brother became King Baldwin I and ruled there for eighteen years beginning 1100 C.E. He was the first to be called "king" in Jerusalem since the days of Herod.

The sacred site on Mount Moriah was turned over to a new organization of soldier-monks known as the Knights Templar, or the Order of the Temple, with the full title: "Poor Knights of Christ and of the Temple of Solomon." It was founded in 1118 under King Baldwin II, who ruled in Jerusalem after Baldwin I.

The name "Temple" came of course from the Crusaders' name for the Moslem shrine, the Dome of the Rock. They referred to the building by the Latin name, *Templum Domini*, and liked to call themselves "Guardians of

Not far from the Temple Mount stands the strange Church of the Holy Sepulcher, containing Crusader tombs from days of the Latin Kingdom of Jerusalem. Tradition has it this Church stands on what was once the Hill of Golgotha (skulls.) Within the limits of the church, it is said, are the places of the entombment and subsequent resurrection of Jesus. An old folktale relates that even Adam's skull once lay there. This Church, a mixture of many styles and periods, is undergoing extensive repair, as suggested by scaffolding in this photo.

the Temple." Its octagonal shape appeared on their seals, their banners, and their armor, and was minted also on coins issued under King Baldwin.

Records of the Templars are lengthy, complex, sometimes contradictory, and often unsavory. At the outset, its warrior monks, garbed in white robes marked by red crosses, were pledged to purity, poverty, discipline, and the military support of Christianity — Roman Catholic Christianity.

Templars were not the only Jerusalem-founded order of this kind. Even earlier the "Hospitalers" had been launched, their formal name being the "Knights Hospitaler of St. John of Jerusalem," their costume a black robe with a white cross on the left sleeve. The order had been formed in connection with the founding of a hospital, and like the Templars, their original purpose had been service to pilgrims: nursing those who were sick, aiding the poor, and protecting them from attack as they traveled between Roman Catholic Europe and the Roman Catholic Kingdom of Jerusalem.

Templars and Hospitalers soon clashed. Each sought to control the profitable "tours" and travel routes of pilgrims who came into Palestine and made their way to Jerusalem. Each order had its own hostelries and controlled its own sacred sites; each also had its own supply of relics and sacred souvenirs to show or sell en route.

Thus the orders of Poor Knights of the Temple and of the Hospital came to hate each other with most impious intensity. Both orders began to concentrate more and more on attacking Moslem strongholds and retaining all that they won. They also solicited contributions from every likely source: the Church, the state, and individuals, rich or poor.

In Syria arose great Templar fortresses where the members of the order lived in luxury, following many oriental practices that they had learned. In the thirteenth century, the order became owner of great feudal estates in Europe also. Whole villages and towns belonged to the Templars.

As their order penetrated Europe, so, too, did its picture of the octagonal "Temple" atop Mount Moriah. It was displayed in their order-churches and chapter-houses in cities such as Metz, Lyon, and London. Even in modern London, Templar-Temple traces remain. London's men of law are traditionally housed in the famous Inns of Temple at Temple Bar. It was once the Templar headquarters, established in 1185, after the order moved from a previous London Temple at Holborn Bar. The octagonal design of the Jerusalem "Temple" (Dome of the Rock) was also repeated in structures erected by the order in Europe.

Early in the 14th century, catastrophe struck the Templars, now grown quite rich and corrupt. Charges of immoral practices and even of satanic orgies were brought against them. Some leaders were tried and executed. The order was suppressed by papal decree in 1312. Its coveted treasures and lands were seized. The final possessors of the wealth of the "poor knights of the Temple" appear to have been their two great foes: the King of France and the reigning Pope.

To Templars and Hospitalers must be added a third and later military-monastic order, founded by Germans among the Crusaders in Palestine. The Teutonic Knights, dating from about 1190, began in connection with a hospital near Acre. They, too, became wealthy, powerful, and aggressive. In northern Europe they even organized great wars of conquest into the Slavic regions later known as Russia.

The Dome of the Rock, though now converted to a Catholic Church for these feudal lords, Templars, Hospitalers, and Teutonic Knights, was not much changed physically. Its Arabic inscriptions remained intact. Atop the cupola, however, appeared a cross instead of a crescent, and within, an altar dedicated to St. Nicholas was either anchored to or cut into the great Rock, around which a grill of wrought-iron was placed by the Crusaders. The Rock suffered other violations. Chips from it were removed as relics given or sold to pilgrims from Europe. Marble slabs were finally placed over the Rock to check this vandalism.

Such souvenir-taking was not restricted to the Rock, however. The tide of pilgrims now flowing to Crusader-ruled Jerusalem carried back to Europe enormous numbers and kinds of relics and miracle-working "souvenirs." In hundreds of European churches and chapels were exhibited amazing or miraculous mementoes from the Holy Land. These included fragments of the True Cross, saints' bones and bits of hair, and other relics.

Other changes were made by the Crusader-conquerors in the Temple area. Godfrey lived for a time in the el Aksa Mosque, until a castle was completed for him on the site where once Herod's citadel had stood. The el Aksa was called, in this era, either the *Palatium* or even the *Templum Salomonis*, thus compounding the confusion with the Temple of Solomon. In the eastern aisle of the el Aksa stood a Christian chapel, complete with rose window. And west of the el Aksa, along the southern end of the Haram area, stood a Crusader armory.

In the great vaults known as "Solomon's Stables," under the southeast corner of the Haram, the Crusaders kept their own steeds, more than two thousand at a time, it is said. On the southern wall, where Solomon's ancient Horse Gate had stood, they built the Single Gate as entrance to the Stables. This has been sealed since the late nineteenth century.

Rabbi Benjamin of Tudela, who saw Jerusalem in the twelfth century, wrote of these stables, which he believed had been part of King Solomon's house: "Enormous stones have been employed . . . the like of which is nowhere else to be met with." Indeed, today, in the last third of the twentieth century, these enormous stones can still be seen in those vast vaults, supported by eighty-eight massive pillars. These "stables" certainly were used by the Romans. In Roman times they had been unroofed. The Crusaders, it appears, covered them over — quite likely to better protect their battle steeds. It is not possible now, however, to be sure whether Solomon actually stabled his horses here.

In 1154, the Sicilian geographer Idrisi wrote a description of the Dome of the Rock, based either on a visit or on what he had picked up from others who had been there. He pays tribute to the "gold mosaic . . . of most beautiful workmanship" overlaying the Dome of the Rock, and tells how visitors may "descend into the lower part" of the Rock, going down "into a dark chamber like a cellar," for which a lamp is needed. This refers to the cave.

Opposite the western gate of the Dome of the Rock, he declared, stood an altar on which "the children of Israel were wont to offer up their sacrifices." And "near the eastern gate" stood "the Church . . . of an admirable size."

The area, in this Christian period, included opposite the northern gate of the Dome of the Rock "a beautiful garden" surrounded by "a colonnade of marble of most wondrous workmanship" with "a place of assembly, where the priests and deacons are wont to take their repasts."

Elsewhere in Jerusalem the Crusaders did much building and restoration. In 1149, the fiftieth anniversary of their taking Jerusalem, they dedicated the rebuilt Church of the Holy Sepulcher. They reconstructed also most of the Byzantine Christian churches that had been there before Moslem rule. During eighty-eight years of Frankish Christian control, about thirty-seven churches were rebuilt or built complete.

Jerusalem as a whole remained enclosed by the Roman wall. Residents and visitors used four gates. That leading north was known as the St. Stephen's Gate, the southern as Zion Gate, the western as David's Gate, and the eastern as the Gate of Jehosaphat.

Gradually, Jews were allowed to come back to Crusader-ruled Jerusalem. Most of them worked as dyers, a privilege for which they had to pay the Christian king. Some historians report that between 1169–75 Jews were expelled once more.

Small industries arose. Money-changing, so necessary in that center of pilgrimages, was operated by "Syrians," as oriental Christians were called to distinguish them from the Europeans. These Syrians and such Jews as could exist there, resided in the district, directly north of the Haram, that came to be known much later as the "Moslem quarter" of the Old City. Rabbi Benjamin of Tudela noted that when he was in Jerusalem in the twelfth century, two hundred Jews were living in a corner of the city "under the Tower of David," today called the Citadel.

Most of the Crusaders who had taken and looted the city went back to Europe, disappointed that they had not found there the land of milk and honey promised by the original preachers of the Crusade. So many arms-bearing men left that the defense of the new rulers was endangered. The population in the city was a mixture: the "Franks" or European Christians, Eastern Christians (Syrians), Armenians, and various other sects. Much interbreeding took place.

Meanwhile, Moslem spokesmen, carrying blood-curdling reports of the horrors following the Crusaders' conquest of Jerusalem, appealed to their ruler in Bagdad. They demanded that their sacred Dome of the Rock be liberated from the unclean hands of the infidels — in this case the Christians. However, the Latin Kingdom of Jerusalem continued to expand by further conquests until it reached from Lebanon on the north, to Egypt.

A small Moslem army under Zangi in 1144 attacked and took some Christian outposts. The next Damascus ruler, Nur u-din, son of Zangi, won further key points and dedicated himself to regain Jerusalem.

In Europe the news of these Moslem successes led to an appeal for a Second Crusade. The famous and influential Bernard of Clairvaux persuaded both the French king, Louis VII, and the German Emperor Conrad II to "take the cross." Masses of supporters were enlisted again. Each monarch, leading an army of his own, set out at Easter time, 1147, destination: Jerusalem once more.

This view of the Dome of the Rock is from the southwest side. Behind the Dome in the distance lies the Mount of Olives. Mount Scopus is along the horizon to the left.

These armies met no resistance when they reached Constantinople. Crusaders, though now much disliked by the Byzantine Christians, were also too much feared. Hardships and battles on the way soon reduced the numbers in both armies. Emperor Conrad reached Jerusalem with only a remnant of his original force; while King Louis, it has been said, got there "with ladies, but no army."

They joined forces now with Baldwin III, then reigning as king in Jerusalem. Under the three-way command, an expedition marched against Damascus. Quarrels, over who should rule that city when it fell, prevented any effective effort to take it. Damascus stood, and from it issued a large Moslem army. It scattered the Crusaders, whose remnants fled to Antioch, Acre, or Jerusalem. Thus, in total collapse, ended the Second Crusade.

A legend rooted in this time blames on the Templars the failure to take Damascus. They accepted, it states, a Moslem bribe to betray the Crusaders. That gold, however, after being stored in their treasure chests, turned to copper.

18

From Saladin—to the End of the Crusades

(1171–1300 C.E.)

The year 1171 brought into this historic arena a new and in many ways more attractive leader. In that year, Saladin dethroned the last of the Fatimid caliphs. By 1175, having unified Syria and Egypt under his rule, he had become the leading Moslem prince and founder of the Ayyubid dynasty. Within nine years more he controlled Mesopotamia also. Now he was ready to move against the Franks in their strange Kingdom of Jerusalem.

Salah-ed-Din-Yusuf (his full name) became known as a wise and moderate ruler, a man of his word, not rabid for wealth, a devout Moslem, and by preference merciful even to enemies. However, he could be hard and ruthless when military needs seemed to demand it. He had learned bitter hatred against the Templars and Hospitalers, and he relentlessly fought to rid Palestine of Crusader rule.

By 1184, he had marshalled one hundred thousand men and soundly defeated the forces of the Frankish Kingdom of Jerusalem at Hattin, north of the Lake of Tiberias. The current Crusader king, Guy of Lusignan, was taken prisoner. Templars and Hospitalers were beheaded. The Franks had carried the so-called True Cross as their standard. It, too, was captured and sent by Saladin to the caliph of Bagdad.

Saladin proceeded now to take more than a dozen of the Franks' fortified towns, including Acre. By autumn, 1187, he was at the walls of Jerusalem. Lacking sufficient Christian defenders, the city was ripe to fall. Some of its citizens came out to plead with Saladin for peace. He replied that he, too, regarded Jerusalem as the City of God, and would prefer not to besiege it. He offered them, however, an alternative: he would hold off during a number of months, allowing the Franks to build up their defenses, cultivate land for some fifteen miles round the city, and even to receive some of Saladin's food supplies. If, at the end of that breathing spell, they still had hope of rescuers coming to their aid, they could fight "honorably" against his attack. Otherwise, Saladin urged, they should now peacefully give up Jerusalem, and he, Saladin, would spare their lives and their property. The delegation rejected this offer. Never, they said, would they surrender the city where Jesus died.

One story says that during the following siege, one of the defending lords of the Franks threatened that they would destroy the Dome of the Rock and other Moslem sanctuaries, burn Jerusalem, and kill their own sons and daughters. This, however, did not take place. In a few weeks Saladin took Jerusalem intact, and by October 2, 1187, he made known his rather lenient terms of surrender. Besides giving up the city, the Christians were to pay a ransom of gold. Saladin resisted those Moslems who urged him to destroy Christian churches. He spared Jerusalem and its sixty thousand captured inhabitants — a stark contrast to the Crusaders' bloody conquest of the city. Thousands of poor people were freed outright. From those able to pay was taken a ransom on the scale of ten gold pieces per man, five per woman, one per child. Some fifteen thousand Christians became slaves.

The Christian rulers had sworn not to take up arms in the future against Saladin. However, when they reached Christian territory, the Church released them from these oaths and they began planning for revenge.

Saladin once against allowed Jews to return to Jerusalem, not only to visit or mourn, but also to live and work there. (Jews have lived there ever since, though from 1948 to June, 1967, they were excluded from the Old City and the Temple mount, then held by Jordan.) Even more typical of Saladin's civilized practice was the fact that he permitted Christian pilgrims to continue to visit Jerusalem, so long as they came unarmed.

Under Saladin, the Dome of the Rock became once again a Moslem shrine and holy place. The Rock itself was washed with rosewater to rid it of Christian taint. As the golden cross atop the cupola was struck down, shouts of joy arose from the victors and groans of dismay from the Franks who watched. Saladin ordered removed the marble covering that the Franks had placed over the Rock.

New inscriptions, in Kufic, an early Arabic alphabet, were placed inside the cupola in yellow and blue tiles. The outer walls were covered with new and lovely mosaics, floral or geometric in design, since the Moslem, like Jewish, tradition excludes human or animal figures.

The el Aksa was restored to its former role: a Moslem mosque, in which the faithful prayed at prescribed times daily. Within it, Saladin placed a magnificent wooden *minbar* (pulpit) which had been built years earlier and dedicated to the recapture of Jerusalem. Its carved wood, inlaid with ivory and mother-of-pearl, was said to have required five years to complete.

This same pulpit was destroyed in August, 1969, by a fire which also damaged the southern portion of the el Aksa Mosque, intensifying already critical Arab-Israeli animosities.

The capture of Jerusalem by Saladin brought dismay to the Christian world of Europe. Now only three cities in the Near East were still held by Crusaders: Antioch, Tyre, and Tripoli.

Pope Gregory VIII issued a call for another Crusade, the Third. He asked each man to contribute a tithe — a tenth of all he owned — to finance it. Kings again became Crusade leaders: Richard I, "the lion-hearted," King of England, and Philip Augustus, twenty-three-year-old King of France. In 1191 they together retook Acre. Later, the French king, ill with fever, returned to his land. Richard, now alone in command, went on against Jerusalem and showed both heroism and military skill in a number of battles against the forces of Saladin. However, the climate proved a foe, too, and finally Richard decided it was no use attempting to defeat the Moslems in this, their own land. Saladin, too, realized that the Christians of Europe and the East could not be excluded from Jerusalem and other holy places of Palestine.

"Co-existence" replaced conflict as the two monarchs at last arranged a truce. The Moslems were to retain Jerusalem, the Christians to control the seacoast between Acre and Jaffa. (Some historians suggest that Italian merchants convinced Richard to accept this plan, since they wished to control the profitable trade of the coastal ports.) Christians were to be assured freedom to go as pilgrims to Jerusalem, with no tax to pay. Both Moslems and Christians were to pass freely into and out of the areas controlled by "the other side."

Among the many anecdotes of that time is one telling that when Richard left to return to England, he wrote Saladin threatening to come back in three years and recapture Jerusalem. Saladin is said to have replied that if he had to give up the sacred city, he would rather lose it to Richard than anyone else.

Leaders of both the Templar and Hospitaler orders, having lost their original headquarters and their sources of profits in Jerusalem, urged continuing the war against Saladin. However, they established themselves instead in Acre, and remained there until about a hundred years later, when, after the eighth and last Crusade, Acre was taken by Sultan Khalil, late in the thirteenth century.

Saladin died in 1193, aged fifty-five. After his death his large empire broke up. The powers in Europe now made new efforts to send Crusaders to

Looking eastward over the Old City of Jerusalem. The great Jaffa gate is left foreground and near it the Citadel, an ancient fort. On the Temple Mount stands the Dome of the Rock, and to its right the el Aksa Mosque. Just this side of the left end of that Mosque is the famous Western Wall. Beyond, across the Kidron Valley, stands the Mount of Olives, and to the left (north) Mount Scopus.

Jerusalem and the Holy Land. The Fourth Crusade, organized by Pope Innocent II, never did reach Palestine. Those Crusaders, instead, were influenced by policies, funds, and supplies from Venice, the great commercial city. In 1204 they attacked — not Jerusalem, but Constantinople, capital of their fellow-Christians of the Eastern (Byzantine) empire. Their sack of that city was fearful. Slaughter and destruction raged. Priceless treasures of art and literature were lost. It is said that even the taking of that same city by the Turks in 1453 caused less loss than this attack by Crusaders on fellow-Christians.

Now Constantinople became a Latin Kingdom, as Jerusalem had been. For the time being, the Greek and Roman Churches were united — or rather, that of Rome swallowed up the other. Jerusalem meanwhile remained safely in Moslem hands.

Next came the fantastic and tragic Children's Crusade of 1212. Thousands of European children, bound for Jerusalem, were tricked by shipowners, sold into slavery in Tunisia and Egypt, or lost at sea.

Three years later, Pope Innocent III once more summoned Europe to a Crusade, the Fifth. Its Crusaders did take the city of Damietta at the eastern mouth of the Nile River. But the war went badly, finally leading to an eight-year truce, obliging them to give back that city and remove all Christian troops from Egypt. They did, however, demand and receive the so-called "True Cross."

Blame for this defeat was placed on Frederick II, youthful emperor of Germany and Sicily who was excommunicated from the Church for failure to join the Crusade. In 1228, he did join a Sixth Crusade only to find, however, when he reached Palestine that the Christian residents there rejected him. They considered him now outside their Church. Frederick, an unusually cultured and imaginative man for his rank and era, was, however, able to make friendly contacts with the Ayyubid leader of the Saracen (Moslem) army and with the new sultan of Syria and Egypt.

Surprising both Christians and Moslems, these two rulers signed a treaty in 1229. It gave to Frederick most of Jerusalem, as well as all Acre, Jaffa, Sidon, Nazareth, and Bethlehem. Islam, however, was to retain the Haram area, the sacred enclosure atop Mount Moriah, where had stood the Temple. Thus for a period in the thirteenth century, Jerusalem again became a divided city. However, the barriers were not complete: Christians were allowed to pray at the site of what had been Solomon's Temple, and Moslems might do the same in Bethlehem.

In Rome, Pope Gregory IX refused to approve this pact. He called it an insult to Christianity. After Frederick left the East, Christian nobles took charge in Jerusalem. They allied with the Moslem government in Damascus, Syria, against the sultan of Egypt. He called to his aid an independent tribe of Turks, the Khwarizmians who had settled in Syria and Palestine after being pushed out of Persia by Mongol invaders under Genghis Khan.

These Turks entered Jerusalem, killing and plundering. Great numbers of inhabitants lost their lives. However, within two months Jerusalem was captured from the Khwarizmian Turks. The victor this time was Baibars, the Mameluke leader, also known as "the slave sultan of Egypt." He had been born a Turkish slave, yet rose to become sultan from 1260–77. Before he regained Jerusalem, he had defeated Crusaders at Gaza. In fact, his rise from slave to sultan is credited to the ability he showed in the constant wars against the Crusaders. In Moslem history he is called the greatest Mameluke sultan and ranked with Harun al-Rashid and Saladin.

Soon after the Mamelukes securely held Jerusalem, a Seventh Crusade was organized by the King of France, Louis IX, also called Saint Louis. He set out relatively alone, for he had been unable to reconcile Pope Innocent IV and Emperor Frederick II. The Seventh Crusade ended, however, when ten thousand Crusaders and Louis himself were all taken prisoner in 1250. He had been ill at the time, and was cured by an Arab physician, then obliged to buy his freedom by a large ransom.

King Louis reached Acre with what was left of his army. There he stayed during four years, vainly appealing to the powers of Europe to give up their quarrels and join him in still another Crusade. Finally, he returned to France in 1254.

Some thirteen years later, after many intervening events, Louis returned to the East again, an old man, accompanied by his three sons. This Eighth Crusade also failed after Louis fell ill and died in 1270 in Tunisia. His final word was said to have been "Jerusalem."

Acre was the strongest center still in Christian hands. Then Christians in Syria attacked and robbed a Moslem caravan and plundered Moslem towns. In retaliation, Sultan Khalil moved against Acre. After a forty-three day siege, he took it and sixty thousand prisoners. All were slain or enslaved. Soon afterward, the Turkish Mamelukes also took the remaining Christian strongholds of Tyre, Sidon, Haifa, and Beirut.

Now all Jerusalem and Palestine were in the strong hands of the Mamelukes. The fantastic ventures called the Crusades were ended. Christian control did not return to the city of the Temple until more than six and a quarter centuries later, when the British under Allenby occupied it in 1917.

19

Mamelukes and Ottomans on Mount Moriah

(1300–1700 C.E.)

The Mameluke sultans continued to rule Jerusalem until early in the sixteenth century. Between 1305 and 1440 they built many Moslem schools and mosques, and restored the dome of the el Aksa. They also removed most of the changes made by Crusaders in the "Templum Domini" and the "Templum Salomonis," though some traces of these changes were found as late as the nineteenth century.

The Mamelukes permitted Christian pilgrims to visit during their regime, though fear kept many away. Those who did come, however, were a source of great profit.

Between 1328 and 1350 greater tolerance was shown the Jews. Some had already returned to Jerusalem in 1190, others had settled there in 1211 and again in 1267. They came also from Egypt and Syria on regular pilgrimages to celebrate their festivals and holidays in the Holy City as in the days of the Temple.

As the Jewish community of Jerusalem continued to grow, the Jews worked chiefly in agriculture, though many were active as handicraftsmen or merchants. Some astronomers, mathematicians, and men of medicine were also among the growing Jewish community.

The Dome of the Rock continued to attract and overwhelm visitors.

One Moslem writer, Ibn Battuta, wrote of it in 1355 as a building of "extraordinary beauty, solidity, elegance, and singularity of shape." He described it as standing in the center of the Temple area, as having four doors and of being reached by a flight of marble steps. Marble was used both in the interior and the area outside the structure. Magnificent decorations and workmanship were apparent everywhere. So great a part of the building was covered with gold, he said, that one's eyes were dazzled by a brilliance which glowed "like a mass of light," or flashed "like lightning."

The great Rock within, declared this writer, was the height of a man. Steps led down to the cave underneath, the size of a small room.

> A Moslem legend substitutes for the cave a giant whale upon which the whole world was said to rest. The head of this "Leviathan," the story goes, is at the place where the sun rises, its tail where the sun sets, with the "Stone of Paradise" (the Rock) resting on the very center of the back of this mighty whale.

Ibn Battuta also mentioned two "gratings" or railings placed as guards around the Rock, one, closest to the Rock, made of iron, the other of wood. Inside the Dome of the Rock, he said, there hung a great "Buckler" (undoubtedly a shield) made of iron which was said to have belonged to Mohammed's uncle.

The influence of the history of Mount Moriah made itself felt in strange ways in Europe during the last half of the fourteenth century. Tarot playing cards, used for games, gambling, and eventually fortune telling, first made their appearance. Two of the cards of this seventy-eight-card deck carried pictures of the free-standing columns, *Jachin* and *Boaz,* which had been placed at the entrance to Solomon's Temple; a third card showed a shattered tower, also identified by some as the *Jachin* column of the Temple. Still another pictured an imaginary idol or devil named Baphomet, said to have been worshiped in secret rites by the Knights Templar. Actually the name Baphomet seems to have been a mangled form of the name of Mohammed or Mahomet.

During the fifteenth century, Christian and Jewish pilgrimages to Jerusalem increased. The average length of stay of these pilgrims from Europe in the Holy City was about ten days.

At this time relics of the Crusader-kingdom still stood in Jerusalem. The tombs of Godfrey and King Baldwin I, the first rulers of the Latin or Frankish Kingdom of Jerusalem, were preserved by the Moslems.

Many accounts survive from this period written by pilgrims who came to sightsee or worship. One of these, Felix Fabri, described the Holy City as standing on a "hilly and uneven" site. He compared it to the city of Basel, Switzerland, naming that city's hills which correspond to Jerusalem's Mount Zion, Mount Calvary, and Mount Moriah. "One goes up and down everywhere through the city," he wrote.

Within the walls of Jerusalem, Fabri commented, were a number of areas occupied by ruined houses used by the inhabitants as dumps for the carcasses of their dead animals. "Yet," he noted, "in the parts [of Jerusalem] where men dwell there are many people gathered together from every nation under heaven."

The Moslem Dome of the Rock most often attracted the admiration of pilgrims. One Christian pilgrim considered it the *only* beautiful building in Jerusalem; another wrote it was "in largeness, height, and sumptuousness . . . far and beyond any work that we ever saw in our lives." Others declared there was "nothing more glorious or more beauteous within sight."

In 1448, its roof was destroyed by fire, but was restored by the sultan "so as to be more beautiful even than it had been aforetimes." Cause of the fire was said by some to have been a thunderbolt, while others claimed the building was set afire by a boy carrying a lighted candle who had climbed under the roof to catch some pigeons.

From a distance, the Dome of the Rock, on its pavement of white marble, appeared to stand "in a pool of quietish white water." It was unforgettable, too, in the darkness of night when illuminated from the interior by many lamps. Their number has been given all the way from five hundred to

To Jerusalem and its Temple site traveled pilgrims, both Christians and Jews, from Europe, Africa, and the Middle East. This early sixteenth century woodcut shows an English pilgrim complete with the traditional robe, staff, and *scrip* or bag for carrying food and other essentials. Pilgrimage required courage and endurance.

twelve thousand by different sources. Felix Fabri described the effect seen through the windows of the Dome of the Rock as of a fire as bright "as though it were a lantern filled with clear flame."

These admiring descriptions were set down even though the sacred area, the Haram esh-Sherif, was then out of bounds for Christians and Jews, who could look at it only from the distant top of Mount Zion or the Mount of Olives. However, there were ways to get around this.

Fabri tells how he and a group of fellow-pilgrims were guided by a Jew "in half secret fashion" close to the Haram on its southern side. They went first to a ruined Christian church; then into crypt-like buildings below the el Aksa Mosque. (They undoubtedly gained access through the ancient Triple Gate which once led to passageways below the el Aksa. This Gate was sealed in the late nineteenth century.) From there they hurried beneath the Haram enclosure itself, and but for fear of consequences, could have "climbed up over the rubbish into the courtyard of the Temple."

One aristocratic German pilgrim bribed a Mameluke who provided him with Mameluke clothes and told him how to speak. Then both were admitted to the Dome of the Rock. He was even able to estimate the dimensions of the Dome of the Rock by pacing them off, to count its pillars, to visit the el Aksa Mosque, and also to steal pieces of copper and wood from the Golden Gate.

Other pilgrims, less bold, would prowl around nearby streets seeking a glimpse of the sacred area and the Dome of the Rock in its center. However, ". . . they were always liable to be shooed off by the jealous Moslems of the neighborhood." After all, Moslems to this day regard this "Noble Sanctuary," (the Haram esh-Sherif) with its Dome of the Rock and the el Aksa Mosque as the third holiest place in their world.

The Egyptian Moslem, Suyuti, mentioned earlier, writing in 1470, speaks of seeing the "footprint" of Mohammed on the sacred Rock within the Dome of the Rock, placed there, he states, when the prophet mounted the steed al Burak for his night ride to Heaven. Most legends state that al Burak was left tied up below at the Western (Wailing) Wall. Suyuti claims this footprint was referred to in the time of the Crusaders as "Christ's Footprint." The Rock itself, he wrote, had acquired speech in order to welcome the Caliph Omar in 638.

> A Jewish visitor to Jerusalem in 1481, Rabbi Meshullam, tells the following tale: Moslem servants, keeping themselves "in strict purity," attended to the lighting of seven candles within the Dome. Every year, Rabbi Meshullam wrote, when the Jews go to their synagogues on the eve of the anniversary of the destruction of the Temple, the 9th of *Ab* (*Tish'ah be-Ab*), all of the candles within the Dome of the Rock go out and it is impossible to relight them. The Moslems then know that it is *Tish'ah be-Ab* and they therefore observe this occasion as the Jews do.

Rabbi Meshullam also described life in Jerusalem in that year, noting that the stones of its very fine buildings were larger than any he had seen.

> "The land flows with milk and honey, although it is hilly and ruined and desolate, and everything is cheap; its fruits are choice and very good. There is a carob honey . . . also date honey, and the honey of bees, and wheat and barley and pomegranates and all kinds of fruits good and fine; and they have good olive oil, but they only eat sesame oil, which is very fine. The Moslems and also the Jews of this place . . . eat out of one vessel with their fingers, without a napkin . . . but their clothes are clean."

Historians tell how the Jewish inhabitants of Jerusalem received permission from the Moslem authorities to build a synagogue on a slope of Mount Zion, a site which contained the ruins of a Franciscan chapel. The Franciscan monks protested to the Pope saying if the Jews were allowed this privilege they might soon take over the Church of the Holy Sepulcher itself. Whereupon the Pope and the Venetian authorities issued orders that no Christian shipowner might transport Jews on their ships to Palestine. Since almost the entire eastern Mediterranean shipping trade was in the hands of the Venetians, this cut off ship passage for the Jews.

However, in 1456, a traveler in Turkey wrote an open letter to the Jews of the Rhineland, Moravia, Hungary, and other regions, urging them to emigrate to Turkey where Jews were treated honorably. The road to Palestine, he pointed out, lay through Turkey. A great many Jews followed his advice, some remaining and becoming citizens of Turkey, others going on to Palestine. As a result of this emigration, and of the Spanish edict of March 31st, 1492, (ordering all Jews on pain of death to leave Spain and the Iberian Peninsula where they had lived for fifteen hundred years), the Jewish population of Jerusalem continued to grow.

The Ottomans under Sultan Selim I occupied Jerusalem after their defeat of the Mamelukes in 1516. At that time, it is said, about one hundred and fifty to two hundred and fifty Jewish families lived in Jerusalem, and more than five hundred families in all of Palestine.

The Ottomans, whose name derives from their founder, Osman (1259–1326), began as a small tribe of Turkish Moslem warriors who had fled the Mongols to settle in Asia Minor. They achieved swift and powerful expansion in Europe and Asia. By 1389 they had conquered almost all the Balkans. In fact, they ruled the eastern Mediterranean countries for about five centuries. In 1453, from a position of power in Anatolia (Asiatic Turkey) they crossed the Bosphorus and took the great Byzantine capital of Constantinople (Istanbul). This ended the Christian Roman Empire of the East. The beautiful Church of Santa Sophia, built by Justinian in 537 C.E., became a mosque, and remains a Moslem edifice to this day.

Sultan Selim I added Egypt to his empire, proclaimed himself ruler over the entire Moslem world, and moved his capital from Cairo to Constantinople.

Selim's son, the famous Suleiman the Magnificent (1494–1566), did much building and restored many Islamic religious shrines throughout his

Jerusalem as it probably looked about 1486 C.E. A woodcut from the German book *Peregrinations* by Bernard Breydenbach. The Dome of the Rock and the Haram are shown here as if seen from the

empire. In Jerusalem today, the Haram area, totalling almost forty acres, is much the same as when it was laid out by Suleiman.

Mount of Olives, hence looking westward. Yet the artist placed the Mediterranean seacoast in the foreground, though it should be in the far distance, unseen beyond the horizon!

Most of the crenellated walls and famous gates which still surround the Old City of Jerusalem, were built or reconstructed under Suleiman. He did very little to the southern wall with its Single, Double, and Triple Gates. The ancient Double Gate was said to have been the main entrance to the Temple area in biblical times. All three gates have been sealed since the late nineteenth century. Suleiman is said by some to have been the sultan who blocked the Golden Gate (on the east side of the Haram) in accordance with Turkish fear or superstition that a Christian Messiah might enter through that portal. Suleiman also built many public fountains and improved the city's water supply.

Suleiman provided the Dome of the Rock with beautiful new exterior mosaics of glazed Persian tiles in various tones of blue, interspersed with yellow, green, white, and grey, which today still adorn the building. Possibly it was easier to import Persian tile-makers than to repair the old broken mosaics. He also had stained-glass lattice windows made which added a lovely diffused light to the interior.

Suleiman (sometimes spelled Solyman, or Soliman) wrote poetry under the pseudonym of Muhibbr. It was under this soldier-statesman-poet that the Turkish Empire reached its peak. Some historians contend that none of the world's rulers of this period was greater than he — neither Charles V, Francis I, Henry VIII, nor Elizabeth. In fact, they assert, it is from the time of his death that Turkish power began to decline.

During his lifetime, as city after city fell to him, he became master of the Eastern Mediterranean. He made of Turkey a European power, one to be reckoned with and feared.

The order of Hospitalers reappears again in this era, about 450 years after the beginning of the Crusades. After surrendering the Island of Rhodes to the Turks, and wandering around the Mediterranean for years, the Hospitalers received from Emperor Charles V, the island of Malta, a barren rock between Sicily and Africa. This they turned into a "garden-fortress," and from there, after a long and bloody seige, were at last, in 1565, able to repulse the Turks. Hereafter, the Hospitalers were known also as the "Knights of Malta," a name which has inspired many writers of fiction.

Jews throughout the world continued to look with longing toward Jerusalem, in spite of the many difficulties of life there and the limits put on their numbers permitted to live in the city. The result was a slow, but steady growth of the Jewish population in Jerusalem and Palestine. It led eventually to the establishment of the present State of Israel. Over the centuries, Jews have toasted each other with the promise: "Next year, in Jerusalem!"

During the Mameluke period, synagogues of Jerusalem had often been destroyed, but the Jews gradually had rebuilt their community life, so devastated by the Crusaders. Later, under the Ottomans, Jews of Jerusalem were able to make contact through traveling representatives with their co-religionists throughout the world. From them they received funds for various projects in Palestine, including institutions for the sick, the needy, and students. Some of the later "fund-raisers" for the Jews of Palestine even collected in North and South America. (Such solidarity has continued to this day.)

During the sixteenth and seventeenth centuries, many Jerusalem Jews worked as dyers (as in ancient days), shoemakers, weavers, or in some form

The detail of the woodcut from Breydenbach's Peregrinations gives an enlarged view of the Haram esh-Sherif. The Golden Gate, to the right of the inscription "Civitas Iherusalem," is shown wholly or partially blocked up even in 1486.

of the clothing craft. Some traveled as peddlers or spice handlers. But most, including rabbis and scholars, were supported by the community and contributions from abroad.

The population of Jerusalem as a whole had sunk to approximately ten thousand — about one-tenth Jews, one-third Christians, the rest Moslems. Jews and Christians, under the Ottomans, were given comparative religious freedom, and while they had no voice in the political life of the city, they were allowed to administer their own marriage, divorce, inheritance, and religious laws.

By the middle of the seventeenth century, the Jews of Jerusalem were sunk in poverty. Poland, once a haven for Jews from Germany and other anti-Jewish countries, had become the scene of horrible pogroms, massacres, and persecution of the "people of the Book." Hundreds of Jewish communities were destroyed, hundreds of thousands of Jews brutally murdered. As a result, monetary contributions from fellow-Jews in other countries were diverted from Jerusalem to Poland to help oppressed Jews there. In addition, Turkish governors of Jerusalem began exacting very heavy taxes and fines on the Jewish population. It was a time of wretched suffering, and many are said to have died of hunger. As a result, some of the leading citizens of the Jewish community left Jerusalem. In spite of this, the lure of the city of David and Solomon remained strong to the Jews of the world.

This is the period in which that colorful, unscrupulous, and most famous of pseudo-Messiahs, Shabbathai Zvi, appeared in Jerusalem about 1666. There, he won followers as he did in many parts of Europe and the East. The leaders of the Jewish community in Jerusalem were completely won over when Shabbathai was able to gain financial concessions for them from the Turkish governing officials. However, when the sultan offered him a choice between death or adopting the religion of Islam, he immediately chose Islam, much to the horror and shame of most of his followers.

20

Two and a Half Centuries of Change—and the Rise of a New Israel

(1700-1967 C.E.)

The Ottoman Empire began to weaken by the end of the eighteenth century, while the powers of the west—England, France, and Russia, grew stronger.

The preceding century was a period of relative quiet for the city of the Temple mount. New groups, especially of the Jewish Hassidic sect, arrived from Eastern Europe adding to the Jewish community of Jerusalem.

In 1798, the brilliant, ambitious French general, Napoleon Bonaparte, then only twenty-nine years old, attempting to cut off Britain's trade route to India, undertook an expedition to Egypt as his first step in this campaign.

On his way to Egypt, Napoleon's fleet seized the Island of Malta, a trade link to the Middle East. This Mediterranean island was still ruled by the Order of the Knights of Malta (formerly the Hospitalers of Crusader days.) They had greatly deteriorated as a group, were most unpopular with Maltese citizens, and were easily conquered by Napoleon's troops.

Napoleon's invasion of Egypt was a rude shock to the Ottoman Turks.

Turkish power had been declining in Egypt, which was administered by their Mameluke governors. Nevertheless, they still claimed that country as part of the Empire controlled from Constantinople. They allied themselves with Britain, whose fleet, under Nelson, practically destroyed Napoleon's navy in the Mediterranean, blockaded the general and his army, and virtually isolated the French in the land they had occupied — Egypt.

Then in 1799, Napoleon invaded Palestine — or Syria, as the Holy Land was then called. It was the first military invasion of Palestine by Europeans since the Crusades.

Napoleon hoped to use Syria as a link between Africa and India. He and his forces made their way by land all along the Mediterranean coast northward as far as Acre. They first captured El Arish (later prominent in the June, 1967, Israeli-Arab war), and then Gaza. At Jaffa, today a suburb of Tel Aviv, Israel, the defenders fought stubbornly before they were defeated. Here occurred a shameful episode of Napoleon's Syrian campaign. Historians relate that the entire civilian population of Jaffa were killed by Napoleon's forces, while the four thousand Turkish soldiers, who had surrendered, were marched to the seashore and shot.

Napoleon was now very close to Jerusalem, but there is no indication that he ever reached that memorable city. He marched instead north to Acre, one-time Templar stronghold, but was unable to take it, so well defended was it by the Turks and Arabs, with help from the British. The continuing battles, together with an outbreak of the plague, reduced considerably the number of troops under his command, and he was forced to retreat to Egypt.

During Napoleon's invasion of Palestine he issued an offer to the Jews of the world — "the patrimony [their inheritance] of Israel." Apparently he had been very confident of victory and intended to promote Jewish settlement. Nevertheless, there is evidence to show that Jews of Palestine fought side by side with Arabs to defend the Holy Land against the French. It is interesting to speculate about the outcome of history had Napoleon's expedition to Syria been successful and he had been able to reach Jerusalem.

One of the only positive and permanent things of value to come from Napoleon's campaign in Egypt and Syria was the discovery by the French of the Rosetta stone — named for the city in Egypt where it was found. French scientists and archeologists gave the world this great key to ancient hieroglyphic writing. After Napoleon's defeat, the stone was claimed by the British and is now in the British Museum in London.

After Napoleon returned to Paris, Egypt and Palestine were once more restored to the Ottomans. The Ottoman Sultan Mahmud appointed Muhammad Ali, one of his generals, as viceroy or governor of Egypt, with title of "Pasha." In 1831, Muhammad Ali rebelled against the Sultan, declaring Egypt independent of the Ottoman Empire. With his son, Ibrahim, he ruled both Palestine and Egypt.

For some ten years Jerusalem was governed by Ali from Egypt. At one point during this period, Palestinian Arab peasants in revolt against Ali's oppressive conscription and taxation measures, took Jerusalem. They were soon defeated, however, and ousted from the city.

Finally, Britain, France, and Russia, all fearful of an expansion by Ali, backed the Ottoman sultan, ousted the Egyptians, and restored Palestine and Egypt once more to the Ottoman Empire.

Muhammad Ali had respected and admired modern European techniques, especially those of the French. During his rule Palestine had been opened to Western travelers. The benefits of efficient administration and economy were quickly learned from the Europeans by Ali and afterwards by the Ottomans when they were restored to power in Palestine. The Ottomans continued Ali's policy of welcoming Europeans. Aided by establishment of the telegraph and the building of better roads, pilgrims, scholars, and archeologists continued increasingly to visit Jerusalem.

The Holy City now had a much more efficient administration. European influences and ideas brought by Western visitors were taking hold all over Palestine. Travelers and non-Moslems were protected by representatives or consuls of the various European powers, most of whom were trying to gain footholds in the Middle and Near East.

To resist this encroachment by European powers, and in order to oversee, maintain, and continue its control of the holy places, the Ottoman Turkish government designated Jerusalem and southern Palestine as a separate district under the authority of Constantinople.

Here, looking eastward along the foot of the Southern Wall of the Haram, careful diggers are going deeper into the past. At left is the wall itself, at right remnants of a great building from the Byzantine era. The full extent and perhaps even the purposes of that building were beginning to become apparent to the scientific archeologists in charge of this work as the authors visited the Temple site in the autumn of 1968.

As thousands of visitors and settlers flocked to Jerusalem each year, the various foreign consulates or missions widened their influence, power, and protection for their subjects. Each foreign consulate representing a western power had its own courts, its own post office, and its own military guard.

In the 1860's began a long series of archeological expeditions to Jerusalem by British, French, Americans, and others. Much has been learned about ancient Jerusalem through their excavations. The British in particular were able to reproduce a first plan of the city through their "British Ordnance Survey." Three important archeological sites were uncovered around the walls of the Temple area and named for their discoverers: Robinson's Arch, after an American biblical scholar, Wilson's Arch for Sir Charles Wilson of Britain, and Barclay's Gate, mentioned earlier. (Modern Israeli archeologists have since made sensational discoveries. Under way at present are further excavations near the walls on the southwestern corner of the Temple mount.)

French scientists were very active, and the French built the first railway from Jerusalem to the sea in the 1880's.

In 1827, there had been about fifteen hundred Jews in Jerusalem. Nearly twenty years later they had grown to be the majority of the population for the first time since the destruction of the Temple by Titus in 70 C.E. By 1873, they formed a community of 10,600 and began spreading out beyond the Old City section. In all of Palestine, however, there were only about twenty-four thousand Jews by 1882, an indication that this one-time land of "milk and honey," was now, in fact, a land where tilling the soil and maintaining life meant bitter hardships. Those Jews who came to settle in Jerusalem and Palestine, however, did not do so to make an easier living. They were escaping persecution, and were drawn, as Jews have been for thousands of years, to the land of their beginnings and the city of the Temple.

As before, a great many Jews, particularly pious scholars, were supported in Palestine by contributions from their fellow-Jews throughout the world. Relatively few during this early or middle part of the nineteenth century succeeded in agriculture. There was little land available for cultivation. Much of it had been devastated in battles between landowners and Bedouins, or neglected for centuries.

Sir Moses Montefiore, a very wealthy English banker and a great humanitarian, visited Palestine some seven times during his life. (1784–1885). The harsh conditions under which his fellow-Jews lived prompted him again and again to try to help them. He attempted to buy or rent land for Jewish families and was at last successful in 1854 in purchasing from the Ottoman sultan some land near Safed — enough to settle fifty-four families.

Similar attempts were made by the French Rothschild family who ultimately supported Jews after the Ottoman sultan banned Jewish ownership of land. As the century wore on, these philanthropic and other projects, plus the influx into Palestine of persecuted Jews fleeing from eastern Europe, launched the concept of Zionism, which later found expression in the modern state of Israel.

In the meantime, the Temple mount was being carefully guarded by fanatical Moslems from Northern Africa who feared the Holy Places of Islam would be profaned if trod by the feet of the "unbelievers." Christians and Jews alike were excluded from the Haram area and needed special permission from the sultan in Constantinople or his Palestinian governor to visit Mount Moriah. Nevertheless, Sir Moses Montefiore and his wife, as well as other notables, visited the Temple area amidst great Moslem ceremony.

Mark Twain, that celebrated American humorist, traveled to Jerusalem in 1867. In his book, *The Innocents Abroad, or the New Pilgrims' Progress*, he told of his visit to Mount Moriah and the Dome of the Rock, or "Mosque

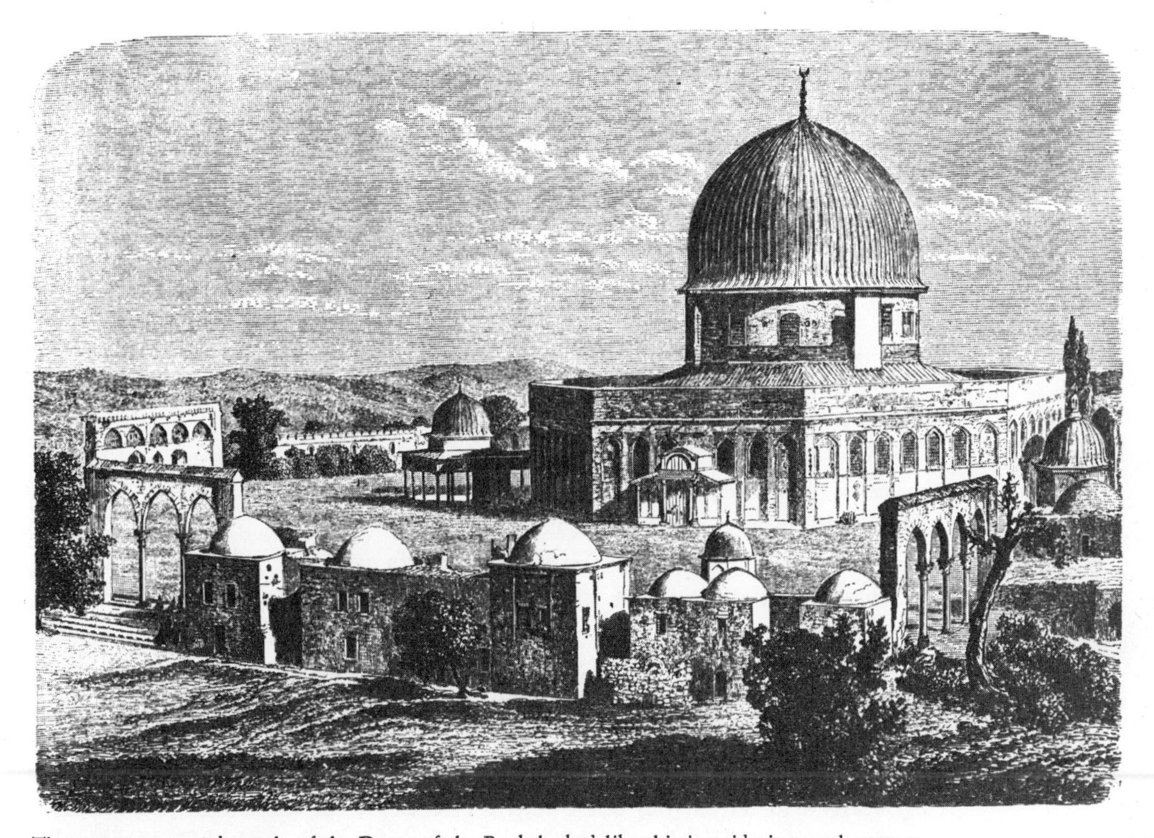

The crescent-crowned cupola of the Dome of the Rock looked like this in mid-nineteenth century, as illustrated in a French work on Syria. Evidences of deterioration and disrepair can be traced in this engraving. The Dome of the Rock in 1969 is in better condition, externally and internally, than it was a century earlier.

of Omar," as his guides then called it. Until just a year or two before 1867, he noted, "no Christian could gain admission to it or its court for love or money." But that ban had been removed, and these American "pilgrims" entered — for a fee. Of the "prodigious rock" under the rotunda, he reported that it was here "that Abraham came so near offering up his son Isaac — this, at least, is authentic — it is very much more to be relied on than most of the traditions, at any rate."

It was also on this Rock, Twain noted, that "the angel stood and threatened Jerusalem, and David persuaded him to spare the city," and here, too, that Mohammed made his ascent to heaven, at which time, "The stone tried to follow him, and if the angel Gabriel had not happened by the merest good luck to be there to seize it, it would have done it. Very few people have a grip like Gabriel — the prints of his monstrous fingers, two inches deep, are to be seen in that rock today."

Even more remarkable, Twain revealed, "This rock, large as it is, is suspended in the air. It does not touch anything at all. This is very wonderful. In the place where Mahomet stood, he left his footprints in the solid stone. I should judge he wore about eighteens."

In the latter part of the 1800's, Jerusalem was also the object of political maneuvers by Kaiser Wilhelm II of Germany. When Wilhelm, known as "*Der Reise-Kaiser*" (the "traveling Kaiser") visited Jerusalem in 1898, it was apparently to be present at the consecration of a Protestant church. At this time he presented to German Catholics the plot of ground on Mount Zion on which was built the Church of the Dormition of the Holy Virgin. The Victoria Augusta Hospice on Mount Scopus, named for the Kaiser's wife, a daughter of Queen Victoria of England, was also constructed after this state visit.

Actually, Kaiser Wilhelm, though claiming to be the leader of Christendom, found it expedient to go out of his way to visit the Turkish sultan in Constantinople and declared himself to be the protector of the Moslem world. One year later, in 1899, this strategy paid off. A German-Turkish alliance was formed, and at the outbreak of World War I, in 1914, Turkey sided with Germany and Austria.

Between 1860 and 1890 a series of books were published on "Zionism" which stirred the desires of much of world Jewry for a return to Palestine and an escape from the anti-semitism, discrimination, and persecution of the countries in which they lived. Some devoutly religious Jews, however, said no such return should take place until the appearance of a Messiah who would lead them back to the Holy Land. The new "Zionists" claimed, however, that it was up to the Jews themselves to take up the struggle, return to Palestine, and transform its barren desert into a fertile Jewish homeland. ("Zionism" or "the return to Zion" was so called in memory of the hill of Zion, David's symbol for the city of Jerusalem.)

Toward the latter part of the nineteenth century, Theodore Herzl, a Viennese playwright, journalist, and a Jew who until then had been somewhat indifferent to his heritage, became keenly aware of the plight of European Jewish victims of anti-semitism. His interest in the now historic Dreyfus Case in France added to his growing concern for his fellow Jews, wandering from place to place in search of a home. In 1896, he published his pamphlet, "The Jewish State," proposing the creation of a national homeland for Jews. Herzl's booklet called for workers, farmers, business men, intellectuals, and scholars to help found a Jewish state. This, and the old religious idea of a "return to Zion," were merged, spurred on by the growing need for a refuge for persecuted Jews. Almost immediately Herzl found himself the leader of the great Zionist organization.

At its first historic Congress in Basel, Switzerland, in 1897, replicas of Bar Kochba coins of the days of the Jewish rebellion against the Romans (132–135 C.E.) were distributed to attending members.

For about seven years Zionists tried in vain to interest the Great Powers of Europe in the idea of a home for Jews. Finally, in 1903, the British government offered to establish such a settlement in British East Africa. Herzl was attracted by the idea, but died (1904) before anything was decided. However, the dream of a return to the land of the Temple was too compelling. The Zionist congress of 1905 rejected the African plan and resolved that their colonization must be in Palestine. They set up a Jewish National Fund and used it to buy land in Palestine wherever they could. Arab and Turkish landowners boosted their prices wildly, but the costs were met, and desert land was acquired for Jewish settlers.

The Jewish population of Jerusalem grew steadily. In 1910, of its sixty-eight thousand inhabitants, fifty thousand were Jewish. Their way of life was beginning to change. The religious institutions for the great numbers of Talmudic scholars, students, and their families, continued to function, but to these were added schools of European influence, public libraries, an art school. Some small industry took shape and a labor force began to grow. There was even in 1907 a strike of workers of the printing trade. Its leader, a young Labor Zionist, Izhak Ben-Zvi, afterwards became President of Israel.

World War I (1914–1918) set back sharply the progress of the Zionist movement. Britain had hoped the Ottoman Empire would join the Allies. Instead, as stated earlier, Turkey sided with Germany, and the Britons faced the Turks as enemies across the Suez Canal.

Jews of Palestine and Jerusalem suffered much during this period. Jews even suspected of sympathy with the British were hanged by the Turks. Zionism was declared illegal, and twelve thousand Jews were deported from Palestine because they were not Turkish citizens. Jerusalem, itself, was beset by famine and plague, and the population sank to less than fifty thousand.

However, during World War I, a brilliant British chemist and ardent Zionist named Chaim Weizmann played a major role in the development of the explosive, TNT, for the British government. In doing so, he helped pave the way for the future state of Israel. His eloquent appeal to the British government to set up a protectorate for a Jewish national home in Palestine was looked upon with sympathy by the British cabinet and especially by Arthur James Balfour, the British Foreign Secretary. Undoubtedly, British desire for a foothold in the Middle East played a part in the decision.

On November 2, 1917, the famous Balfour Declaration was issued in the name of the British government. It stated that country would use its "best endeavors" to help establish a national home for the Jews in Palestine, with the understanding that the civil and religious rights of non-Jewish Palestinians or the rights of Jews in other countries, would not be injured.

On December 9, 1917, five weeks after the Balfour Declaration, Britain's General Sir Edmund Allenby marched into Jerusalem at the head of his troops and occupied the city in a bloodless conquest. Jerusalem was restored to Christian rule under the British. Except for the period of occupation by the Crusaders, the city of the Temple had been under Moslem domination nearly thirteen hundred years. Palestine remained under a "mandate," an arrangement which made Britain the ruling authority for the time being.

Encouraged by the Balfour Declaration and supporting statements by world leaders, large numbers of Jews, mainly from eastern Europe, emigrated to Palestine after World War I.

As its population grew, Jerusalem's economic and intellectual life made rapid strides. In 1925, the Hebrew University, a medical center, and a national library were established on Mount Scopus. New Jewish living quarters arose in the Old City, west of the Temple site and as near as possible to the "Wailing" Wall. In contrast, the expansion of the non-Jewish population was slow.

At the same time, Arab nationalism and resentment grew in opposition to the British Mandate, increasing Jewish immigration, and the whole Zionist movement. In Jerusalem in 1922, 1929, and again between 1936 and 1939, bloody riots took place spurred on by Arab political and religious leaders. The riots culminated in a six months general strike which left the city divided into an Arab and a Jewish sector.

The rise of the German dictator Adolf Hitler in 1933 — even before his wartime slaughter of six million Jews — brought additional floods of refugees fleeing from persecution to Palestine's shores.

In 1939, persuaded by the violence of Arab protests, the British government under Neville Chamberlain published a "White Paper" limiting and practically putting an end to Jewish immigration into Palestine. During the war against Nazi Germany (1939–1945) many Palestinian Jews fought side by side with the British against the Nazis. However, after the war, the new Labor Government of Great Britain upheld the White Paper, dashing the hopes of the Jews. Jewish opposition to British policies in Palestine took the forms of non-cooperation, of so-called illegal immigration by running the blockade of British ships, and in some instances of retaliatory attacks upon British buildings and personnel. British attempts to deal with the situation failed, and they finally turned to the United Nations to settle the conflict.

On November 29, 1947, that body voted to partition Palestine into separate Jewish and Arab countries. The Jews of Jerusalem rejoiced. But the following day the Arab Legion began a series of attacks, bombing and destroying buildings in the new Jewish sector, killing dozens of people.

In the days that followed, and aided by many British from the Mandate Government, the Arabs succeeded in blocking the road which carried supplies

The lion of Judah, also known as *Ariel,* was chosen for the seal of the city of Jerusalem. The rampant King of Beasts is set against a background of great blocks, suggesting the Western Wall, and surrounded by olive branches, symbolic of Shalom (peace) akin to the root of the name Jerusalem — a city that has enjoyed far too little of that condition during its three millenia of history.

to the city, and in destroying its water pipeline. Arab forces gained control of the Hebrew University and the Hadassah Hospital on Mount Scopus, as well as over the Jewish Quarter in the Old City, close to the Temple area and the Western Wall. But the Jews of the rest of Jerusalem held out, and convoys of food and supplies finally reached them. (Today, looking down on Jerusalem from above, one can see the countless water tanks on the roofs, built and kept filled against any other possible emergency of this kind.)

On May 15, 1948, the official date for the end of the thirty-year British Mandate over Palestine, the Jewish provisional government proclaimed the independent State of Israel. At first, the Jews succeeded in opening the road to the old city of Jerusalem, but immediately the Arab Legion attacked from every direction in overwhelming numbers and with powerful modern war weapons. After fierce fighting, they again took the Jewish quarter in the old walled city of Jerusalem which includes Mount Moriah. The Jews stood their ground in the new city, suffering tremendous bombardment from Arab forces who began a siege in hopes of starving the defenders. The Jews, however, were able to open a new road to the coastal plain, and food and ammunition began to flow to the city.

The odds against the new Israel seemed overwhelming. However, this War of Independence was fought with courage and spirit, plus powerful determination to hold the land so newly proclaimed a sovereign state.

There followed a series of armistices, with attacks and battles interspersed between the truces. In the final armistice, 1948, Jerusalem became a divided city: The Old City, the Temple mount, and some adjoining areas, were held by Jordan, the Arab nation to the east. Once more, Jews were forbidden access to the site of the Temple, and, in disregard of the terms of the armistice agreement, were also denied the right to worship at the Western Wall.

Not until June of 1967 was this situation ended by events — sketched in the first chapter of this book — which led the men of Israel back to the Western Wall and to the site of their unparalleled Temple beyond time.

PROTECTION OF HOLY PLACES LAW 1967

Given below is the text of the special Law passed by the Knesset (Israel's Parliament), shortly after Jerusalem's reunification in June 1967. The Law guarantees the inviolability of the Holy Places, proper reverence and respect for them, and free access. It prescribes consultation between the competent Israel authorities and denominational representatives for fulfillment of its terms.

1. The Holy Places shall be protected from desecration and any other violation and from anything likely to violate the freedom of access of the various religions to the places sacred to them or their feelings with regard to those places.
2. (a) Whoever desecrates or otherwise violates a Holy Place shall be liable to imprisonment for a term of seven years.

   (b) Whoever does anything that is likely to violate the freedom of access of the members of the various religions to the places sacred to them or their feelings with regard to those places shall be liable to imprisonment for a term of five years.
3. This law shall add to and not derogate from any other law.
4. The Minister of Religious Affairs is charged with the implementation of this law and he may, after consultation with or upon the proposal of representatives of the religions concerned, and with the consent of the Minister of Justice, make regulations as to any matter relating to such implementation.
5. This law shall come into force on the date of its adoption by the Knesset.

LEVI ESHKOL
Prime Minister

ZERAH WAHRHAFTIG
Minister of Religious Affairs

SHNEOR ZALMAN SHAZAR
President

Brief Bibliography

Works published since 1920

Aharoni, Yohanan. *The Land of the Bible.* Philadelphia: Westminster, 1967.

Aharoni, Yohanan and Avi-Yonah, Michael. *The Macmillan Bible Atlas.* New York: Macmillan, 1968.

Ausubel, Nathan. *Pictorial History of the Jewish People.* New York: Crown, 1953.

Avi-Yonah, Michael. *The Holyland from the Persian to the Arab Conquest.* Grand Rapids, Michigan: Baker, 1966.

Avi-Yonah, Michael. *The Madaba Mosaic Map.* Jerusalem: Israel Exploration Society, 1954.

Avi-Yonah, Michael (editor). *Jerusalem.* New York: Arco, 1961.

Boudet, J. (editor), *Jerusalem, a History.* New York: Putnam's, 1967.

Boyd, James P. *Bible Dictionary.* New York: Ottenheimer, 1958.

Cragg, Kenneth. *The Dome and the Rock: Jerusalem Studies in Islam.* London: 1964.

Durant, Will. *Our Oriental Heritage.* New York: Simon & Schuster, 1935.

Durant, Will. *The Age of Faith.* New York: Simon & Schuster, 1950.

Dubnov, Simon. *History of the Jews.* New York: Yoseloff, 1968.

Ginzberg, Louis. *Legends of the Jews.* Philadelphia: Jewish Publication Society, 1938.

Hanauer, J. E. *Folklore of the Holy Land.* London: Macmillan, second edition, 1935.

Hitti, Philip K. *History of the Arabs from Earliest Times to the Present.* London: Macmillan, sixth edition, 1956.

Join-Lambert, Michel. *Jerusalem.* London: Elek Books, 1958.

Le Strange, Guy. Palestine Under the Moslems. Beirut, Lebanon; Khoyats, 1965. (a re-issue of the original 1890 edition.)

Parrot, Andre. *The Temple of Jerusalem.* New York: Philosophical Library, 1955.

Runciman, Steven. *A History of the Crusades.* New York: Cambridge University Press, 1951.

Stockoll, Solomon. *The Gates of Jerusalem.* New York: Praeger, 1968.

Wilnai, Zeeb. *Legends of Palestine.* Philadelphia: Jewish Publications Society, 1932.

Watzinger, C. *Denkmäler Pälastinas.* Germany: 1933-35.

Wollman-Esamir, Pinchas (editor). *Graphic History of the Jewish Heritage.* New York: Shengold, 1963.

Works published prior to 1920

Archer, J. A. and Kingsford, C. L. *The Crusaders: The Story of the Latin Kingdom of Jerusalem.* New York: 1894.

Doré, Gustav. *The Doré Bible Gallery.* New York: 1894.

Fergusson, James. *Temples of the Jews.* London: 1878.

Graetz, Heinrich. *History of the Jews* (six volumes). Philadelphia: 1891-93.

Hosmer, J. K. *Story of the Jews.* New York: 1887.

Perrot, G. and Chipiez, C. *History of Art in Sardinia and Judaea.* London and New York: 1890.

Schmidt, Emmanuel. *Solomon's Temple.* Chicago: 1902.

Suyuti, Kamal (or Shams) ad Din as Suyuti. "Description of the Noble Sanctuary at Jerusalem," *Royal Asiatic Society Journal.* London: 1887.

Index

ACKNOWLEDGMENTS

The authors gratefully acknowledge the following sources for illustrations which appear in this book: On pages 19 and 155, Israel Government Tourist Office; page 21, Matson Photo Service; page 28, J. K. Hosmer, *Story of the Jews;* page 53, Bibliotheque Nationale, Paris; pages 85, 93, 113, 124-25, 143, 151, 160, Israel Information Service; page 4, Dr. Michael Avi-Yonah, with the permission of the Holyland Hotel, Jerusalem; page 102, Pinacoteca di Brera Gallery, Milan, Italy; page 104, Rosenwald Collection, National Gallery of Art, Washington, D.C.; page 105, National Gallery, London; pages 110-111, UCLA Library, Department of Special Collections; page 128, Spencer Collection, New York Public Library; pages 130 and 137, James Fergusson, *Temples of the Jews;* pages 168-169, Rogers Fund, Metropolitan Museum of Art; page 171, British Museum; page 175, M. C. Klein.